# BAJA TO PATAGONIA

# BAJA TO PATAGONIA
## Latin American Adventures

▲

LARRY RICE

Fulcrum Publishing
Golden, Colorado

Chapter 1, "Paddling Through Patagonia," and Chapter 6, "Lake Titicaca," appeared in abridged versions in *Canoe* magazine. Chapter 5, "In the Land of Lauca," appeared in an abridged version in *Américas* magazine.

Library of Congress Cataloging-in-Publication Data

Rice, Larry.
    Baja to Patagonia : Latin American adventures / Larry Rice.
      p.   cm.
    Includes bibliographical references (p.  ).
    ISBN 1-55591-113-7
      1. Latin America—Description and travel.  2. Natural history—
Latin America.  3. Ecotourism—Latin America.   I. Title.
F1409.3.R53    1993
918.04'33—dc20                                93-23088
                                                    CIP

Book Design by Jody Chapel

Printed in the United States of America

0  9  8  7  6  5  4  3  2  1

Fulcrum Publishing
350 Indiana Street, Suite 350
Golden, CO 80401-5093
(800) 992-2908

*To all those individuals and organizations who are striving to preserve Latin American wilderness and wildlife. As Aldo Leopold observed, "I am glad I shall never be young without wild country to be young in. Of what avail are forty freedoms without a blank spot on the map?"*

# Contents

ACKNOWLEDGMENTS     ix
INTRODUCTION     xi

1   Paddling Through Patagonia (Chile)     3
2   Island at World's End (Chile)     31
3   The Elusive Spires of Fitzroy (Argentina)     53
4   The Circuito Magnifico (Chile)     75
5   In the Land of Lauca (Chile)     95
6   Lake Titicaca—An Andean Oasis (Bolivia)     121
7   Lost Worlds and Limitless Horizons (Venezuela)     143
8   Ten Degrees North of the Equator (Costa Rica)     169
9   Baja's Southern Reaches (Mexico)     191

SELECTED BIBLIOGRAPHY     215

# ACKNOWLEDGMENTS

THANKS TO Jack Miller for giving me a koan, Lan-Chile Airline's Chicago office for their patient assistance and enthusiastic support, the Consuls General of Chile and Bolivia in Chicago who were gracious representatives of their countries, and the friendly and knowledgeable staff at the South American Explorers Club.

Also Lost World Adventures, Montaña, Ríos Tropicales, and Baja Expeditions, adventure travel companies whose guides took obvious delight in showing others the natural wonders of their countries.

I owe a great debt to Carmel Huestis, my editor at Fulcrum, for seeing merit in this work. Thanks also to Bob Erickson, my neighbor and friend, who did the maps; and to Mike Peyton, who made sea kayaking in Baja a genuine delight, despite his avowed distaste for the heat.

A special note of gratitude to Judy Bradford, my wife and first editor, without whom the book could not have been written. She shared the journeys with me, was often forced into the role of interpreter, and didn't even disown me when, in Spanish, I accidentally told an acquaintance that she was my mother.

Finally, I want to acknowledge my sister Ronna and her family. During the time I was writing this book, I came to realize that my life is enriched not only by freedom and travel, but by the pain and sorrow, the joy and comfort of having those ties that bind.

# Introduction

AS I SIT AT MY CLUTTERED DESK in rural Illinois, tapping out these words on my computer, I am far away from the areas I write about in this book. I can sit back and reflect for a moment, unaffected by the rhythms, excitement, and, sometimes, frustrations of traveling.

I'm occasionally asked why I keep going down to South America, Central America, or Mexico when there is so much to see at home in North America. My first response is because things are so *different*, so entirely unfamiliar, so unexpected. Take buying a broom handle, for example—as mundane a chore as ever there was. In Punta Arenas, Chile, the search took half a day, poking into this shop and that as I was directed from one merchant to another. Instead of being upset over the loss of time, as I would have been at home, the task became a challenge, an opportunity to practice my Spanish and to learn more about this city on the Straits of Magellan. I finally did locate a broom handle, but I never was able to convince the clerk that I wanted the stout stick for hiking in the mountains.

Another reason for visiting Latin America is that its natural settings are among the most exotic and spellbinding on earth. From its rain forests to its coastal deserts, from its river basins to its mountain peaks, Latin America is a composite of superlative wonders. Within the nearly eight-thousand-mile stretch from Mexico to Cape Horn are the world's biggest river (the Amazon), its driest desert (the Atacama), its longest continuous mountain range (the Andes), and its highest waterfall (Angel Falls). And for someone whose passion is wildlife, I was continually delighted with the strange and wonderful creatures I found south of the border. South America boasts the greatest variety of life forms of all the continents, and new species are constantly being discovered.

On my first trip (to Patagonia), I found not only the rugged wilderness I was seeking but also a new way of appreciating the world. Maybe because I was so inexperienced, I was forced to rely on strangers, to be open to offers of assistance. And from that position of inferiority, I did not find (on the whole) people who were rude, or conniving, or deceitful. Instead, I found kindness and generosity and infectious joy. I enjoyed the cities as much as the backcountry—quite a turnaround for someone used to seeking solitude.

Latin America is a huge expanse, and I do not purport to know it well. Few foreign travelers do, since even today this fascinating region inspires myth, controversy, and speculation. Latin America's burgeoning population is pushing back its wilderness frontier, but despite an onslaught of deforestation and industrial development, it is still a far more virgin frontier than anything that exists in the continental United States. That fact is not being lost on developing Latin American countries who are desperately in need of tourist dollars. Many of the elements that hampered the economic development of Latin America are the very things that appeal most to visitors. Stretches of deep, untrammeled jungle and vast, lonely deserts, grassy plains, and mountain ranges still survive from Mexico to the tip of South America, as do the mysterious, nearly hidden ruins of cultures that may date back to the time of the Egyptians.

Wilderness preservation is spotty at best in Latin America, but progress is being made. South America alone claims more than 160 national parks and reserves, and there are scores of others in Central America and Mexico. At the turn of the century, these areas were unknown, out-of-the-way places, accessible only by weeks of arduous travel. Not so any more. Whether for good or ill, every area visited in this book, from the Baja peninsula to Isla Navarino on the Beagle Channel, can be reached within a couple of days of leaving the United States. Yet these same areas, particularly the *altiplanos* of Bolivia and northern Chile, and the Guyana Highlands in Venezuela, still seem more than a bit remote from a world of instant travel and communication.

My initial trip to South America led to another, then yet another—on foot, in canoe and kayak, and even by mule. These journeys are the basis of this book. The grandeur of Latin America's landscape and the friendliness of its people lie thousands of wandering miles away from me as I write. But I will encounter them again, in places I have never seen before. I know the joy of making new discoveries in the wild, and the sadness of having to leave so soon places so much enjoyed.

My only advice for those planning to visit Latin America's wildlands is to read as much as you can before you go (a selected bibliography appears in this book). Don't concentrate on where to find the least expensive hotel (as seemed to be the quest of many travelers we met along the way); read also about the cultures, the history, the wildlife. Hone up on the languages (or hope your companion knows Spanish better than you do). And, while you're likely to find hospitality, don't expect it. Plan your trip to be self-reliant; allow for changes and delays, and count on being confused much of the time. As they say in Spanish, *Vale la pena*, "it's worth the trouble."

# BAJA TO PATAGONIA

Glacier
Grey

ARGENTINA

Torres del Paine
Cuernos del Paine
Lago Pehoe
Lago del Toro
Rio Serrano
Mt. Balmaceda
Seno Ultima Esperanza

Lago de
Grey

Puerto Natales

Rio
Gallegos

CHILE

Straits of Magellan

Punta
Arenas

ISLA
GRANDE
DE TIERRA
DEL FUEGO

Cabo de Hornos

ATLANTIC OCEAN

PACIFIC OCEAN

N

# 1.

# PADDLING THROUGH PATAGONIA (CHILE)

WE WERE HALFWAY ACROSS Lago Pehoe, near the base of the Paine mountains in southern Chile, when a cold gust, immediately followed by a whispering roar, gave notice of a williwaw avalanching off the Andean peaks. "Paddle hard! Head to shore!" I yelled to Judy. Too late. In seconds, the calm blue Patagonian lake was furrowed with white foam.

Funnel spouts skipped and danced across the water. Clouds boiled up above mountainsides. "Faster!" I ordered. "Faster!" We paddled furiously toward a protected cove and were almost there when I heard a snap. Our two-person folding kayak suddenly became unmaneuverable.

I frantically unclipped the sprayskirt. The problem was obvious: A wire cable connected to the rudder assembly had popped loose. Without a rudder in these waves, the straight-tracking kayak was nearly impossible to turn into the wind.

The creaking wood-and-canvas boat wallowed in the middle of the lake. Steep curlers broke over the deck, dumping buckets of icy water into my lap. I barked instructions to Judy. She was in a better position to refasten the fouled cable at my feet. Handing me her paddle, she swiveled around in her bowseat and went to work. The whitecaps grew steeper. A gust almost tore both paddles from my hands. I scanned the shoreline for possible help, but the ridges and foothills were deserted and there were no other boats on the lake. Only an Andean condor wheeling overhead showed any interest in our predicament. The great black bird resembled a feathered crucifix crisscrossing the sky.

Another wave spilled overboard, drenching me from the head down. "Hurry up, will you?" I implored. My wife growled something unintelligible from under the deck. Finally, she straightened. Her long dark hair streamed back from her head; her bright-red rainjacket glistened with spray. "Okay, move!" she shouted, as I shoved a paddle back into her hands.

Inside the snug inlet, we slumped in our seats, humbled and chastised by the powerful and unpredictable winds. The boat nudged against the shore. Unclenching my grip on the paddle, I grabbed a stalk of grass undulating in the shallows and focused on my surroundings. Through sheets of rain I could make out the Horns of Paine looming more than a mile directly above. In the valley below the peaks was a moor of scarlet flowers and a thin fringe of trees bent nearly over.

The morning had been mellow: sipping hot cocoa while watching a family group of guanaco, the wild cousin of the llama and the alpaca, graze the soft rounded hillocks behind camp. Now we were soaked, disheartened, and not even close to where we wanted to be. But during the lulls in the wind I could hear the call of the lark and the trilling of an austral thrush. The ferocious howling and the sweet trilling were typical of the contrasts of Patagonia.

▲

A week earlier we had arrived in Punta Arenas, a large and well-developed city situated at the very end of the Chilean mainland, across the Straits of Magellan from Tierra del Fuego. Self-declared as the "southernmost city in the world," Punta Arenas (population 130,000), offers a blend of frontier atmosphere and urban amenities. With its tidy brick homes and fair-skinned residents, Punta Arenas looks more like New England or Scandinavia than Latin America. Founded in 1848, Punta Arenas might have remained nothing more than a small military town had it not been for the increasing use of steamships during the second half of the last century. Since the Panama Canal had not yet been built, Punta Arenas became a port of call for giant sailing ships and a coaling station for steamships rounding Cape Horn. Migrants, mostly of British and Yugoslavian ancestry, were part of the cargo. All around the city there are monuments honoring these early settlers and farmers who pioneered the area.

The locals say that if you wish to see Patagonia, all you need do is stand still on any street corner in Punta Arenas and it will blow past you. During our visit, the city suffered one of its worst hurricanes in years: Fishing boats were tossed inland; cars were turned over; we had to hang onto lampposts to keep from getting blown off our feet. I liked the place. Its location made it a convenient jumping-off point to the Patagonian marvels I had long dreamed of seeing.

In college I had read Darwin's *Voyage of the Beagle*—to my mind, one of the best travel books ever written. The scientist-explorer's keen eye for observation and his sharp, idiosyncratic mind bring alive the many exotic places and animals he encountered during his five-year voyage around the world. His account of Patagonia, virtually unknown to the outside world in the 1830s, always stuck with me. Still, I was over thirty before I seriously thought about traveling there.

But dreaming about adventure travel is one thing; transforming those dreams into reality is quite another. Judy and I had more than a dozen wilderness journeys to Alaska behind us, plus others to Africa and arctic Canada, but we were neophytes when it came to Latin America. Judy's sole excursion to a Spanish-speaking country had been a brief visit to Colombia, when the country was known more for its beautiful beaches, mountains, and coffee than for drug cartels and rampant terrorism. My only foray south of the border came during my senior year at the University of Arizona when a classmate and I haunted Mexico's Sierra Madre for a few weeks looking for vampire bats.

I started planning for the journey a full year in advance. What I learned sounded good. One source described Patagonia as Alaska at the bottom of the globe. Occupying the southern cone of South America, Patagonia is a huge area larger than Texas that is shared by Chile and Argentina. It is generally considered to be made up of the wedge of low, semiarid steppes that stretches south from the Pampas and east from the Andes to the Strait of Magellan, the channel that separates the island of Tierra del Fuego from the mainland. The first European to discover Patagonia was Ferdinand Magellan of Portugal, for whom the strait is named. In 1519, he sailed down the Atlantic coast of what is now southern Argentina, searching for a passage to the Pacific. The sailors named the place *patagones*, a word that means "big feet," possibly in reference to a race of large Indians they encountered whose footwear consisted of bulky skin coverings wrapped around their feet.

My research also revealed that Patagonia offers some of the most monotonous scenery in Latin America, as well as some of the most spectacular. Several of the world's finest mountain ranges lie in the western margin of the region, along with glaciers, forests, and enormous lakes. I decided this was where we should go—by kayak, if possible—and I started doing my homework.

I contacted the Chilean consul general in Chicago, LAN-Chile Airlines, my U.S. senators, and anyone else I thought could supply me with information, letters of introduction, and general assistance. I joined the South American Explorers Club and eagerly studied its members' trip reports—interesting stuff for trekkers and general sightseers but of limited value for someone who wanted to paddle through Patagonia.

I found a series of articles about Patagonia by Jack Miller, a mountaineer and all-around adventurer from Colorado. He was the one who suggested to me (after much correspondence) the route that we were following. I still have never met him, but were it not for his encouragement, I'm not sure I would have ever begun my travels in South America.

▲

It took nine hours by bus to cover the 250 miles north from Punta Arenas to Torres del Paine (pronounced TOR-ehs del PIE-nay) National Park. We passed through a dun-colored, windswept plain reminiscent of eastern Wyoming or Montana. The few trees and bushes were stunted and twisted by the wind. Isolated, weather-worn homesteads were the only signs of civilization, except for a few small inns and the intermittent police checkpoints. Occasionally we passed another vehicle, but for the greater part of the journey the land seemed empty.

If I needed a reminder that we were in a foreign land, however, the sight of large flightless birds, South America's version of the African ostrich, easily sufficed. Flocks of ñandú, known also as Darwin's rhea, dashed helter-skelter across the plains when we rumbled near. At other times, they remained at the roadside, pecking at the grass stubble as calmly as overgrown chickens.

The entrance to Parque Nacional Torres del Paine was heralded by a simple wooden sign alongside the gravel road. A little farther was a small booth manned by two park rangers attired in brown trousers and shirts, black leather boots, and short-brimmed caps. A handful of backpackers stepped off the bus, paid a small entrance fee, and began slogging up a nearby trail. The rest of us signed the register and returned to our seats. The bus rolled on.

The landscape grew wilder and more spectacular with each passing mile. The road wound west between undulating hills whose folds contained two large lakes: Nordenskjold, a turquoise blue with the Paine mountains beyond, and Sarmiento, over thirty miles wide. A light rain started to fall, flattening the dust and casting rainbows over the countryside. Paine's dark, shining mountains grew steadily in size. I craned my neck to see the granite peaks, slender and sharp as fangs, poking through the ragged clouds.

I had heard that Torres del Paine is the sort of park against which all other parks can be measured. Indeed, the place had the magnificence of a Yosemite, a Yellowstone, or a Glacier without the intrusiveness of road traffic, curio shops, and crowds. Established in 1959 with little fanfare, the nearly six-hundred-thousand-acre Chilean park straddles the central spine of the Andes, thus encompassing one of Latin America's most unspoiled areas. Climbers worldwide have long been drawn to the spires of sheer stone that rise more than a mile above the southern Patagonian steppes. But this United Nations biosphere reserve is also noted for its less lofty attributes, including glacial lakes of varying sizes and colors, trout-filled rivers and streams, meadows and forested hills, as well as herds of guanaco, the elusive puma, flocks of pink flamingo, and condors and rheas, amongst much other wildlife. Our plan called for spending a few days hiking the foothills in Paine, an acclimatization of sorts, before beginning our "real" trip: paddling from the base of the Paine mountains to the sea.

The bus delivered us to the Hotel Pehoe, which is located about fourteen miles within the park. Built on a tiny island in Lago Pehoe and connected to the mainland by a wooden footbridge, the inn is small and simple and offers a stunning view of the mountains over the lake. The few remaining passengers had reservations there, but Judy and I were headed to an established campground about a mile away. A mile may not seem like a formidable hike, especially for a couple of relatively fit thirty-five-year olds about to embark on a journey into the wilderness. But with about 230 pounds of gear between us, which included three weeks' worth of food and the folding kayak, it was far more preferable to take the bus. The driver clearly let us know that the hotel was the end of the line; however, he acquiesced when Judy and I begged for a ride to the campground. We had no trouble finding a campsite. The thirty or so clearings were only half-occupied. After lugging our gear from the road to a spot near the lake, we pitched the tent beside a screen of wind-flagged shrubs and gnarly beech trees. To the north, appearing to leap into the clouds from the floor of the valley, lay the Cuernos del Paine (Paine Horns, 8,530 feet), two massive peaks of pinkish-gray granite made exceptionally striking by their steep, slightly concave sides and caps of several hundred feet of onyx-black slate. Overlooking the Cuernos was Paine Grande (10,007 feet), the highest mountain in the park. The contrast of the stark Paine massif with the opal-green water was dramatic.

It was ten o'clock by the time we finished dinner and squared everything away for the night. Evenings are long at this high latitude in January, the height of the Patagonian summer. Under a roseate sky, we crawled into our sleeping bags, exhausted from our long day of travel. From outside the nylon walls came the sounds of fellow campers cutting firewood, softly playing guitars, and conversing in Spanish. For the first time since leaving our rural Illinois home I began to truly relax. As far as I was concerned, the most difficult part of our trip was just getting here; now it was time for fun.

▲

We woke at 8:30 A.M., which is unspeakably late for me, but not for Judy, the night-owl. In four years of marriage, we still had not managed to synchronize our biological clocks. This morning, though, we were both feeling groggy until we squirmed around in our bags and unzipped the tent flap. The spectacle before us was as rousing as a faceful of cold water: the Cuernos shone gemlike through a dark curtain of clouds; patches of blue sky snapped open and shut, beautiful but menacing.

I threw on my clothes and stepped outside to reinforce the tent guylines and to secure any loose odds and ends that could blow away. Not five minutes later we were in the grip of what was to be our first of many Patagonian williwaws, or sudden fierce windstorms. The flimsy hedgerow offered scant protection against the squall. Our dome-shaped tent rocked and shuddered, bending the aluminum poles close to the breaking point. The north face VE-24 is built for adverse conditions, but from past experiences in the arctic I knew that it could be flattened, even rolled. We braced our backs against the vibrating walls, hoping that the williwaw would be short-lived.

Ten minutes passed, a half hour. If anything, the wind grew more violent. We were about to settle in for a long, desperate siege when suddenly the gale sputtered and died. An eerie calm returned to the campground. I heard shouting, laughing, zippers sliding, car doors slamming. Someone from a neighboring campsite strummed a cheerful tune on a guitar, another broke out in song.

"I can't imagine why everyone's so cheerful," I said, peeking out the door. Our tent was the only one still standing. The others, mostly simple A-frame models, were squashed flat with their occupants wiggling inside them.

Later, after breakfast, the birth of a seventeen-foot kayak from a couple of nondescript duffle bags attracted a small crowd. The adults looked on quietly, but the children's curiosity got the better of them; their delighted giggles made me feel as if I were putting on a magic show. Slowly, the kayak's wooden skeleton frame materialized out of a jumble of girders, ribs, and rods that snapped together. The assembled unit was then slipped into the canvas-decked and rubber-hulled superstructure. Final touches included inflating the air chambers (which run the length of the boat and make it virtually unsinkable), installing the rudder and foot-pedals, fastening the seats and backrests, and lashing on a spare break-down paddle. A half hour later, Judy and I stood beside our trusty German-made Klepper. First manufactured in 1907, Klepper boats similar to ours have proven themselves on expeditions worldwide. First a tent that survived the williwaw, now a boat-in-a-bag. What other tricks could this gringo pull out of his pack?

We were busy stuffing gear under the deck when a yellow motorcycle whined into the campground. Straddling the knobby-tired dirt bike was a man about my age dressed in the familiar brown park uniform. "*Buenos días*," the dark, muscular ranger said as he strolled up to us and surveyed our gear. "I see you are about to go on a journey. Do you mind telling me where?"

The ranger listened attentively as Judy and I summarized our route in basic conversational Spanish. Using a topographic map, we explained that we wanted to explore the western side of Lago Pehoe for a couple of days, then paddle back down the lake to the Río Paine, which would quickly lead us to Lago del Toro and the head of the Río Serrano. About forty miles miles long and hemmed in by mountains, the Serrano would empty us into Seno Ultima Esperanza, or Last Hope Sound, which we'd then follow for forty more miles to the seaport town of Puerto Natales. We had allotted three weeks for the trip—sufficient time, we figured, even for some side trips and weather delays.

The ranger wrinkled his brow and nodded thoughtfully when we finished. Being a park ranger of sorts myself, I sensed what he was thinking: The Río Serrano and Last Hope Sound are rarely frequented; no place for a couple of inexperienced kayakers. One kayaker, an American, had already disappeared without a trace in these waters. Do these people know what they're doing, or will we have to mount a search in a month or so when *they*, too, turn up missing?

"*Bueno*," the ranger finally said. "Sounds good." Swinging a leg over his bike, he instructed us to report to the park administrative center at the edge of Lago del Toro before heading down the Río Serrano. "I'll radio your itinerary to my supervisors, but when you get there you'll have to tell them again and fill out some forms." Shrugging, he added in English, "There is much red rope."

As soon as the ranger was gone, we slithered the heavily laden kayak off the shingle beach and onto the lake. Judy wiggled inside the cockpit first. At five feet four inches she was the optimum size for a fully loaded Klepper, unlike my own six-foot-two-inch frame, which was cramped among an assortment of dry bags and gear. A Chileno camper we had befriended gave us a helping shove as we waved goodbye.

After years of kayaking together, we automatically reached a steady paddling rhythm—pull with the bottom hand, push with the top, Judy setting the pace. The Paine mountains grew in stature at each stroke. I began to annoy my partner with frequent requests to stop paddling so I could take another photograph, but the range of light never looked the same twice. Entire peaks were visible from base to summit, with billowy clouds drifting across the top. Through a notch in the massif I could see the tips of three monolithic towers. These fingers of steep, sheer stone—the *torres* from which the park received its name—are magnets for climbers from all over the world.

The big picture was so grand it was a relief to focus on small things closer to earth. A kestrel-like falcon hovered above a clump of golden grass, waiting for a mouse or insect to appear underwing. Ducks and geese dabbled in the shallows for aquatic vegetation. A pair of amorous, long-necked grebes swam past, more interested in each other than our boat. And working their way from branch to branch among the wind-stunted thickets were small songbirds: flycatchers, thrushes, wrens, blackbirds, sparrows. Unable to locate a proper field guide for the region, I was frustrated not to know their names.

Gouged by glaciers into the base of the mountains during the Ice Age, Lago Pehoe is only about two miles across and five miles long. Thus our first stint on the water lasted just a few hours. By midafternoon we had camp set up at the far side of the lake near a meadow surrounded by rolling open foothills. This lazy day of paddling suited us fine. We traded rubber boots for running shoes and went for a hike.

It took an hour to reach the ridgeline overlooking camp. Standing on the flat treeless bench, wiping my face with my tee shirt, I declared that there was no finer weather on Earth than a calm and sunny midsummer day in the Patagonian Andes. Reclining on a moss-covered rock ledge to soak up the warmth, Judy was in total agreement. "Not even a mosquito," she sighed contentedly.

I scoured the area with binoculars, examining the high peaks, the grassy hills dotted with small ponds and crossed by rivers, and the groves of beech in sheltered valleys. It appeared as if we had the entire park to ourselves, but ambling back to camp we discovered otherwise. The *refugio*, or mountain hut, located a few hundred yards inland from our tent, was now occupied. One of five refugios in the park, the hut was a simple log structure with wooden bunks and a wood-burning stove. A young mop-haired man sat on a stool in front, making repairs on a combat boot. He greeted us in heavily accented English when we walked past.

"How long you been in Paine?" he asked. "Not long," we replied. "Oh, then you must have missed the big storm." He told us of a hard-hitting gale that raked the area a week earlier. "It was a bastard. Lasted several days," he said, pausing to light a cigarette. "Everyone was wet and shivering. This place was so crowded that my girlfriend and I had to sleep sitting up on the muddy dirt floor."

"Sounds like fun," I said.

"It was okay," the man shrugged. "Are you staying here tonight? I'm by myself. My girlfriend left. There's plenty of room."

Some people love the camaraderie of it, but I'm not enthused by the thought of sleeping with a bunch of strangers in a cramped building if I don't have to. "Thanks, but we've got a tent," I explained.

Back at camp, we plopped down beside the kayak and dug out one of the freeze-dried dinners we had brought from home. Lasagna, my favorite. A chocolate bar and mint tea would be dessert. It didn't seem like much, but we never lost weight.

From our "dining room" we watched the sun set over the Cordillera del Paine and saw the massif turn fiery orange in the alpenglow. The fading light brought out the wildlife as well. A pale and ghostlike barn owl coursed over the meadow and perched on a dead tree a short distance away, blending with the background until only its heart-shaped white face remained. A black-and-white *zorrillo,*

Chile's version of a skunk, snuffled past in the spiky grass, its fluffy tail billowing against the cool mountain breeze.

But it was the guanaco that made my day. We were enjoying our last sips of tea when a solitary big male gamboled past. This relative of the camel, and tallest of South American mammals, survived until recently throughout the Andes and the west coast of South America in areas ranging from sea level to an elevation of thirteen thousand feet. Due to unregulated hunting and competition from livestock, its numbers have been so severely reduced that it no longer exists in many of its former habitats. The Paine mountains are one of its last major strongholds. With its tawny brown-and-white coat, periscopelike neck, and thin legs, I was struck more by the guanaco's grace than its oddness. The animal assumed a rigid pose, looking us over with an air of haughty intelligence, its soft dark ears erect. Then, with a high-pitched bray, it slipped silently away.

Dawn broke overcast and breezy. We slipped on pile pants and jackets and crawled outside into spotlight shafts of sun. Instant oatmeal and cups of hot chocolate erased the chill as we prepared for our hike to Grey Glacier, seven miles away.

The trail leading to the glacier was well worn and easy to follow. We passed through a dry rimrock canyon replete with small bands of guanacos in the brushy draws and condors soaring in the sky above. Soon the trail entered a dense forest of evergreen and deciduous beeches; a hushed and eerie place dripping with moisture and jungly with moss and ferns. Green-backed hummingbirds no larger than my thumb buzzed by Judy's red jacket. By contrast, thrushes and other drab brown birds melted into the darkest parts of the forest at our approach.

Climbing higher, we emerged from the dim forest onto slippery mountain ridges. The trees and shrubs grew smaller here, contorted into grotesque shapes by constant battles with the wind. A sudden beating of heavy wings startled us. Disturbed from its roost, a solitary condor staggered into the wind and whirled overhead. We were amazed that a bird weighing as much as twenty-five pounds could fly at all. It looked as big as a sailplane.

Grey Glacier is today a mere remnant of its original size, but ample reward for our long hike. Born in the southern Andean ice cap, the mile-wide glacier flowed down like a river between the shoulders of two mountains. At its snout, where the ice cliff was several hundred feet high and blue crevasses glimmered through the mists, the glacier reached down into the water: fifteen miles of ice disgorging a procession of icebergs that floated across Lago Grey's milky surface.

We ducked into a pair of small ice caves nearly hidden along the glacier's leading edge. The dripping caverns emanated a cobalt-blue light from deep within their scalloped ceilings and frosted sides. Suddenly the air reverberated with a sharp crack like a rifle shot, followed closely by booming thunder. We scurried out of the cave and made a hasty retreat to the trail, reaching it just in time to watch as a cube the size of a four-story house broke away and collapsed into the water. A shower of ice and spray was fired out sideways like an explosion. Breaking waves jostled the floating pack ice.

Feeling very tired and rather footsore, we didn't make it back to camp until nearly dark. The hike convinced me that I wanted to plan a return visit to Paine. According to the *South American Handbook*, that bible-sized guide to travel in Latin America, the hike around the Paine range is one of the best scenic walking tours on the continent. The loop trail was said to be endowed with mountains, lakes, waterfalls, and glaciers—clearly a fine place to backpack.

Later, ensconced in our synthetic cocoons, shielded from the cold rain falling outside, Judy listened as I jabbered on about this future trek. There were logistical and equipment considerations, expense, time off from our jobs. Finally, she tuned me out by pulling up her hood and turning on her side. "The *circuito* sounds great, Lar, really," she groaned. "But how about we finish this trip first, all right?"

▲

It had been three days since the williwaw blew us off the water. Pinned down by a succession of storms, we were still holed up in the same cove along Lago Pehoe's north shore, a disappointing two miles from our last camp near the refugio. We were concerned about the delay and eager to get moving. Our destination was a long way away.

We clipped the sprayskirt onto the gunwales, snugged up our lifejackets, and shoved off. The lake was smooth until we reached the mouth of the inlet. It was blowing quite hard from the west and swells hissed under the boat. There was no protection along the rocky shoreline, and I felt hesitant about making a direct crossing. Still, we couldn't stay where we were and I couldn't stomach going back.

We surged ahead, cranking out smooth, steady paddle strokes, marshalling our energy for the long haul across the lake. Looking over my shoulder, I watched as our tiny campsite cove receded. Ahead, the waves began to build. Clear water lapped over the deck and squalls shrouded the distant mountains. A rainbow curved across the lake and the light reflected from the water on the blades of the wooden paddles.

The boat surfed forward atop each crest, followed by a stall as it slipped back into the trough. "This is kind of fun!" Judy hollered when we gained the middle of the lake. I thought so too, but not for a second did I lose my respect for the wind. I had been told of three British climbers whose inflatable raft had capsized while attempting to cross nearby Lago Nordenskjold. None of them survived.

The wet ride came to an end when we pulled ashore at Pehoe's southernmost arm. Now the real work began. We had to carry everything over a hill and around a twenty-foot-high waterfall that separates the lake from the lower Río Paine. Unlike open canoes, sea kayaks are ill-designed for portage; our Klepper had no carrying yoke and must have weighed eighty-five pounds empty. It took four carries and a couple of hours before we got the boat and all our gear across the quarter-mile divide.

Stopping only for a quick snack of trail food, we loaded back up and pointed the kayak downstream. It felt wonderful to be on the water again, especially water that wasn't about to erupt at any moment. The Río Paine was wide and smooth, its gentle current the only thing that distinguished it from a narrow lake; however, our peaceful float between low canyon walls ended too soon. After a couple of miles, we entered a long, wide arm of Lago del Toro close to the southeastern boundary of the park. Near a small pier on the right bank was a cluster of old wooden buildings, barns, outbuildings, corrals, and grazing horses. Judging from the peeling paint, the structures had long ago been painted bright red.

On the dock a small boy, the son of a park employee, informed us that the area was a working ranch before being bought by CONAF, the Chilean governmental agency that administers parks and reserves. He said that the administrative center for Torres del Paine was a short walk down the road. We thanked him and were about to pay a visit to the park office—when shyly and in Spanish— he asked us a two-part question: Was our boat a submarine and did we want to sell it?

"The chief ranger is in a staff meeting," the receptionist said when we announced who we were and where we were going. "Please wait. He wants to meet you."

Two hours later, the chief ranger welcomed us into his spartanly furnished office. He and his aides immediately put to rest our anxieties about bureaucratic blockades. There were the obligatory permits to fill out but the rangers were mostly concerned for our safety. They pinpointed on our map the location of a dangerous cascade and other noteworthy landmarks on the Río Serrano. They also radioed the port captain at Puerto Natales of our expected arrival.

The rangers were interested in the folding kayak. I asked the chief if he wanted to go for a quick spin. He was a quick study on the use of the double-bladed paddle, but when the waves slopped over the deck, soaking his dress uniform, I could tell he was ready to hit the shore. After a brief photo session, Judy and I shook hands all around and waved goodbye. A minute later we were off the lake and heading west on the Río Serrano, a deep, milky-blue river known for its remoteness and record-sized brown trout.

The first few miles of the Serrano took us past long, sweeping grasslands that melded into the distant Paine mountains. At every crook and bend, flocks of ducks and geese drummed into the air, quacking and gabbling then settling back down when we cruised past. A pair of black-necked swans swam lazily out of our way, their cygnets riding safely on their backs between their wings. There were buff-necked ibises and some new species of grebe, half the size of those on Lago Pehoe, that quickly dove when we glided too close.

Within the hour we came upon a developed campground on the right bank. A couple of men fished from shore. A few families huddled behind tarpaulin lean-tos, cooking dinner over wood fires. A forest of beech offered shelter from the wind, and there were clean, grassy clearings where we could pitch a tent. "Might as well stay here," I suggested. "It's not exactly the wilderness, but it's six o'clock and what I see looks pretty good."

Later that night, by the light of my headlamp, I scribbled down the day's highlights in my journal. I couldn't have been more content. I was warm and dry in my sleeping bag, well fed, and had just spent several hours with one of the most hospitable families I had ever met. Father, mother, grandmother, and three teenage children had driven up from their home in Punta Arenas on a camping holiday and had virtually adopted us as soon as we arrived. Grandma kept dishing out hot biscuits until I felt I was going to explode.

Judy jotted a few notes of her own, then riffled through her Spanish-English dictionary, looking up words that she had come across or stumbled over during the day. "It's so frustrating," she lamented. "I know my Spanish is improving, but sometimes I feel like such an idiot! I couldn't understand half of what the family said, and I'm sure they didn't understand me very well."

*Judy standing at the shore of the Río Serrano next to the Klepper and gazing back at the Cuernos del Paine (Paine Horns, 8,530 feet).*

I was sympathetic. I had spent at least an hour each day for six months before the trip trying to teach myself Spanish out of a book, and I still had trouble getting a cup of coffee at a restaurant.

▲

The Río Serrano twisted west, then south. There was a sprinkling of snow on the tops of the hills nearby which hid the peaks of the Andes. Ahead of us was a steep valley of forest and moor and bog, of wilderness and uncertainties.

Since leaving the campground earlier that morning, we had been searching for the mouth of the river whose source was the iceberg-choked Lago Grey. I was beginning to think we had missed the Río Grey among the brushy islands and braided channels, when suddenly an abrupt line formed on the Serrano with chalk-colored water merging in from the right bank. A couple of days ago we were standing at the glacier where this water was born. Now we would follow it to the ocean.

The Serrano grew wider and wilder as we drew closer to Mount Donoso, a 4,818-foot peak to the west. Donoso's lower slopes supported dense stands of southern or austral beech, a deciduous tree with a copper tinge to the leaves. There were also many smaller flowering trees and bushes, such as the aptly named fire bush with its red blossoms and the calafate bush with its yellow flowers and edible blue berries. The saying is that if you eat calafate berries you will always return. I was eating them by the handful despite the fact that they weren't very sweet.

The spectacle of the surrounding mountains was exhilarating, but I was wary of the power they could unleash without warning. Hidden among the peaks, forty-three hundred feet above sea level, was the Patagonian ice cap, forming the second largest expanse of ice outside the polar regions and one of the least explored wildernesses in the world. Its two sections almost fill a three-hundred-mile trough between twin cordilleras. Great pockets of cold air trapped on the icy plateau are notorious for triggering fierce winds. Many times the Serrano's surface would suddenly smoke with whitecaps. All we could do was hug the deck and hang onto our paddles until there was a lull.

It was close to sunset when we landed near the mouth of the Río Tyndall, a braided glacial stream that has formed a mile-wide gravel bar covered with long green ribbons of shrubs and small trees. A couple of miles away, just inside the park's southwest boundary, lay

Lago Tyndall, which we couldn't see, and the Tyndall Glacier, which we could. The serrated lobe of blue-white ice filled the wrinkles of the mountainside—a shrinking reminder of the Ice Age.

We set up camp inside a grove of dwarf beech whose short gnarled trunks leaned over beds of ferns and purple violets. The upper boughs of the trees were draped with lichens that fluttered in the breeze. And some trees were festooned with manes of a yellowish-orange parasite, *Myzodendron punctulatum*, a flowering plant of the same order as mistletoe. There was something spooky about this place. We stood inside the small alcove, not speaking, listening. For what? The forest seemed empty of animal life. Yet etched in the damp sand near the kayak was a large four-toed pug print that couldn't have been more than a few hours old. I kneeled for a closer look. "Puma," I announced reverently. "No doubt about it."

In nearly twenty years of roaming the North American backcountry, I had seen my share of grizzly bears, wolves, and wolverines, but the closest I had been to a wild mountain lion was the time I helped release one into the desert when I was a student at the University of Arizona, and I figured that really didn't count. Except for the jaguar, the puma is the largest feline in the Americas, and the widest-ranging. Although its numbers have been greatly reduced, the big tawny cat can still be found from British Columbia to the tip of mainland South America; and despite continued persecution it appears to be holding its own in the southern Andes. I'd have to be incredibly lucky to spot a puma—or *león*, as it is called—but that didn't stop me from scanning the surrounding wall of vegetation, looking for a set of amber eyes staring back.

That night I almost did come to believe that the woods were haunted. I was awakened from a deep sleep by a harsh noise inches from my head. In my confused state, I thought Judy was snoring or having a nightmare. I prodded her with my elbow, hoping that would muffle her.

"Stop it!" she responded angrily.

"I thought you were making some strange sounds."

"Funny, I thought it was *you* making strange ..."

Suddenly, a piercing yip! yip! yip! cut short her words. Grabbing my headlamp, I went outside. It took only a moment to unmask the stranger: a *zorro*, or grey fox, sat on its haunches behind a fallen tree. The size of a small dog, the animal seemed indifferent to my presence. I walked in an arc toward its glowing eyes, which were reflecting the beam of my flashlight. I got within ten feet, and then I made the wrong move by swatting a mosquito on my neck. In a heartbeat, the fox vanished into a hole in the ground. As the mosquitoes hummed merrily around my head, I dove back into the tent, the mystery solved.

▲

A cold front pushed through during the night, bringing with it a light rain and brisk winds. But since this was a layover day we could afford to be lazy: no packing a wet tent; no squashing gear into too-small stuff sacks; no scraped knuckles squeezing everything into the kayak. Snuggled in our sleeping bags, we spent a few pleasant hours reading paperbacks, completely lost in someone else's adventures instead of our own.

By about eleven o'clock we decided that rain or no rain we were going to get in some hiking. We tossed some stuff into daypacks and carried the kayak to the river's edge. A quick ferry across the Río Tyndall brought us to a gravel bar. Nearby was a dense clump of bushes where we stashed the boat. Without the Klepper it would be a long walk back to civilization.

I glanced at the map for a final compass check. Three miles due west was Lago Tyndall. We planned to spend the day there looking for wildlife. I had noticed some cow tracks in the soft sand; if there were stray cattle maybe there was also a puma.

A hundred yards into our hike we saw them, or rather they saw us. Three men on horseback, riding abreast, broke out of the forest and galloped directly toward us.

I don't know why, but I immediately thought the worst. Maybe it was because these scruffy *caballeros* were not your typical dude ranch cowboys. Or maybe it was simply natural to be wary of strangers carrying machetes. In any case, before we could take evasive action (running for the kayak was an option) the horsemen reined up in front of us and blocked our escape. But instead of asking for our dollars, the trio deftly dismounted their steeds and walked over to shake our hands.

Our new acquaintances looked as though they had sprouted right from the earth in their drab, well-worn wool and denim. The spokesman of the group was a short, stocky, black-bearded fellow with two missing front teeth and an enormous bone-handled sheath-knife strapped to his belt. He asked where we were from.

"Ah, *norteamericanos!*" he nodded approvingly to my reply.

"Illinois," I specified.

"Illinois?" he repeated quizzically.

"Near Chicago," I added helpfully, and waited for the usual response.

"Ahh! Chee-CA-go!" he cried. "Al Capone!" All at once he and his mob blasted the air with imaginary Tommy guns.

As soon as the "bullets" stopped flying, we explained where and how we were traveling. The three horsemen solemnly nodded their heads. "It is very unusual to see people in these parts," the leader said as they followed us back to the river to check out the kayak. "We were rounding up stray cows when we spotted you. You are easier to spot than the cows."

The chief gaucho smiled when he saw the Klepper. He remarked that five years ago a man from New York City and his three sons had paddled similar boats down the Serrano and had stopped in at his *estancia*, about five or six miles downstream, just outside the park's southernmost border. "I have always wondered about them, whether they made it safely out," he said. "I never did receive the postcard they said they would mail me."

Menacing dark clouds rolled in. The rain, which had stopped, resumed. "We must go," the rancher said, gathering his horse. "But please, I would like you to meet my family." He pointed to a distant bend in the river, near the base of a solitary, dome-shaped mountain. "My wife will be happy to see you."

The Chilean cowboys saddled up and leaned over to shake our hands goodbye. "*Hasta luego,*" they called out, wheeling their horses around and riding into the forest.

▲

The morning ushered in overcast skies that seemed to promise more rain. We ate our granola bars in the tent and quickly packed, eager to get back on the river.

Our pace slowed considerably as we drifted down with the current. Large flocks of upland geese, white and grey and chestnut, honked and lifted off the water as we passed, settling back down on gravel bars and backwater pools. On a deadwood snag at the river's edge, a dozen cormorants stood shoulder to shoulder, jostling each other for room. There were also many kinds of duck: teal, widgeon, pintail, shovelers. Though I didn't know the species, I felt right at home since waterfowl management is a large part of my job along the Illinois River.

As we approached Mount Balmaceda, a sixty-six hundred foot peak draped with glaciers and gossamer waterfalls, we caught sight of a small white house set back from the right bank. The question of whether or not to stop had been nagging us since we received the rancher's invitation; we had no idea what was socially "correct" in Patagonia. Was the rancher merely being polite when he asked us to his home, as is frequently the case in our own culture, with the assumption we wouldn't show? And if the offer was sincere, would his wife be expecting us? If she was, then would it be rude not to stop?

We tied the kayak to shore and climbed the bank. The house was a hundred feet away. No one was around. "It's not too late to leave," I joked, taking a step backward. "Oh, yes it is," Judy replied, grabbing my arm. From a chicken shed out back scrambled a small, stout woman dressed in black wool pants and a loose grey sweatshirt that barely concealed a huge bosom. Two rosy-cheeked children squeezed through the door behind her; a young teenage girl and a boy about nine.

"*Buenos días, buenos días,*" the woman chirped, in friendly greeting. "My husband is away, but please, come inside and rest; you must be hungry."

The rancher's wife smothered us with hospitality. We shared hot biscuits, black coffee, and conversation while sitting around the kitchen table of their tidy frame house.

"We have a good life here," the mother said, pulling more biscuits from the wood stove and coating them with honey and jam. "It is hard work, but much better than living in town. The only thing I don't like is that my children have to go away for school; nine months of the year they live with relatives in Puerto Natales."

Currently at home on summer vacation, and obviously enamored with country life, the daughter smiled bashfully when she explained that to get to school she and her brother have to row a boat across the river, ride a horse for four hours to the nearest dirt road, then meet a vehicle for the long drive to town.

I asked if it gets lonely out here, miles from the nearest neighbor, with no television, no telephone, no two-way radio, no electricity. The mother shook her head. "Oh, no," she said. "I have my music for company when the children are gone and my husband is out working." She nodded toward a small battery-powered AM radio belting out scratchy pop tunes in English and Spanish from a station in Argentina.

The mother asked us to spend the night. It was tempting, but the port captain in Puerto Natales was expecting us within the week and we weren't certain how many more days our trip would take.

Judy and I were about to leave when the children asked us to wait. They ran off to a corral behind the house and a moment later came galloping up on their horses. "Would you like to ride them?" they asked, as they hopped off. I balked. I hadn't sat on a horse since I was ten years old, and that was at an amusement park where the pitiful nags were led around in circles. Furthermore, these feisty mounts didn't have saddles, and I was rather uncertain what to say to a horse in Spanish.

"Go on, Jude," I insisted. "You've got more horse experience." With the mother and children giggling at our clumsiness, I gave Judy a lift by pushing on her butt. "Heecht! This is so embarrassing!" she muttered as she struggled up onto the mare.

I wasn't exactly the Cisco Kid either. It took me three tries to get mounted, and once on top I didn't know what to do. Fortunately, the boy did. He took the reins and led me in circles around the front yard, exactly like they did when I was ten years old.

▲

We left the Río Serrano behind the following afternoon when we entered Puerto Toro, a wide-mouthed bay off Last Hope Sound. The contrast between the river and the sea was distinct. The forest rimming the sound was a deeper green and virtually impenetrable. The mountains rose higher and steeper. The wind brought with it a whiff of kelp and the taste of salt spray.

In no time at all we were humbled. A brief foray into open water resulted in a tense struggle to regain shore when sudden, powerful downblasts raked the bay. Waves sloshed over the cockpit. The boat pitched and yawed. A wall of swirling mist enveloped us, eclipsing the sun.

"Lar, I'm scared!" shouted my wife, who has faced off Alaskan grizzly bears, canoed whitewater rivers, and jumped out of airplanes. "Let's go back!"

"I'm trying to!" I yelled as another sea spout spiraled over us, driving stinging rain into my face. "Paddle hard. Give it everything you've got!"

It took fifteen minutes to cover a hundred yards, fighting the williwaw every foot of the way. We were sapped of strength when we finally reached the leeward side of Mount Balmaceda. Its bulk provided us with temporary shelter and a chance to rethink our plans.

I was angry with the wind, and frustrated because I was powerless against it. I couldn't think of another time when the wind had been such a potent force during one of our wilderness journeys. I wanted to make a side trip to Lago Azul, a glacier-ringed cove at the end of Last Hope Sound, ten miles to the west. But with conditions as they were, it was clear that we might have to postpone, even cancel, paddling deeper into the mountains.

We had lunch at the outflow of an ice-cold torrent, its source a tiny blue lake perched a few hundred feet away beneath a hanging glacier. Despite our most recent battle, it was hard to be glum as we picked through our bags of M&Ms, raisins, and nuts—not with scenery as magnificent as this. Several miles wide, Last Hope Sound glittered blue and inviting one moment, lead-grey and forbidding the next. Rugged mountains swathed in gloomy, wet forests rose from the sound to an elevation of two thousand feet, where they gave way to alpine tundra, bare rock, and finally to snow-covered peaks. It was a lonely scene, an utterly primitive place. The last thing I expected was another human being.

"*Hola!*" came a voice behind us. I dropped my precious bag of trail mix in surprise. A tall, thin man dressed in oily coveralls and carrying a five-gallon plastic bucket stood a few feet away; his approach had been drowned out by the gurgling of the stream. After filling the bucket with clear runoff, he told us that he was from the *21 de Mayo*, a boat that takes tour groups from Puerto Natales to the Balmaceda Glacier during the summer months. "We're moored at a jetty about a hundred meters away," he said. "You probably didn't hear us arrive because of the wind." He added that the boat almost turned back several times because of the choppy sea.

"Well," the deckhand said, grabbing the bucket. "I must serve lunch." He laughed as if he had just told a joke, and then explained that most of the passengers were seasick.

"This is too weird," Judy said after our visitor had left. I agreed. We had to go see this mysterious tourist boat.

The deckhand had already alerted the captain about us, so he wasn't caught off-guard by a couple of brightly garbed gringos appearing suddenly out of the woods. The tour group was on shore, looking a little green, poking listlessly at sandwiches and sipping cokes.

Since the captain had done many successful trips on Seno Ultima Esperanza, we thought we could get some information about our route and any hazards we might encounter. Maybe it was a lack of understanding, but each of my queries was met with the same reply: "*No problema.*"

The captain tooted the boat horn three times to alert his passengers that it was time to leave. "You want to come with us?" he asked. "No charge." It would have been so easy to say yes: We'd be back in civilization by nightfall; no more dreaded wind. We declined and thanked him for the offer.

The captain shrugged his shoulders and went about his business. The tourists—Germans, Swiss, a few Japanese—stared at us as they reboarded. I wasn't sure whether they admired our adventurous spirit or thought we were crazy. The *21 de Mayo* chugged away from shore and entered the wind-whipped sound. The boat's bow lifted and plunged and rolled. Plumes of white spray shot high over the wheelhouse. The topdeck was empty except for a few brave souls who hung onto the rail and leaned over the side.

▲

"I'm getting sick of this," I complained, out of sorts from nearly forty straight hours in the tent. After breakfast, I donned my parka and bolted outside into the pelting rain, next to the same glacial torrent where we ran into the deckhand. The seascape was the same; windswept and whitecapped. From the looks of things, we would be stuck here for another day at least. I was regretting our refusal of Captain Alvarez's offer of a ride. A good hot restaurant meal and a soothing hot shower were creeping into my fantasies.

Together, Judy and I ambled through the dripping forest, stretching our legs and clearing our minds. A courageous little tree-creeper, its feathers ruffled against the rain, scolded us loudly from its perch on a branch. If a bird can look miserable, this one did. A pair of Patagonian firecrowns—a species of hummingbird that is believed to go into a state of torpor, or temporary hibernation, during very cold periods—chased each other at high speed around a red-flowered fuchsia, then disappeared. At least the somber woods offered some serenity for these extraordinary little birds—beyond, there was none.

During the night the storm finally blew itself out. Flashlight beams flickered as we stuffed and packed, trying to be ready at the first tinge of light. I wished I could push a button and the kayak would be instantly loaded. I didn't want to waste a minute of the calm. I wanted to make some miles.

I took a moment to study the fjord. I couldn't believe how different it looked. Not only was the sea benign, the cold dawn was showing huge streaks of blue, the first color other than grey or black we had seen in three days. We headed for the main arm of the sound. From there we would turn west to Lago Azul. I wanted to tell Jack

Miller—my mentor from Colorado, the mountaineer who put me onto this trip—that at least we had tried.

Everything was going well; nature was putting on a gallant show and we had box seats. Waterfalls cascaded into the sea. Condors circled lazily far up in the sky. Flightless steamer ducks flailed the surface of the water with their stumpy wings, making a commotion and a good deal of spray as they rushed out of the way. And although it was early February, still the middle of Patagonia's summer, fresh snowfall blanketed the peaks, further dramatizing the beauty of this remote area.

We cruised past a dark line of trees that straggled up from a steep shore. Just a little farther and we would round the mountain and be on our way toward Lago Azul. That was the plan; however, waiting for us around the bend were the jaws of another quickly building williwaw.

"I don't believe it!" Judy protested. "Doesn't this place ever run out of wind?"

The incoming black cloud thundered down the narrow channel. I felt like the fjord was a bowling alley and we were the pins. Suddenly we were heaving up and down on waves as tall as our heads. We tried battling into them but a half-hour later we had gone nowhere, and actually may have lost a little ground. Finally, we admitted defeat. The winds were getting stronger. Lago Azul was history.

We paddled back to the first thin strip of beach inside the bay. It wasn't much of a refuge, but at least it wasn't pounded by waves. Judy rummaged beneath the spray skirt and pulled out a small waterproof bag. "Here, have some breakfast," she said, trying to sound cheerful. Inside the Ziploc was our daily ration of granola bars and Fig Newtons.

We studied our options. We could return to our previous camp and wait for a break in the weather; or we could make a direct crossing of the bay with the wind at our backs. I voted for the crossing. Judy abstained. Democracy ruled.

The mile-and-a-half-wide estuary was rough but manageable. What we feared most was that things might get worse. Facing an uninviting windward shore, we sprinted between headlands, stopping to rest behind rocky promontories. It was midafternoon, and our previous camp was about five miles away, when we followed a pair of plump steamer ducks into a U-shaped cove edged by a gently sloping shingle beach.

"Good spot for a break," Judy said, as we nosed to shore.

"Good spot to dry out," I added. My clothes were soaked despite my expensive "waterproof" rainwear.

We stripped down to shorts and tee shirts and draped the polypro long underwear on some box-leafed barberry, the familiar calafate. Although the sun was out, it was far from balmy. The thermometer dangling from my life jacket registered forty-four degrees Fahrenheit.

To generate some body heat, we took a brisk hike to a large bowl-shaped meadow nearby. It didn't take an ecology degree to deduce that the grassy valley had once been covered in old-growth forest. Charred stumps and cow pies littering the ground were evidence that the area had been cut and burned to make room for cattle.

At the clearing's edge was a deserted cabin with a picket fence. A little farther on was a one-hole outhouse that straddled a small swift creek, a no-frills sewer system designed to flush human waste directly to the sea. We peeked inside the cabin. It needed a paint job and some general clean-up, not to mention windows, doors, and furniture. Otherwise the place was in halfway decent shape. Lying on the floor was a brown and brittle Punta Arenas newspaper, nine months old.

Since it was getting late, we returned to the kayak with the idea of pitching camp nearby. A brief exploratory paddle led us to a grassy area midway between a babbling stream and a rock face softened by leafy ferns and wildflower bouquets.

"Great spot, eh?" I bubbled, pacing like a real estate salesman about to close a deal. "Flat tent site, great scenery, drinking water, no bugs ... ."

"Okay, enough already!" Judy implored. "You've made your point. Let's unload the boat and put up a mailbox."

To the side of the cliff was a twisty, muddy cattle trail that burrowed through a thorny thicket to a precipice overlooking the sound. The view from above was glorious, even by Patagonia's high standards. To the east was a more or less straight watery canyon; somewhere at the end of that long blue line was Puerto Natales. To the west was a range of angular peaks heavy with glaciers; tucked in there somewhere was Lago Azul. I told Judy about my regret at having had the opportunity to paddle into the heart of the Andes only to turn back. Judy was not feeling philosophical. "I'll be glad when this is over," she declared. "Paddling here has got me spooked."

We were enjoying a hot chocolate after dinner when I noticed something was amiss in the air. The thrushes in the woods had stopped trilling, the wind swirled across the fjord, and the tent started shaking. "Please, not again," I moaned.

Dropping my cup, I held the tent down while pegs popped loose and guylines shuddered. Judy tossed loose stuff into waterproof bags and shoved everything inside the kayak. Chaotic waves turned the surface of the sound into whitish foam. Water spouts a hundred feet high danced and wiggled across the channel. In its present state I doubted that even the *21 de Mayo* could stay afloat.

The only good thing about some williwaws is that they disappear as quickly as they appear. A short time later the wind tapered off and the fjord settled down. The thrush resumed its singing. We crawled into bed.

▲

The night was not made for sleeping. Sometime after midnight we were hit by a deluge. I jammed foam plugs in my ears to dull the drumroll on the tent. I sank deeper into my sleeping bag. I pulled the hood around my head. Sleep was impossible. Too many "what ifs" raced through my brain. *What if* the stream overflowed? *What if* the wind kept blowing? *What if* I returned to my government job a couple of weeks late?

When I next checked my watch it was 6:30 A.M. The rain had diminished to a drizzle. The inside of the tent glowed a little in the grey morning light. Judy was still asleep. Her eyelids twitched. She was probably having nightmares about williwaws, I told myself, laughing.

I sat up and stretched. "That's odd," I thought. The tent floor was damp and kind of puffy like a waterbed. I leaned over and felt the foot of my sleeping bag. It was soaking wet.

"Jude, get up, quick. We're getting flooded! C'mon, hurry! We've got to get out of here!"

I unzipped the door and saw that our perfect campsite was now a shallow lake. Water sloshed against the tent walls and was seeping inside. The kayak was afloat, still tethered to a tree. "We won't have to carry our gear to the beach," I said sourly. "We can load the boat right from here."

We retreated to the deserted cabin. There was no point in traveling, not with half our gear soaked and the weather showing no signs of improving. That evening, after a day of drying out and exploring the uplands, we joked about our earlier misfortune. Our frenetic wake-up already seemed a hazy memory. I couldn't wait to see the photos I took of Judy as she waded outside the tent.

▲

February 10 was our last backcountry morning. I awoke at seven, huddled in my sleeping bag against the cold. Filaments of frost coated the inside of the tent. It was calm, without even a suggestion of wind. The night before we had seen the lights of Puerto Natales flickering at the end of the fjord. In the still air of this workday dawn I could hear heavy trucks grinding through their gears down a distant gravel road.

The last few days on Last Hope Sound had been a medley of disparate experiences. Struggling with the wind was taxing both physically and mentally; there were times we vowed never to paddle here again—too risky, too uncertain. However, when the seas calmed and sunlight streaked through the clouds, we couldn't have been happier. We were seeing a part of the world we had long dreamed about, and we were doing it under our own power.

Instead of wistful daydreams, I turned my attention to the present. Now only five miles from journey's end, the rolling countryside, in the rain shadow of the Andes, was dry and dusty; the soil, always sparsely vegetated, was eroded by wind, runoff, and sheep farming. Knee-high scrub hid skinny hares—descendants of animals introduced from Europe during the last century—that now plague parts of Patagonia.

When the fog burned off and the temperature climbed, we hiked up the escarpment behind camp for a final view of our route. The Andes formed a line of snow-covered peaks to the west. One of them was Mount Balmaceda, easily identified by its icy dome glowing in cold shades of pink and red.

Birds were all around us. They seemed to welcome the interlude of pleasant weather as much as we did. A hundred or so black-necked swans dabbled at the edge of the channel, their broad backs as white as snow. Cormorants flew past our perch in an endless stream. Condors, caracaras, harriers, kestrels, ducks, geese, grebes, plovers, oystercatchers and swallows augmented the avian biodiversity.

We were on the water by nine, cruising directly into the glare of the sun. A mile out of town, the *21 de Mayo* sailed past, its reflection perfectly formed on the mirrorlike surface. The horn blasted, and as we looked, the people on deck began cheering and clapping. We laughed and waved back.

# 2.

# ISLAND AT WORLD'S END (CHILE)

MY SEATMATE, a scholarly looking man who had introduced himself as Frederick, motioned for me to look out the airplane's window. On our right, a thousand feet below, I could see a row of jagged mountain peaks. "They are called the Teeth of Navarino," he pointed out in Spanish. "We are very fortunate to see them."

Judy and I could vouch for that. During our first visit to Isla Navarino—a Chilean island across from Tierra del Fuego on the Beagle Channel—we had not glimpsed the mountainous interior even once in four days because of low dreary clouds. This time we were prepared to stay in Navarino's backcountry for a week, one leg of a ten-week tour in Chile and Argentina, hoping to learn more about this island at the "uttermost part of the earth."

An hour earlier we had embarked from Punta Arenas, our stomping grounds of last year, for the flight south. Our route took us across the Strait of Magellan, down Canal Whiteside, and over the Cordillera Darwin, the last major range of the Andes, an impenetrable wilderness of forest and snow. Airplanes in this region have to be superbly maintained, pilots first-class. The orange-and-white Twin Otter looked okay, but I wasn't so sure about the pilots. Minutes after takeoff, the captain of the twenty-seat plane lit a cigarette and turned around to chat with a woman in the first row. The copilot, meanwhile, rummaged through a leather briefcase on the floor, pulled out a newspaper, and was soon immersed in a crossword puzzle as he brought the aircraft into the clouds at eleven thousand feet.

The flight passed quickly, thanks in part to Frederick. A lecturer on forestry and ecology at a Chilean university, he couldn't resist giving me a crash course on Isla Navarino and other aspects of his country. In heavily accented English, he explained that CONAF, or the National Forest and Protection of Renewable Natural Resources Corporation, had contracted him for the summer to study the floral composition of Isla Navarino. "The government is embarking on a far-reaching plan to reduce the population pressure in our major cities, where masses of poor, unemployed people are arriving every day to try and find work. The cornerstone of this scheme is to relocate families in the hinterlands. Isla Navarino is under consideration."

Isla Navarino is located only fifty miles to the north of Cape Horn, the storm-blasted extremity of South America, and is one of the largest islands in the Beagle Channel archipelago, measuring forty-five miles east to west and twenty-five miles north to south. Vegetation in this cold climate ranges from dense beech forests and boot-sucking bogs to somber moorlands and lichen-covered crags above treeline. According to Frederick, a vanguard of a dozen families were being sent to Navarino. CONAF was supposed to learn how these families might earn a living before the relocation occurred. Preliminary studies on the island suggested that the soil was poor for farming and ranching, and that a self-sustaining logging industry would be marginal.

I asked whether it would be better to declare Isla Navarino a national park. After all, a park would draw tourists and tourist dollars meant jobs. "Chile already has enough national parks!" he replied indignantly. "What's more, Isla Navarino is not unique. There are many such islands in the archipelago."

"But none are accessible," I pointed out. "Navarino is." On the island was Puerto Williams, the most southern settlement in the world, barring those in Antarctica.

Frederick smiled condescendingly. "National parks should not be accessible," he said unequivocally. "Too many foreigners, especially Germans and Israelis, come to Chile looking for cheap places to stay. They leave all kinds of litter and trash in our national parks and are careless with fires. They wouldn't dare act this way in their own countries, but here they act like slobs. As an American, you surely must know what I mean." I didn't know whether to take that last statement as a compliment or a gibe.

The airplane lurched and shuddered as we began our descent. Judy gave me a weak smile from her seat across the aisle. I glanced toward the cockpit. The copilot had put away his crossword puzzle and was back at the controls.

A frequent flyer to these parts, my seatmate was unfazed. "Since you are American, there is one other matter I'd like to discuss. The trash we get from the U.S. is disgusting! Do you know the average Chilean watches so much American TV he hardly reads at all? Who are the morons who think these shows up? They are guilty of horrible crimes. It is a cancer destroying the education of our people. It is not like that in Russia. In Russia everyone reads all the time, on buses, on trains."

"Maybe that is because they have such rotten TV," I responded, cinching up my seatbelt.

Heavy winds bucked the tiny plane up and down and from side to side. A few hundred feet below, the Beagle Channel was alive with whitecaps. Raindrops streaked against the windows. Everyone tensed for the final approach. A baby awoke and began to cry. The guy on my right held a plastic puke bag to his mouth. More importantly, the pilot kissed his girlfriend on the cheek and returned to the cockpit.

Crabbing down the runway, the plane hit hard, bounced a few times, then settled onto its nosewheel. It braked to a stop with several hundred feet to spare before sliding into the ocean. Everyone aboard, except Frederick, clapped and cheered. He was too busy telling me how he hated American movies.

▲

Puerto Williams is not your ordinary Chilean town. It is a naval base where a few hundred civilians reside among an undisclosed number of military personnel. A sign warns visitors that taking photographs of the airport and port is strictly prohibited; however, the only items of strategic importance I saw were a lightly armed destroyer escort moored to the dock and four howitzers guarding the airstrip.

The sole reason for a military presence here is Chile's long-standing feud with Argentina. For nearly forty years Puerto Williams has been waving the Chilean flag at the toenails of its neighbor. In 1983, the two countries nearly went to war over territorial disputes in the Beagle Channel. The Pope intervened before shots were fired, and new boundaries were drawn; but Chile and Argentina still harbor a mutual distrust of each other.

As a military garrison, Puerto Williams is under the jurisdiction of a naval commander who also functions as the civil governor. We went through his office for permission to trek into the mountains.

On the walk over from the airport, we agreed that Judy should do most of the talking when dealing with the bureaucracy. My Spanish had improved after long hours of home study, but remained mired in the preschooler stage. More often than not, my efforts merely provoked laughter or looks of bewilderment. Judy, however, was fresh out of a language school in Mexico. Though far from fluent, her Spanish had improved dramatically after intensive, structured lessons and living with a Mexican host family. I promised myself that one day I, too, would attend a language school. In the meantime, I'd keep stammering away in Spanish, hoping Judy was nearby to bail me out.

Leaving our backpacks outside the spartan little office, we took a deep breath and prepared to meet the island's boss. Instead we were greeted by the commander's adjutant, a crisply dressed officer in starched whites with a round, stern face and a black Clark Gable moustache. He curtly informed us that the commander was away, but that he would radio our request to him. With a precise about-face he disappeared into a back room.

I paced the foyer, growing increasingly anxious as the minutes lapsed into a half hour. Judy sat calmly in a straight-back chair under the stern portrait of a nineteenth-century Chilean naval war hero.

Finally, the adjutant marched back into the entrance room with an official letter of authorization, plus a stern warning for us to stay clear of a particular tract of forest south of Puerto Williams. We also obtained permission to camp next to the Hostería Wala, a small inn that we passed on the road in from the airport. We thanked the officer and shook his hand, promising to drop in and see him upon our return.

"See, that wasn't so bad," I said to Judy as we slipped into our brutally heavy packs. "What did he say as we were leaving?"

"I think he warned us that it gets cold in the mountains, and that we shouldn't forget our *pisco*." Pisco is a fiery local spirit, and it wasn't among our camping supplies.

▲

Perched on the edge of beautiful Lauta Bay, the *hostería* was tucked away in a thicket of stunted, lichen-draped *lenga*, or high beech, bowed and broken to the shape of the sheltering contours. We found an ideal campsite in a grassy clearing, but first we had to shoo off a herd of overly friendly cows to make room for the tent. Although the inn was only a twenty-minute walk from town, it felt as if we were already on the edge of the wilderness. The Beagle Channel glittered nearby. Farther inland were Los Dientes—the Teeth of Navarino—just as foreboding and alluring as I had imagined them to be.

"Interested in a bite of real food before we go freeze-dried?" Judy asked when camp was squared away. It had been a long time since our toast-and-coffee breakfast at the Hotel Ritz in Punta Arenas, and an appetizing Chilean lunch sounded better than the trail food we had carted from home.

Trying to improve our appearance (a hopeless effort), we strolled up the cow path that led to the hostería's front door. The two-story hotel is owned by the navy, but instead of battleship architecture and a messhall motif, the place is spacious and comfortable with a roaring fireplace, locally made furniture, and soft furnishings. What really made the place a standout, though, was the combination dining room and bar that looked out onto the Beagle Channel. Somehow it seemed fitting that classical music played softly in the background.

The sole guests at the inn were an energetic French couple who had made a side trip here from Punta Arenas; a young German architect who was on a year-long journey to see the world; and two college students from Santiago, Chile, who had won an all-expenses-paid, four-day vacation to Puerto Williams for capturing first prize in a music talent contest.

Over hot dogs and potato chips, the only meal on the lunch menu that day, the young hostería manager told us that the island's location and subpolar weather keep outsiders away. Those who do venture here, he explained, are usually tourists who stay for two or three days, sailors voyaging the southern oceans, and Antarctic cruise ship passengers who drop in just long enough to mail postcards.

"No, Navarino is not for everyone," he sighed, sipping at his Polar beer. He pointed to the two students sitting at the bar. "See what I mean?"

From the looks of the young men's faces, it was apparent that Puerto Williams was not the destination they would have chosen for first prize. They were glued to a television set, watching Lindsay

Wagner in one of her vintage performances as the "Bionic Woman." I wouldn't admit it to him, but Frederick, the guy from the plane, was right: Hollywood is trashing the globe.

Our departure for the mountains wasn't until the next morning, so we spent the afternoon wandering around town. The "business" district consisted of a central block of shops and offices, plus there was a post office, church, and museum. A few sailors walked briskly between military buildings, but there were also a few foreigners. One in particular who stood out was an Asian man alone with his suitcase at the pier. Encased in a shiny red jump suit with a matching hood pulled tightly over his head, he could have passed for a character out of an old Flash Gordon TV show.

He didn't look the outdoorsy type, but we learned that he was an accomplished, world-traveled scuba diver. James was traveling aboard the *Argonauta*, a small tourist freighter way past its prime, that spent each night in a different cove, allowing him access to dive spots that had probably never been explored before. "Diving is my passion," he said, positively buoyant. "I don't look that old, but I wrote the first scuba diving manual in Chinese back in the fifties."

A specialist in magnetic resonance imagery with postdoctoral studies, James was part of a group of Hong Kong scientists invited by the Chinese government to visit their new Antarctic research station. The Chilean Air Force had volunteered to fly the Hong Kong delegation from Santiago, Chile, to Antarctica but there had been repeated mechanical delays. James had been using the time to travel, visiting Robinson Crusoe Island, Torres del Paine National Park, and now Isla Navarino.

The white Wala Inn van pulled up beside us. "My ride," James said, grabbing his suitcase.

Before he left, I mentioned that Judy and I were also scuba divers, but we had never seen an outfit quite like the one he had on.

"Ah, you like it?" he beamed, running his fingers over the glossy, metallic high-tech fabric. He explained that it was a NASA space suit designed to be worn under a conventional wet suit. "It's made of Ko-Tex."

"Gore-Tex?" I asked.

"Yes, Ko-Tex," he repeated. "Made in America."

We were on our way back to the hostería ourselves when we met a woman from Switzerland who was looking for a telephone. She had just returned from a three-week cruise to Antarctica aboard the sailing yacht *War Baby*. Already we knew the basics about the town and informed her that the telephone office was closed until morning.

"Oh, well," she said, brushing a strand of long blond hair out of her eyes. "I've waited this long to tell my parents where I am, what's another night?"

We were curious about Antarctica and asked about her travels. "I can't describe how beautiful it is there," she said softly. "It's like being on another planet. What's more, we had calm seas the entire time, which is rare and lucky, since I am the cook and I don't cook well when I am seasick."

However, there were some disconcerting aspects to their voyage. They had sighted only two whales, when historically the area has teemed with cetaceans. Also, the number of pleasure boats at the bottom of the world was far greater than they had expected. "We sailed for nearly a month in the fjords of southern Chile without seeing anyone," she explained. "But in Antarctica, where one would expect to be alone, we routinely saw cruise ships and other sailboats."

The *War Baby*'s crew was having a celebration party at the hostería that evening, but we weren't invited. Just as well. The next morning we were heading up the mountain and needed to get an early start.

▲

After nine hours of sleep I was ready to climb, but the weather told me to make other plans. The mountains were socked in tight with clouds, and a wet, cheerless mist drooped to nearly sea level. This was the Isla Navarino Judy and I had known the year before.

We made the most of the gloomy day by going for a long hike along the Beagle Channel. Following a lightly used gravel road that hugs the island's north shore, we made our way to some small bays and shell-lined beaches a few miles west of town. The bleak land in the latitude of Cape Horn supports few animals, yet the waters are among the richest in the world. Floating masses of giant kelp fringe the coast, providing shelter for an abundance of small fish, shellfish, and other species which, in turn, are food for a variety of birds. We had found a field guide this time, and with a little patience were able to identify neotropic cormorants and black-crowned night herons, buff-necked ibises and great skuas, kelp geese and flightless steamer ducks, kelp gulls and South American terns. Rich in krill, the channels also support southern sea lions, dolphins, Magellanic penguins, and the occasional whale, but these were species we were not likely to see from shore.

Large breaking rollers pounded against the beach. The wind was cold and constant. We huddled behind a clump of green scurvy-grass that grew over the old shellfish middens of former Yahgan Indian encampments. During many of his journeys in this region, Darwin came into frequent contact with these nomadic canoe Indians who occupied the bleak southernmost channels and offshore islands of Tierra del Fuego. He was amazed, as were visitors before him, that anyone was able to make a living in this inhospitable place. He described the Fuegians at great length and was clearly shocked by what he saw. "These poor wretches," Darwin wrote in his journal in 1832, "were the most abject and miserable creatures I anywhere beheld ... stunted in their growth, their hideous faces bedaubed with white paint, their skins filthy and greasy, their hair entangled, their voices discordant, and their gestures violent. Viewing such men, one can hardly make oneself believe that they are fellow-creatures and inhabitants of the same world."

These "wretched natives,"—the southernmost inhabitants of the planet, occupying lands remote in the extreme—were decimated by European-introduced measles and hunted like animals. We were told that the last people of identifiable Yahgan Indian descent lived in a small enclave of several houses on Isla Navarino, a short distance east of town. There were only two or three left, the youngest being a woman in her nineties.

We gazed across the channel, exhilarated by the region's rawness and the tangy sea breeze. A score of dark giant petrels, or fulmars—fierce scavenger birds of prey whose habit of feasting off carrion on sea lion colonies has earned them the nickname of Stinkers—skimmed back and forth above the waves, riding the wind without ever flapping their long bladelike wings. Sharing air space with the petrels were several black-browed albatrosses, among the world's largest flying birds. Head down, sailplane wings outstretched, they cut across the water in lazy curves.

I tried to imagine what it would be like aboard a cramped wooden vessel for days on end in these heavy waves. Darwin, though impressed by the "savage magnificence" of Tierra del Fuego, found it a somber and gloomy place. Of course, being continually seasick while aboard the HMS Beagle didn't help matters. While I liked the notion of cruising the southern seas and am fascinated by others' accounts, I am not a sailor. But kayaking along Patagonia's southern coast—now that was a possibility! I discussed with Judy circumnavigating Isla Navarino and seeing more of the archipelago, or paddling west to the Darwin Range with its tidewater glaciers and remote fjords, or even taking several months to round Tierra del Fuego itself. But when? It couldn't be next year since we already had plans to visit other areas in South America. And after that? Asia, Australia, Europe, Africa, and a million places in our own country beckoned.

I reminded my mate that we would both be thirty-seven years old this year, and that if we wanted to see the world we had better get busy. She mulled that over for a minute before she replied. "I don't feel the urgency that you do," she said, leaning back into the grass. "Hopefully we'll always be fit enough to travel. But with you babbling on about making another kayak trip down here, especially after the wind in Paine, well, it's going senile first that worries me."

▲

It was 6 A.M. when we braced ourselves to meet the day. The front must have passed on through, for it was clear and warm, a combination we were beginning to think wasn't possible in these parts. At fifty-five degrees south, the same latitude as the Alaska panhandle is north, the Beagle Channel archipelago is similarly rainy, foggy, and blustery for most of the year. Fuegians say they have two seasons: winter and February. But, as we had learned, even in February (the month of our visit) the island's weather can be decidedly unsummerlike. Caught between two tumultuous oceans, winds can be hellish and unpredictable; snow can fall in the mountains at any time. We broke camp quickly, eager to start our trip while the sun shone.

We set out at seven o'clock, struggling under the weight of our fully provisioned packs. The first hour took us along a spur road that gradually climbed upward into the slopes behind the town. The dirt track was narrow and winding, cutting through a wall of evergreen beech. Unseen birds called from within. There was a breeze blowing, but its tendrils couldn't touch us here.

A few military vehicles rumbled by on their way to some hidden installation in the forest. Some of the rifle-toting marines waved from the trucks and gave "thumbs-up" signs, but most merely stared.

The next hour took us over rougher ground. We reached road's end and picked up a faint forest path adjacent to a mountain torrent. We had learned of this path from the curator of the natural history museum in Puerto Williams. "It is very steep," he had warned, "and not often used. I have climbed it a few times while looking for rare birds, but have never been to the end. With no assistant, I am required to spend most of my time in the museum. When you return, you can tell me what I have been missing."

It took only a few steps after leaving the road to realize how fortunate we were to have a trail. The cement sack on my back didn't allow for much more than shuffling one foot ahead of the other. Trudging up the muddy footpath, I cringed when I recalled how the baggage handler at the Punta Arenas airport had cursed while hoisting my frame pack onto the scale. I knew the Kelty was heavy, stuffed as it was with all the essentials for camping plus food for eight days. But I didn't know *how* heavy until the worker informed me that it weighed in at thirty kilos (sixty-six pounds), and that didn't include a fanny pack with binoculars and camera gear.

The woods were dark and eerie, what I would envision if I had stepped into a Tolkien *Hobbit* fantasy. Ancient moss-covered trees with smooth grey bark and bearing small triangular nuts sighed in the breeze. These southern beech are the largest and most domi-nant trees in Magellanic forests. They stand up in the wind by leaning strongly eastward with all their branches on one side. Nevertheless, many of the big trees, some well over sixty feet high, had toppled. Trees trunks and limbs lay everywhere. We labored ahead, helping each other over the obstacles, rather than sidetrack around them. Walking would have been twice as hard without our trusty hiking sticks—broom handles we'd bought in a Punta Arenas hardware store.

Tap, tap, tap … tap, tap! I looked up, startled at the loud drumming sound. Directly ahead, glued against a dead standing tree, was a black crow-sized bird with a bright crimson head and crest. Bark flew in all directions as it hammered its chisel-shaped bill into the soft wood. Glad of any excuse to take a break, I dropped my pack.

The *Carpintero negro*, or Magellanic woodpecker, is similar to the pileated woodpecker that frequents the woods near our central Illinois home. Spiralling the snag in clockwise hops, its stiff tail feathers assisting it in climbing, the big male woodpecker neared the top where it let loose an ear-piercing rattle. The harsh cry was answered immediately from deeper in the woods. With a final squawk and pumping of wings, the bird flew off to find its mate.

This flashy woodpecker wasn't the only bird that helped take our minds off the upward slog. Most conspicuous were the noisy little thorn-tailed *rayaditos*, or spinetails, similar to North America's brown creeper; and the *cachaña*, or austral parakeets, common to these parts but more easily pictured in a steamy equatorial jungle. Flying in flocks of a dozen or more, the reddish-green parrots swept through the tree tops, their raucous chattering continuing long after they disappeared.

We exited the forest at midday. My map was vague and not very accurate, but I guessed the elevation to be around two thousand feet. Beyond the treeline, the mountainside was matted with short yellow grass and scattered knee-high shrubs.

A half-hour later we reached the Chilean flag on a flat, open ridge. I had to admit, it was unique; I wasn't aware of too many four-by-eight-foot sheet metal flags swaying atop a steel pipe on the side of a mountain. According to the hostería manager, the military erected the grandiose affair a few years ago with the aid of a helicopter; it was a message to Argentina about Chilean sovereignty along the Beagle Channel. In its prime the flag must have stood tall and proud, but high winds had snapped all of the cable guy lines and had bent the pole nearly to the ground.

We slipped off our packs and sat down, slumped against the pole, trying to get our second wind. It made little sense to come this far if we couldn't soak up the view. And the view was superb. To the north lay the Beagle Channel, serene now that the wind had died down. Through binoculars, we watched a couple of small fishing boats tending crab pots as their boats zig-zagged from one watery station to another. Considered a delicacy and exported all over the world, the *centolla*, or southern king crab, was once abundant in this area, but is now overfished and overpriced.

On the far side of the Beagle Channel, in Argentina's slice of Tierra del Fuego, we could see a chain of coastal sierras three to four thousand feet in height. Some of the peaks were mantled with perpetual snow, others glistened with icy glaciers. Below the bald ridges and the whiteness was one great, dusky-colored forest, which covered the mountainsides to the water's edge. It looked a very wild and lonely place. "In these still solitudes," wrote Darwin, describing this outlying part of Tierra del Fuego, "Death, instead of Life, seemed the predominant spirit." Some things are unchanged by time.

Far to the west along this range, appearing as just a smudge in our magnified vision, was the dim outline of Ushuaia, Argentina's regional economic center. Today Ushuaia is a modern, duty-free port of concrete houses and tourist accommodations, sprawling up hills overlooking the strait and whipped by cold winds that sweep in from every side. When E. Lucas Bridges was born here in 1874—the son of British missionary parents who became Tierra del Fuego's first permanent white settlers—it was one of the most forbidding locales on Earth, virtually unknown to the outside world and inhabited by hostile tribes.

A tall, weather-beaten man, Bridges lived at the tip of South America most of his life, exploring the area by horseback, boat, and foot, one of the first white men to do so. As a boy he worked in his father's fields and played with Yaghan Indian children from whom he learned Yaghan customs and language. Later, Bridges became friendly with the Ona tribe, fierce nomadic hunters of the Fuegian plains who resisted any encroachment on their hunting grounds. Gradually, he won their trust, eventually becoming a fellow tribesman, adviser, and protector. He was a kind of "White Chief" among the Fuegian Indians and was looked upon by many as the uncrowned king of Patagonia.

Bridges's autobiography, *Uttermost Part of the Earth*, was published in 1949, the same year he died. Not only is it an ethnographic work about the Indians of Tierra del Fuego, who are now virtually extinct, it is also a fascinating true adventure story that reads more like a historical novel. *Uttermost* was essential reading for us before traveling to Patagonia, ranking right up there with Darwin's *The Voyage of the Beagle*. Now that we were in view of Bridges's birthplace, I wished I had a copy of his book in hand. Just what I needed— another pound and a half in my bulging pack.

As a cold damp breeze swirled over the high country, Ushuaia vanished beneath a low-lying cloud. We hoisted our packs. Sitting under a creaking metal flag on a bare mountainside was not the place to be.

We traversed the ridge to a wind-scoured plateau where the only plants underfoot were ground-hugging mosses, lichens, and forbs. With darkness settling in, we decided to spend the night on the mountain top and pitched our tent in the lee of a boulder field, the only sheltered site we could find. Aluminum pegs were useless in the hard ground, bending when I pounded them with a flat stone. Instead, I guyed the nylon dome with a dozen heavy rocks, knowing full well that even these anchors wouldn't be worth much in a typical roaring forties gale.

The view from the tent door that evening made up for our bumpy beds. We watched a flock of white upland geese and speckled teal swim lazily in the reedy shallows of a small nearby tarn. A few drab sparrowlike pipits pecked for seeds among the wind-blasted stones as a reddish-pink alpenglow set the surrounding summits afire. With sunset came an eerie silence. The air, already cold, chilled a few degrees more. The change was instantly perceptible, and I wondered how much colder it would be by midnight.

▲

At daybreak there wasn't even a flutter of wind. Not a single peg had been needed to hold the tent down, let alone a couple hundred pounds of stones. The sun crested the mountains and warmed our camp. Enveloped in my sleeping bag, with the hood cinched tight and only a breathing hole for my mouth, the rise in temperature felt good. It had dropped to below freezing during the night; the tarn was rimmed with ice. Fortunately, Judy had remembered to put our water bottles inside the tent. I hastily pulled on my pile jacket and lit the stove to brew coffee.

"Wake me when it's ready, okay?" Judy mumbled. "No hurry."

The continued calm weather was making me nervous. We set out as soon as we had had a bite to eat and walked briskly to get warm. Soon we were at the brink of a steep bowl-shaped basin oriented northeast to southwest. Glaciated mountains rising up several thousand feet encircled the deep valley. Most notable of these was a range of reddish peaks in the west, exceptional for their sawtooth forms: Los Dientes.

Rocks and shale avalanched beneath our feet as we slid down the loose rubble that had been stripped from the mountain by glacial and freeze-thaw erosion. There was a brushy bench about five hundred feet below, midway to the valley floor, that looked as if it might make a good base camp. From there we would be able to reconnoiter the area, since now that we were here we didn't know exactly where we were going. The best map of the island I could lay my hands on was a Chilean nautical chart of the Beagle Channel and Cape Horn at a scale of 1:200,000 (1 inch = 3.2 miles). Isla Navarino's land mass was depicted in ochre along with six or seven significant blue lakes. Los Dientes was the only range of peaks named; the mountainous interior before my eyes was barely acknowledged by the cartographer. This lack of terrestrial detail may be enough for sailors; for hikers with heavy backpacks all those blank spots on the map mean potential trouble.

We were following each other, concentrating on watching our feet, when we were startled by a loud WHOOSH! I looked up just in time to see a condor, barely above us, its impressive wingspan of perhaps eight or nine feet almost blocking out the blue sky.

Found only in the Andes, this largest bird of prey in the world has been known to soar effortlessly to eighteen thousand feet on upcurrents of air, covering enormous distances with little exertion in its search for carrion. Maybe it thought we were potential pickings, because it glided back for a second pass to investigate us, so close this time that it seemed I could reach up and touch it with my hiking stick. I knew I had nothing to fear; there is no record of a condor ever attacking a living human being. Still, there was something very sinister about this scraggy bird with its naked, wattled head, viciously hooked beak, and loose, creepy wrinkles about the eyes—he seemed to be waiting; waiting for one of us to die.

In less than a minute, four more condors appeared out of an empty sky. They floated high over the rocky ledges, then in gradually diminishing circles, zeroed in on us with heads and necks turned inquisitively in our direction. Only when we reached the bottom of the rock slide unscathed did the great black shapes whirl off in search of something already dead.

The bench was the only level ground on the slope. You would think that in an area the size of a football field there would be a multitude of tent sites, but a thorough reconnaissance revealed only one tiny patch with flat, dry turf and some protection from wind. With the selection made for us, we established camp near a thicket of matted dwarf trees fringed by moor and bog. There was no sign of human occupation in the whole landscape. I could envision settling here very happily for the next several days. To celebrate our good fortune, we had a late lunch of grilled cheese sandwiches and hot tea—an unbeatable combination on a cool mountain afternoon.

▲

Of the several treks we took from base camp the next few days, the most challenging was the one into the basin and back out over the high plateau that divides the island in half. Sliding downhill was no problem. When we reached the lower forest, our body weight and gravity helped us shimmy through the entangling stand, which was almost tropical in appearance and lushness. But waiting for us in the poorly drained valley were sluggish streams, ponds, and sphagnum moss bogs. Composed of thick dome-shaped mats of mosses, lichens, liverworts, ferns, and a few reeds, the bogs were soft and spongy underfoot; if not careful, it was possible to break through the surface into deep layers of treacherous, oozy mud and organic debris. It became a game as we crisscrossed the valley trying to keep our feet dry. Eventually we gave up and resigned ourselves to wet boots for the remainder of the hike.

We scrambled over bog and tussock for an hour. Edible berries gleamed in the moss at our feet and the water tasted peaty. At last we reached a copse of wind-shaped Antarctic beech that crept up from the floor and clung to the sides of the steep valley. One of two deciduous southern beeches, their leaves were just beginning to show the brilliant reds, yellows, and browns of fall.

Above the straggly forest, barren cliffs and sparsely vegetated rock slopes formed an amphitheater around us. The air was close, hushed, fragrant. There wasn't a scrap of litter, no old fire rings, no tent rings, not a footprint. It was a lost world, but instead of pterodactyls and stegosauri, we found a large population of buck-toothed rodents imported from North America.

I have always been a staunch defender of beavers—a family of *Castor canadensis* patrols a river inlet in my front yard at home. But while beavers are a natural component of North America's biodiversity, in the Fuegian islands they are out of control. Near Puerto Williams we had seen some evidence of the animals when the road went through a beech forest, a portion of which was being drowned by the incursion of ponds. However, it wasn't until we reached the hidden valley that we saw the full impact of this exotic species. Throughout the basin entire groves of beech had been gnawed. Virtually every rivulet, creek, and stream was dammed with trees, branches, stones, and mud. The smallest dam we measured was a foot wide and a half-foot high; I estimated the largest to be 225 feet across, and it was taller than I am.

According to a local naturalist, beavers were introduced to Tierra del Fuego's streams in the 1940s by an Argentine entrepreneur who hoped to become wealthy marketing their pelts. When beaver coats became unfashionable no one bothered to trap the beavers, and with abundant food and virtually no predators, they have flourished throughout the region. Meanwhile, a decline has been observed in the native species, *Myocastor coipus*, which is similar to the beaver but smaller and with a muskrat-shaped tail.

We climbed out of the valley to see what lay beyond. Even with a light daypack, this was not an easy task. A confusion of low, crooked trees separated us from the open ridge. Crawling and pulling, we bashed and tunneled through the woody maze.

At last we reached the treeless heights. We rested on a flat rock ledge. Once our breathing had returned to normal we were struck by how clearly the sound of water trickling over stones rang out from a nearby stream. There was no other sound. The panoramas were wild and sublime, similar in many respects to the Scottish moors or Alaska's tundra-covered hills, many thousands of miles to the north. Mountains blocked our view of the island's south shore; however, five inches on our map indicated that it was roughly sixteen miles away. Originally we had contemplated backpacking to the coast, but upon seeing the kind of country we would have to traverse it didn't take much to change our minds. We had heard of an old Indian trail through the lowland forest and patchwork of bogs, but had no idea where it was. It was easy to rationalize not undertaking the long hike. "We don't have time," I said, ticking off the days before we had to return to Puerto Williams. "Not enough food," Judy said, slitting open another wheel of Gouda cheese to go with our bagels.

I leafed through my journal as I munched nuts and M&Ms. My records showed that during our trek to date we had positively identified twenty-six species of birds. This wasn't much; fewer, actually, than the number that visit my backyard bird feeder in winter. But unlike our last visit to Chile, we now had a field guide to confirm our sightings. In return for lending us the guide, the museum curator wanted us to look for the *carancho negro*, or striated caracara, and a species of seedsnipe. He suspected they both lived in the mountains where we were headed, but no one was sure. "I need proof," he had said. "I will be most grateful if you'd get me a picture of either bird."

Birdwatching can be a tricky pursuit: rewarding and challenging but sometimes excruciatingly frustrating. After nearly a week of beating the bush, I concluded that if these birds were in the mountains I wasn't going to be the one to identify them, let along get near enough to snap their portraits.

Judy touched my arm and pointed to the far side of a beaver pond about a hundred yards away. Among a jumble of boulders were two adult guanacos and a young foal or *chulengo*. Guanacos were reported to be relatively rare on Isla Navarino, their most southerly range in South America. We could understand why when we heard that local officials bragged of killing guanacos with their revolvers and watching them fall off the cliffs when shot.

We hid behind the rocks and remained motionless, camera and binoculars at the ready. Sure-footed as mountain goats, the animals picked their way through the boulder field to a crumbly ravine, stopping every few steps to turn their heads and stare. The leader gamboled down the muddy chute, followed closely by the *chulengo*, but the adult at the rear slipped and slid halfway down on its rump before recovering without missing a beat.

The family group was angling beneath our perch when suddenly a horrific *whumpf-whumpf-whumpf-whumpf-whumpf* rent the air. Two olive-green helicopter gunships skimmed over the valley, threading their way toward a pass to the south. The guanacos panicked and bolted across the plateau as the Vietnam-era Hueys whirred by. Judy and I didn't run, but some instinctive response prompted us to take cover until the high country was silent again.

I hate the noise of choppers in the backcountry. What were these guys doing? More than likely they were resupplying the naval crew at Cape Horn or something equally as harmless. But the cynic in me saw a group of trigger-happy young soldiers getting their kicks by shooting down guanacos and condors with automatic rifle fire.

▲

We spent the morning reading and staying warm. The weather had changed during the night, dropping to well below freezing and turning every few minutes from sleet to rain to hail. The only constant was a blustery west wind and an overcast sky that held the threat of snow.

My beat-up Polarguard sleeping bag just didn't do the trick any more; whatever loft it once had held had been smashed flat with repeated use. Only when I put on a pile sweater and pants over my longjohns was I able to warm up.

Snug in our rock-solid tent, I thumbed through the bird guide and caught up on my journal. I tried to write every day; otherwise it was far too easy to forget what I had seen and done and the people I had met. Pulling out my old pocket notebooks, reading my chicken-scratch scrawls, trips taken a decade earlier come to life as if they had happened only yesterday.

The brunt of the storm was over before lunch. Though still windy and wet, there was a promise of sun amid the greyness. During a long trip I sometimes miss the comforts of our life at home: the woodland view from our back window, reading the local newspaper, watching the nightly news, playing volleyball with friends. But "comfortable" was a state of mind I could easily postpone. We had only two days left in the backcountry, and the best mountain hikes had been saved for the end. We tossed our journals and books aside and meted out the essential day-tripping supplies.

At the start, the gradient was gentle and the ground firm and easy to walk on. The next mile was more difficult: Twice we had to climb down into the bottom of the bowl, with its mucky peat beds and swampy beaver ponds. Then it was a scramble out again before continuing upwards, our bushwhack impeded by clinging shrubs, brittle rock, and patches of old snow.

We could see we were making progress, however, because Los Dientes inched closer and closer. Nearly thirty-eight hundred feet above sea level, Los Dientes are not the island's tallest summits (a peak to the west is a few hundred feet taller), but without question they are its most dramatic. I shot frame after frame of the toothy sierra as the changing light played over its stark, fractured surface.

"If this place isn't national park quality, then what is?" I asked, thinking back to my conversation on the airplane with the argumentative forestry professor. "In its own way, it's every bit as spectacular as Torres del Paine."

"Or anywhere else we've been," Judy added, taking it all in.

The wind grew in intensity the higher we went. The surface became barren, stripped of vegetation, deeply incised and weathered. We steadied ourselves with hiking staffs while treading up the narrow ridge toward the base of Los Dientes. On either side were precipitous slopes terminating in gullies strewn with large chunks of shattered rock. A step in the wrong place meant a long slide to oblivion.

The slope increased unpleasantly. The wind tore at our bodies and threatened to knock us over. We crawled straight up to a sharp jagged point from where we could go no farther and collapsed behind a pile of burnished rock. I ripped off my flapping parka hood. Now for the first time I could take in the amazing scene of desolation before me. Across a deep divide, a range of slender pinnacles soared hundreds of feet above us—the Teeth of Navarino. In the valley below their flanks were lifeless rubble and a string of blackwater tarns. Ice and snow lay unmelted between the rocks where the sun couldn't reach.

My eyes searched for something familiar, something green, something alive in this geologic chaos. I found it to the north. A thousand dizzying feet below were several stream and river valleys as verdant as the peaks were barren. Somewhere in these green corridors were parakeets, hummingbirds, and woodpeckers. Still farther north was a reminder that despite our feeling of isolation, civilization was never far away. In the middle of the Beagle Channel were three small warships coming in from a patrol on the Atlantic Ocean. It had to be an uncomfortable ride for the sailors aboard, with the boats plunging and riding over every wave.

Through a slot in Navarino's Teeth, Judy pointed out a wedge of flat, marshy-looking ground, our first glimpse of the island's south side. The land merged into broad Nassau Bay, and then the Drake Passage; the whitecaps must have been enormous to be visible thirty-

*Looking down from a mountaintop in the Dientes de Navarino, on Isla Navarino.*

five miles away beneath the claw of South America. A smattering of islands loomed on the hazy horizon: Isla Grevy, Isla Wollaston, Isla Hoste. All uninhabited, these are some of the loneliest places in the world, where one can expect only one day in a hundred of calm weather and sunshine.

Though out of sight, Cape Horn also lay in that direction; the broken headland where the Andes finally give up their struggle to rise above the sea. A British party kayaked round the Horn in 1977, becoming the first to do so, setting the stage for several other paddling, rowing, and even windsurfing expeditions seeking their own recognition. While I admire these adventurers' pluck, I am content not to be among them. The gales that sweep the straits round Cape Horn have an evil reputation.

Some conception of these seas, where countless ships have foundered, can be gathered from the journal of George Anson, a British naval commander who led an expedition to the region in 1741. After rounding the Horn, he wrote: " ... we had a continual succession of such tempestuous weather as surprised the oldest and most experienced mariners on board, and obliged them to confess that what they had hitherto called storms were inconsiderable gales compared with the violence of these winds, which raised such short and at the same time mountainous waves, as greatly surpassed in danger all seas known in any other part of the globe, and it was not without great reason that this unusual appearance filled us with continual terror."

Looking south, I found it hard to believe that Antarctica was only 650 miles from where we stood. I wanted to visit that frozen continent, to see its penguins, seals, and whales and to experience firsthand the dazzling spectacle of its huge masses of eternal ice moving through waters so rich with life. But I didn't want to go as part of a crowd aboard a tourist ship, and I wasn't about to row there. I wondered if the *War Baby* would be sailing to Antarctica again next year, and whether they might possibly need an unskilled deckhand.

Freezing rain plinked against our jackets. The cold of the mountain began to bite. We headed back to camp; we would have to hurry to get there before dusk. Tomorrow we would climb again among Navarino's Teeth for one last look at the other side.

# 3.

# THE ELUSIVE SPIRES OF FITZROY (ARGENTINA)

EIGHT HOURS AFTER LEAVING Punta Arenas, our bus rolled into Río Gallegos—a new city, a new country: Argentina. From this dusty, wind-blown town on the Atlantic coast, our plan was to head inland to Parque Nacional Los Glaciares, which encloses twenty-three hundred square miles of forested mountains, immense lakes, and one of the great glacial regions of the world. But the bus to Calafate—a small settlement on the south shore of Lago Argentino, and the starting point for any visit to the Andean park—didn't depart until the following afternoon. We'd have to spend the night in a hotel, which, at the southern tip of the Patagonian peninsula, can be more daunting than the wilderness.

For $16 U.S. per night, we got a dark, basic hotel room with a horribly sagging double bed and a sink that gurgled and belched a foul-smelling stench. On the wall over the old-fashioned crank-chain toilet was a holographic painting of a space capsule on the dimpled surface of the moon, with an astronaut planting a U.S. flag; over the bed was a somber rendition of the crucifixion.

The only thing we knew about Río Gallegos, other than that it is the capital of the province of Santa Cruz, was what a guidebook had to say, and it began with the caveat, "If you have the misfortune to be stuck in Río Gallegos for a day ... " The main street outside our hotel looked and sounded like a dragstrip. *Halloween III*, a slasher import from the States, was the only movie playing at the only movie house. Tinny dance music blared from loudspeakers affixed to gaudy storefronts. We were glad to be leaving the next day.

The bus to Calafate left at 3:00 P.M. sharp. The first thing to remember about riding buses long distances in Latin America is to have short legs; there's not much space between the seats. The next thing to remember is to sit in the back seats; some of these bus drivers are a danger to the human race.

The road out of town soon turned to gravel. I was becoming mesmerized by the emptiness of the country blurring past when I noticed a larger, newer bus pulling alongside us on the narrow washboard road. We were going at least eighty kilometers per hour, already in excess of what I thought was prudent, and this idiot next to us was jockeying to pass.

Our driver—a small, rotund man pushing fifty—wasn't going to give up without a fight. Pulling down his black beret, he flipped the other guy an obscene gesture and gunned the old diesel for all it was worth. Passing on narrow two-lane (or less) roads is a very macho competitive sport. Our flamingo-colored coach lurched back and forth, swaying from side to side. Every time we hit a chuckhole the frame slammed hard onto the axles, producing a screech of metal on metal. I glanced at the newspaper on my lap. Plastered across the front page was a gory color photograph of Argentina's most recent bus crash, the third such tragedy in the last two weeks.

The buses nearly scraped. If my window had been open, I could have passed a Coca-Cola to my bug-eyed counterpart in the next lane. Our driver downshifted and pulled ahead going up a hill. The other driver was manic, but at least he wasn't totally suicidal. He blasted his horn in surrender and darted in behind us.

The rest of the ride was uneventful. We were passing through the monotonous expanses of Argentina's flat, semiarid steppes, which lie in the rain shadow of the Andes. I doubted that even a lizard could survive among the sparse growth of low, hardy shrubs, but then suddenly, four guanacos appeared in the middle of the road, forcing the driver to swerve. The animals dashed to safety and didn't look back until far up a distant ridge.

About six o'clock, we rumbled into Esperanza, the first "town" since leaving Río Gallegos. A lonely outpost of life, Esperanza in its totality consisted of a few houses and a single ramshackle inn that also served as the bus depot. Out of the inn walked a tired-looking young couple with beat-up backpacks. They boarded the coach and flopped down without saying a word.

Gradually, we began to leave the flatlands and ease into rolling, treeless hills. Far to the west, across a sea of eroded brown caprock, floated a row of billowy white, clouds; a giveaway that our mountainous destination lay somewhere ahead.

Seven long, bumpy hours after leaving Río Gallegos, we lumbered into Calafate, with the Andes towering behind us. Only one more bus ride separated us from the wilderness, but we were crestfallen to learn that the bus wouldn't be leaving until the day after next. "Two nights in Calafate," I groaned, as we stood under a streetlamp in front of the deserted station. "Who ever said traveling is fun?"

We shouldered our backpacks and wandered over to the municipal campground a few blocks off the main street. About the size of a soccer field, only with hard-packed dirt instead of neatly manicured grass, the place contained an amalgam of different camping styles and modes of transportation that reflected the international gathering. There were Volkswagen vans, expensive European mountain tents, grimy mountain bikes, modified school buses, pop-up trailers, Japanese motorcycles, and cheap tube tents that looked ready to blow over in the first breeze. Italian, German, French, Hebrew, Portuguese, and Spanish were being spoken. The only English we heard was from an Australian curled up under his touring bicycle, who asked me what time it was.

A young Argentine woman who had been on our bus was already at the campground. She unrolled her sleeping bag right in the dirt, crawled inside without undressing, and immediately went to sleep. While in the bathroom, Judy overheard a group of Spanish-speaking older women carrying on about how brave, or foolish, the girl was. "Imagine," exclaimed one of them, "to travel by herself all the way from Río Gallegos!" "Ayy!" cried another. "How could her mother let her do such a thing?"

We were charged six australs, nearly ten dollars, to set up camp. A bit steep, I thought, especially when I noticed the burly woman attendant charging another couple, obviously not North Americans, only one-third as much. But it was too late, and I was too tired to care about it. We pitched the tent next to some others and fired the stove for a quick dinner of soup and bread.

At midnight, serenaded by howling dogs, a neighbor's boom box, and trucks and cars clattering down main street, I read a few pages from Larry McMurtry's western saga *Lonesome Dove*, then drifted off to a nightmarish sleep dreaming of maniacal bus drivers.

▲

At 5:30 A.M., while it was still pitch-black outside, I woke Judy and we quietly gathered our things and slipped out of camp. The minibus to Fitzroy, the mountainous realm on the north side of the park, was scheduled to depart at 6:50. If we missed it we'd be stuck in Calafate another four days. We were at the station before it opened.

The sun was just breaking over the horizon as we rolled out of town. Going to Fitzroy with us were a half-dozen others, including some German and Swiss tourists we recognized from the campground. Since this was a "tour bus," as opposed to regular public transportation, we had the services of a guide who would be explaining the natural history of the region. Taking his place in the sunken step near the front door, the tall, paunchy fellow curled his black upturned moustache and looked us over with dark, sleepy eyes. He greeted us with a hearty grin.

"Who speaks Spanish?" he bellowed in English. The Germans and Swiss (obviously trilingual) raised their hands. "For you others (he looked at Judy and me), if you don't understand Spanish I can say it in English, but I must warn you," he smiled mischievously, "no es-speak so good."

For the first hour or so, the road skittered across the grasslands. A few hares bounded out of the way, luckier than some of their brethren who lay splattered on the pavement; flat as doormats. Caracaras, those carrion-eating members of the falcon family, perched patiently on fenceposts every few miles, evidently mindful of the fact that sooner or later another free meal would be delivered.

On our left appeared sweeping views of Lago Argentino, an enormous body of water that formed at the base of the mountains at the end of the last Ice Age. Clicking on his microphone, the tour guide cleared his throat and turned to face us. But instead of pithy anecdotes and facts about the country, we got a Cliff's Notes synopsis of the park brochure; and he didn't even feign enthusiasm.

"Not very enlightening," Judy commented.

"I'm not surprised," I said. "He's got more important things on his mind."

Lighting up another cigarette, our guide was totally focused on the two unattached, young women sharing a seat in the front row. Passing them his *yerba mate* (a herb tea) was a first move. The silver inlaid cup with a communal metal straw was an especially good touch; but the kicker came when he clicked the microphone back on and serenaded the embarrassed lovelies with an out-of-key Spanish ballad.

The bridge spanning the Río Santa Cruz marked the beginning of the wildlife-rich Andean foothills. The noise of the bus surprised a group of ostrichlike rheas. They rose from their camouflaged resting places and hurried off like clockwork feather dusters, their heads low to the ground and puffs of dust exploding at their feet. We counted a herd of twenty guanacos grazing the hilly ground. Ducks, geese, and swans gave glossy life to an otherwise lonely lake. A pair of condors soared above with hardly a wing movement until they were specks lost in the sky.

It was nearing lunchtime when we rattled past a sign marking the park boundary. But instead of glorious mountain views and continued sunny weather, we were greeted by a cold steady drizzle and low grey clouds. The tour guide stared dolefully out the window, having given up on his amorous quest. Even the picture-snapping German sitting next to me seemed subdued; his twin Leicas hung limply around his neck.

Fifteen minutes later we approached a cluster of buildings in a river valley surrounded by grass- and tree-covered hills where sheep and cattle grazed. "Welcome to Fitzroy Village," the guide announced as the bus stopped in front of a small hostería. "We will stay here until three o'clock. You can do what you want: hike, take pictures, whatever. But *please* be here when we leave. The next bus out is in four days."

Although everyone was keen to view Cerro Fitzroy, Argentina's equivalent to Wyoming's Grand Tetons, it didn't look as though the mountain was going to appear anytime soon. We followed our leader en masse into the warm, cozy inn.

One side of the inn was set up with tables and chairs, the other with a bar and stools. Memorabilia of climbing expeditions adorned the rough wooden walls: snowshoes, ice axes, crampons; commemorative posters, flags, photographs, and inscribed plaques; intricate wooden carvings done while at base camps waiting out storms.

About fifteen people were already enjoying the crackling fireplace when we walked in—a sensible place to be on such a dreary day. A group of blue-jeaned, college-aged men and women sorted through climbing gear and coiled a rope. A pair of middle-aged, out-of-shape women, dressed as if they were at Chamonix, sat in the lounge laughing and sipping drinks. A few chain-smoking men sat by themselves at the end of the bar, haggling over some card game. Our guide announced that lunch cost twelve australs, then bellied up to the bar to order a drink for himself.

Judy and I were not returning with the group. We would be hiking in the area and returning in a week or so. We stood near the doorway a bit befuddled. We asked the tour guide if he knew where the trailhead to Cerro Fitzroy was located. The guide said he didn't know, but he assured us that the hostería employees knew everything about the trails. "Don't ask the *guardaparques* (park rangers)," he advised between sips of his *aguardiente*, a potent sugar brandy. "They are lazy and useless like all government workers." I didn't mention that I was a government worker myself.

"I'm sorry, I don't know," the young worker waiting tables replied when we asked him about the trails. "But the owner, he knows."

"Good. Can we please talk to him?"

"Yes, of course, but he's not here. He is in Calafate picking up supplies."

Okay, how difficult could it be to find the trailhead to one of Argentina's most famous mountains? And we did have a crude, hand-drawn map copied from an outdated guidebook. We crossed the new bridge over the Río Fitzroy. Before the concrete span was installed, the crossing was considered hazardous due to the knee-to-thigh-deep glacier water and rounded rocks. I'm usually opposed to making the wilderness more accessible, but as I stared down at the rushing green current I felt guiltily grateful for this little improvement.

A road of sorts led toward a ranch in the cleft of the valley. The guidebook stated that there was "usually a gaucho around who is able to give directions." It also warned that his dogs sometimes drive hikers off, "unless the gaucho prevents them, as he sometimes does, by beating the hell out of them."

The guidebook failed to mention that before reaching the gaucho's hut we would have to hike through the Twilight Zone. In the valley bottom, hemmed in by steep ridges and mountains lost in the fog, was a flat clearing about thirty acres in size. This was the spanking-new town of Chalten, except there were no buildings, no roads, no people, only simple plywood signs stuck in the ground marking the future location of the police station, hotel, tourist office, gas station, bank, mechanic shop, and grocery store. A white wooden cross indicated where the church would eventually be.

According to an Argentinian we met, who may or may not have had cause to stretch the truth, the story behind Chalten began about ten years earlier when the Argentine army killed twenty-five Chilean homesteaders a few miles from where we stood. In retaliation, Chile vowed to occupy this undeveloped section of the Andes, one of twenty-two disputed pieces of land along the two countries' thirty-one-hundred-mile mountainous border. To block Chile's move, the Argentine government hastily scratched out Chalten to help consolidate, by virtue of colonization, Argentina's claim to the area. Free land was being offered to any citizen in the Fitzroy region. "That's fine," our source said disgustedly, "but what are these people going to do when they get there? How are they going to make a living in the winter? There are only so many days they can look at pretty mountains without food in their bellies."

Beyond the "Town of Tomorrow," as our acquaintance sarcastically called it, we found a crossroads of sorts: one sign said "camping," pointing off to the right; another said "*salto*," or waterfall, pointing straight ahead; and the third read "Río Blanco," pointing to a trail on the left that headed northwest through a corral. I studied the map, then studied the signs. "I think Cerro Fitzroy is to the left," I said uncertainly.

We scooped up a handful of stones in case the bloodthirsty curs suddenly appeared, then entered the corral and strode across the field as fast as we could. As it turned out, there was no cause for alarm. There was no helpful gaucho to offer directions, and no menacing dogs. In fact, since leaving the hostería, we hadn't seen anyone or anything except a few skinny cows.

We continued steadily west and upward. The path was well trodden and easy to follow through the big trees. The forest was similar to others we had seen during our travels in Patagonia. Eerie, moss-covered old beech with green, copper-tinged leaves formed a solid canopy overhead. The spongy and wet forest floor hid the true rough and rocky nature of the land. A few small birds darted in and out of the jungly underbrush, but I was in no mood to whip out my binoculars with a heavy backpack biting down on my shoulders.

We found a brook gurgling down the mountainside—a good thing since we had started our hike with only a few swigs left in our water bottles. Stopping for a refill, we dropped our packs and broke out some chocolate and fig cookies for quick energy. I glanced up the trail into the clouds, and back down through a hole in the mist to the valley below. Apparently Judy was on the same wavelength as I was because when I proposed camping where we were, she readily agreed.

With the rain and fog, we weren't exactly seeing much of the countryside anyway.

We pitched the tent far enough from the trail so that someone would have to look hard to see it. Folding our wet gear near the door, we tossed the rest of the stuff inside and crawled in behind it. I let out an exaggerated sigh of relief as I pulled off my squishy leather hiking boots and slipped into dry wool socks. "Life doesn't get much better than this!" I said, doing my beer commercial imitation. But it was true. It was positively wonderful to be out of the weather, in our own tent, by ourselves, far from cars, buses, hotels, radios, other tourists, and lovesick tour guides.

What was left of the day was spent reading, eating, talking, and listening to the rain. Dusk had fallen when we suddenly heard Spanish voices. We quietly unzipped the tent flap and peeked outside. Six bedraggled backpackers in muddy jeans and tattered plastic ponchos marched down the trail toward the road. They looked grim and definitely in a hurry. I waited until they passed then zipped the door back up, wondering who else was up in the mountains, in the cold rain.

It was a good thing we had a snug campsite because the next day a hard nonstop rain pinned us down. The tent held up well, except for a small puddle near the door that our sleeping bags managed to mop up.

Fortunately, we had three long books for Argentina. I don't know how anyone can travel without a book, yet I know that some true wilderness freaks believe that having a book is a distraction because it keeps you from focusing on everything happening around you. That it does, which of course is why I like books; they provide escape from "cabin fever."

Later, the deluge was replaced by a bone-chilling drizzle; birds started to call for the first time in twenty-four hours. We listened to a flock of parakeets, a kestrel, spine-tails, wrens, and finches.

A horseman passed camp, leading a loaded packhorse down the slippery trail. The guy was wearing a thick black woolen poncho and long, pleated trousers that were gathered at the ankles and covered the tops of high leather boots. A wide-brimmed black hat was tilted low over his head. Maybe he was the gaucho from near Chalten, the one with the killer dogs.

After sunset, I was looking out the tent, watching the gloomy darkness settle in, when all of a sudden three more soaking wet backpackers came plodding down the trail, abandoning a sinking ship. These were not happy campers—I know, having been in their boots. But did I feel guilty as I eased back into my sinfully warm and dry sleeping bag? Not a chance!

▲

The rain finally slackened during the early morning hours. The wind diminished to a whisper. The forest was very quiet, very still. Lying in my sleeping bag, I listened to a bird call. The sharp, repetitive screech could have belonged to an eagle or a falcon, but since it was still dark, more than likely it was that of an owl. A minute passed, maybe two, then another sound seared the woods, much closer to the tent. I jolted upright, cringing at the agonizing squeal of a creature in pain, most likely a rabbit or hare in the throes of death. The cry stopped. The owl had made a kill. The forest was very quiet, very still.

The sun rose over the ridge, casting a powerful spotlight across the tent. Outside the thermometer registered forty-six degrees Fahrenheit; inside our nylon womb we began to swelter. We had a cold breakfast and were on the trail with the day still young. The path dipped and climbed then leveled out, weaving between stands of dripping wet trees and small grassy clearings. I scanned for pumas, foxes, guanacos, condors. The best the wilderness could offer this morning was a solitary backpacker who had stepped off the trail to lighten his load.

Startled at our sudden appearance, the man quickly pulled up his pants, shouldered his pack, and walked over to meet us. Tall and thin, with plastic bread bags wrapped around his socks and a thick wool balaclava on his head, the hiker introduced himself as Dieter, a German from Bavaria. His Spanish sounded perfect to us, but he instantly switched to English when he realized we were unilingual Americans.

Dieter told us he had camped the past four days near the Río Blanco, the same place we were headed. "It rained the entire time," he said. "My friends left yesterday evening. Their tent got flooded and they got soaked." Now Dieter was returning to the hostería where his companions were drying out. "I hope you have better weather," he said. "To come all this way and leave without seeing Fitzroy is a real bummer."

Too bad Dieter couldn't have stuck it out a day longer. Trudging up the trail, we emerged at the treeline onto a grassy plateau. Directly ahead was a beautiful towering peak—a sheer, tooth-shaped spire where nothing but condors and intrepid climbers might dare to tread. Glaciers and snowfields and spectacular lesser peaks added the necessary backdrop to make this a world-class mountain scene. This was the Fitzroy range.

The sight of so much mountain majesty hurried us on. We were afraid that at any moment another storm could track in and the range of summits would be gone. We dropped into a poorly drained valley flooded with small lakes and meandering creeks. The recent rains had inundated the trail, forcing us to make long detours around submerged sections. Sometimes there was no going around, and we had to take off our socks and boots and wade.

More of a problem were the streams that were so deep and fast that they could only be crossed using makeshift log bridges hauled in by previous hikers. One of these tottering structures was about fifteen feet across, six inches wide, and six inches above a gusher that I preferred to avoid. With Judy offering encouragement from the sideline, I unbuckled the waist-strap of my pack, steadied myself, and gingerly stepped off the brushy bank onto the waterlogged timber. Using a long crooked stick for support (we had stupidly left our broomsticks behind in Punta Arenas), I was more than halfway across when a low overhanging branch snared the crossbar of my pack frame. I was cool. I was calm. I was stuck.

Judy shouted useless instructions and began to laugh as I flailed and teetered. I was not amused. With a desperate, twisting lunge I broke free of the branch, wobbled for a second over the water, and caught myself with the stick. Once I was upright I managed to do a shaky dance across without falling in.

The path rose out of the spongy ground and entered a strand of dense woods where we found another trail intersection sign. We leaned our packs against the post and investigated our options. The trail to the right led to an overused campsite centered around a communal cooking shed. The camp was empty, but the place was dirty and unappealing. Straight ahead was a high rocky bank overlooking the Río Blanco. The trail led to a rickety log bridge that spanned the river then snaked up a steep, open slope in the direction of the Fitzroy massif.

With a little bit of hunting, we discovered a perfect, unused campsite about a hundred yards off the trail. The site not only provided excellent protection from the prevailing winds but also offered a view of Fitzroy, which was just about to disappear in the clouds. We hadn't come far (it was only twelve-thirty); but with a spot like this to ourselves we didn't hesitate to make camp. Good timing. A gusty rain began to whip through the valley, rattling tree branches and sending shivers up our backs.

Rain or no rain, as soon as the tent was up we hiked back to the Río Blanco and followed it upstream. A massive amount of chalky-white rocks and boulders filled the wide river bed, but the river itself

*A solitary backpacker going across a grassy field toward the snowy peaks of the Fitzroy range.*

was no more than twenty feet across—twenty feet of foaming, ice-cold glacial water which without a bridge or some exotic rope system would be impossible to cross.

We retreated into the forest to escape the wind. The big beech provided a welcome screen, but this wasn't the place to linger, not with the steady crack of dead branches and tree limbs overhead. Judy found some orchids in bloom—delicate yellow flowers with slender stems. A little farther on, clustered in a seep, was a bouquet of wildflowers: gentians, daisies, and lupines. The flower bed also harbored a complete guanaco skeleton, picked clean by scavengers.

A sizeable tributary of the Río Blanco stopped us about a half-mile into our hike. Over the years, the side channel had evidently busted out of its banks more than once. A ghostly forest of bleached grey trees leaned drunkenly away from the wind, their bases smothered in heaps of river gravel and rocks.

The rain had reached a crescendo by the time we reached camp. Despite being shielded, the tent took some blows from the erratic williwaw. We positioned boots, water bottles, anything of weight, around the edge of the floor to help hold it down. The far-off hum of the wind would begin up the valley then increase in volume and tempo until the blast "whooshed" through the tree tops, sounding exactly like the fly-by of an F-16 jet fighter.

After a couple hours of listening to rock falls, or ice falls, and the crazy wind, our nerves began to fray. We began to think of leaving. With this weather, a dingy hotel was starting to sound good.

▲

By the next day we were decidedly sick of our smelly yellow tent interior. The skies remained leaden grey, but we battled listlessness and went outside. Our leather boots were already wet, but to keep them from getting thoroughly soaked we wore only running shoes with no socks. The temperature was a hypothermic forty-two degrees Fahrenheit but, as long as we kept moving, our shriveled-up feet would be all right.

We reached the Río Blanco in a few minutes. The watercourse was swollen and milky-white, lapping at bushes that normally would be high on dry ground. I tried first to cross the two parallel logs that someone had wired loosely together and laid across the stream. The tall, stout branch I was using as a third leg broke only a few steps into my traverse and was swept from my hands.

"I think I'll try a different approach," I said, jumping back to shore. On my hands and knees, I baby-crawled over the logs a few inches at a time. Judy studied my technique, knowing that her turn was next.

The trail climbed out of the river bottom and immediately entered a fringe of woods. The footpath was a wet, eroding mess. Leaving our hiking boots behind was the right choice; we were soon wading ankle-deep in the rivulets of icy water that were running down off the mountain. We laughed at each other's appearance: rain pants rolled up above the knees, revealing pale white skin riddled with goose bumps; below the waist we were streaked with mud.

We had hiked only a short distance into the forest when we stumbled upon a crude log shack. Two smaller hovels were farther off to the rear. The place looked like a set from the movie, *Swiss Family Robinson*. There were gutters fashioned from hollowed-out tree limbs, water spouts fabricated from rubber tubing, chairs and benches made from stumps and logs, and windows of clear plastic sheeting. We were about to walk quietly past and continue up the mountain when a tall, muscle-bound man with a bushy black beard and black curly hair suddenly stepped out of the main hut and hailed us in Spanish. He invited us to hot tea.

José and his partner, Luiz, were here in hopes of being the first Brazilians to stand on Cerro Fitzroy's fabled spire. For the past twenty-one days, however, they had gone nowhere.

"The weather has been horrible," José lamented, while Luiz put the tea kettle on a little twig fire near the door. "When we arrived we had six days in a row of storms; then three days when it let up, just long enough for us to cache supplies part way up the approach glacier." Staring outside the doorway, he added glumly, "The past eleven days have been continuous rain, wind, and low clouds. Like it is now."

Four other climbing parties had arrived at the same time they had, José said, "but they all called it quits after the first week." Only one group, from Spain, had climbed the spiked peak the entire summer. José explained that though Fitzroy was first climbed in 1953, and has since been climbed several times by teams from many different nations, the region has not lost any of its compelling mystique. "In part," he said solemnly, "this is because several climbers have died attempting to scale Fitzroy and nearby peaks."

We talked away the afternoon. For Judy and me, the relatively roomy hut and the conversation offered a pleasant change from sitting in our tent and reading. In English, José nonchalantly told us about some of his climbing feats. In 1984, he became the first South American to solo Alaska's Mount McKinley. More recently, he had climbed the third highest peak in the Himalayas; and next year he hoped to join a Polish expedition to climb Everest.

The two men said they would take as long as necessary to reach Fitzroy's summit. "Except we are low on food," Luiz announced. "We are returning to Calafate tomorrow to get resupplied for another three weeks."

While in town they planned to pick up some reading material. "We brought only two books, and we read them the first week," Luiz laughed. "After a while, even the best of friends get tired of talking about about food and the weather." Judy and I exchanged glances: Yes, we knew *exactly* how they felt.

We still had to cross the river again, and I was afraid if we waited much longer the log bridge would be underwater, or gone. Before leaving, I asked José and Luiz if they would pose outside the shack so that I could take their photo. That was the last we saw of them. And we never did learn if they were successful in their climb.

▲

An hour before sunrise, the temperature had dropped to well below freezing. After taking a quick glance outside, and seeing nothing but a lacquer-black sky pierced with stars, I put another stocking cap over the one I already had on and curled into a tight ball in my sleeping bag.

At 6:30 I awoke and looked outside again. What a way to greet the day! Fitzroy and its neighbors were bathed in soft golden light. The sky was a robin's egg blue, marred by only a strand or two of pinkish clouds. Even more remarkable was the absolute absence of wind.

I slipped out of my bag, climbed quickly into my clothes, and stuffed my daypack with everything I might need for a long day in the mountains. Judy was still half-asleep, but I told her that I was going to climb to the *laguna* below Fitzroy's east face. If she wanted, she could meet me there later.

"Okay, I will," she mumbled. "Have fun."

The mountain shone in the sun as I started off, but the blue sky turned grey in the short time it took me to reach the Río Blanco. The sun vanished behind a bank of clouds. The strong, warming light of before was now a pale hazy yellow. At least the mountains were still visible, but I didn't have much hope that the view would last for long.

I forded the river and passed the base camp. The place was deserted. Following the steps of many a famous climber circling for a good route to tackle Fitzroy, I emerged quickly out of the forest to begin my own "ascent" of the mountain's flanks.

Although flabby from too much sitting in buses and idle days in the tent, I managed to make it to the promontory directly beneath Fitzroy in about one hour. But I did need to catch my breath, which was fine, because the view from the plateau was worthy of slow and methodical examination. To the southeast, far below, was enormous Lago Viedma—grey-blue and calm, covering over four hundred square miles of Patagonia. Like many of the lakes in the region, its oblong basin was carved out by huge sheets of glacial ice. Rough, rolling, grass-covered steppes—the preferred habitat of guanacos, rheas, armadillos, and rabbits—stretched eastward to the horizon. And to the southwest were more high peaks, just as rocky and rugged as the one I was on. Somewhere over there stood 10,263-foot Cerro Torre, a pillarlike mountain once rated as unclimbable and con-quered only after Everest. Nowadays, weather permitting, the world's best mountaineers clamber up and down this peak in two days, though several have died trying. I looked for a route across the plain that would lead us into the next valley, since we planned to pay a visit to Cerro Torre the following day.

Despite the cool air, the exertion left me sweating. I stripped off a layer of clothes and stuffed them into my pack. A swig of ice-cold water and a granola bar sufficed for breakfast. A few minutes later I crested a boulder field and gazed up on one of the most stunning sights I had seen during our travels in the Andes. A small cobalt-blue lake was set in the midst of a bench of grey rock and rubble. Looming over the laguna was a gleaming white, heavily crevassed glacier. And above that was Fitzroy itself, a dagger of granite leaping more than two miles (11,073 feet) into the sky. The mountain's name seemed particularly fitting, since it honors the captain of the *Beagle*, in which Darwin made his voyage to the southernmost Andes in 1832.

I studied the mountain through binoculars, looking for two spidermen moving up its face. Maybe the Brazilians had chosen to forget about supplies in Calafate and instead were making a dash for the peak. But I saw no one, nor any trace of where they might have been. While I have done some minor rock climbing, and have enjoyed the physical and mental stimulation of it, the thought of struggling up a big wall, pitch after pitch, left me with far more doubts than desires. What kind of inner fire did these Brazilians possess to maintain their tireless vigil with such a slim chance of success? What kind of extraordinary abilities enabled them to climb a peak that, even in ideal weather, appeared to be impossible to conquer? Where the simplest mistake could mean death; where several climbers had already died?

Mulling these things over, I tightened the straps of my daypack and moved on. I focused on a narrow-ridged peaklet ahead. It would do just fine for my own climb.

The line of ascent was rotten and crumbly, the handholds less than secure. Still, after an hour of steady climbing I found myself standing on the peak. I gaped downward for a thousand precipitous feet from a perch no larger than a tractor seat. A misplaced step or an unexpected strong gust could send me plummeting into another laguna that had remained hidden until now. The small lake was the color of chalk, not surprising since a steady stream of stones and ice chunks clattered off the glacier above it.

I clicked on my wide-angle lens, held the camera at arm's length, and snapped a self-portrait with Fitzroy over my shoulder. It was an act of vanity, but I wanted some record to show a climbing friend at home. I put the camera back in my pack, took a long lingering look at the mountain then began to pick my way down. Judy was cresting the promontory below the small peak and I didn't want to miss her. It would be nice to get a picture of both of us looking out over Patagonia.

The evening turned sour again, with rain and howling wind. In the morning we were ready to leave for Cerro Torre, but it made no sense to pack up only to be socked in with more of the same crud. By noon, the thermometer had risen to only thirty-five degrees, considerably below the average summer temperature of about sixty degrees. Fresh snow dusted the mountainsides, dropping the snow level to its lowest elevation since our arrival. We stayed in the tent, trying to stay dry and warm. The local wildlife was also taking shelter from the elements. The only creature I saw all morning was a sorry-looking sparrow that hopped in front of the tent to pluck red berries growing in the heath.

We read, talked, snacked, and napped in a kind of funky malaise. We exhibited the first symptoms of cabin fever. We talked about people at home that we would normally go out of our way to avoid. We thought we would invite them to dinner when we got home. We were thinking of everyone we knew. Let's face it, we were tired of each other's company.

"Okay, forget the party," Judy snapped, annoyed at my unwillingness to participate in planning some dinner I knew we wouldn't want to have. "I gotta get out of here!"

We put on our rain gear and yanked on our boots. I was about to unzip the door when we heard an English voice outside: "Knock-knock ... Hello ... Is anybody home in there?"

I undid the flap and found a lanky, parka-clad stranger with wire-rimmed glasses and a week's worth of whiskers leaning over in front of the door. "Oh, hello," he said, in an accent that almost sounded British. "I'm Peter. My wife and I have a camp by the river, and we wondered if you want to come have a cup of tea."

"Sure!" Judy answered without hesitation. "Give us five minutes to get ready. We'll meet you over there."

After Peter left, we giggled and acted like a couple of goofy teenagers about to go on a first date. For some ridiculous reason, we suddenly wondered what we should wear (as if we had a choice), and if we smelled (which went without saying). "I know," Judy gushed in a frenzy of activity. "Let's take some chocolate bars and Fig Newtons as our contribution."

Their camp consisted of a small mountain tent and a tarp stretched tightly between two trees to help shield them from the wind. It was more sheltered than our site but darker being secreted in the forest. "Here, have some *mate* with a spot of brandy," Peter offered, handing us steaming hot cups when we strolled in. "I don't know if the Argentines drink it this way, but we do."

Two more genial people we never could have met. They were both "Tassies" from the island of Tasmania off southeast Australia. Peter was a fisheries biologist by profession. Jan was studying to be a teacher. They had arrived the previous evening during the storm. This was Peter's second trip to Fitzroy; three years earlier he spent a week camping and hiking in the area with a friend. "We had fantastic weather the entire time," he said with a wry grin. "You wouldn't believe what this place looks like when there's sun."

We'd have to take his word for it. As we spoke, the rain turned to sleet, then spitting snow. A small cooking fire in front of the tarp gave off just enough heat to warm our hands and toes.

▲

The next day the weather moderated enough for us to break camp. There were still flurries and grey skies, but at least it wasn't raining and the winds were not so fierce. It was now or never if we wanted to hike over into the next valley. But first we had to say goodbye to our friends. When we got there, their tent was sealed tight and there wasn't a sound.

"They should be up by now," I said, glancing at my watch. "It's ten o'clock."

"Ssshh! They might be sleeping. Let's just leave a note and be on our way."

There was a rustling inside the tent. A murmuring of voices. The door was unzipped and thrown open. "G'morning," Peter croaked. "Did I hear you say it's ten o'clock?"

Both he and Jan were in their sleeping bags, puffy-faced and bleary-eyed. Judy apologized for waking them, specifying that it was my idea.

"That's quite all right," Jan said good-naturedly. "We should be getting up."

"That's right," Peter echoed, stifling a yawn. "We don't want you to think that we Tassies do nothing but drink *mate* and sleep away the day!"

For the next two hours we bushwhacked through marshy areas and between steep forested slopes to reach the Río Fitzroy valley. Eventually we hit the path that would take us along the river and to Cerro Torre itself. The route climbed above treeline and onto ridges of bare rock. It was a gentle walk, apart from one point near the start where we had to ease ourselves along a narrow ledge of a cliff face. Lago Torre (the source of the Río Fitzroy) was on our left, azure-tinted water overshadowed by grey gravelly mountains. In the distance were the Torre and Grande glaciers rising into the mists, their twin crevassed snouts reminding me of cat's paws waiting to strike. Cerro Torre, exceptional for its needlelike form, was lost in the clouds, as were all the high peaks and towers around it. Hidden just behind the mountains was the Patagonian ice cap. And beyond that, a mere thirty miles away, lay the Pacific Ocean.

Pausing to rest, we listened to the clattering rock slides, the steady din of cascades and waterfalls, and the deep percussion of cracking and growling glaciers. "Too bad I didn't bring a small tape recorder," I said. "I could replay it whenever I miss the Andes."

An hour later we entered a sparse stand of beech trees that overlooked the lake and the tongue of the glacier. This was the end of the line for the trail and the last place to pitch a tent. On a small patch of level ground near a babbling brook was the Cerro Torre base camp. As was the case at Fitzroy, the place was empty except for a couple of alpinists ensconced in a ramshackle hut.

While Judy searched for a campsite, I mosied over to the hut to be sociable. There was no language barrier this time, since both climbers were mountaineering instructors for the American Alpine Institute in the state of Washington. I had read about the exploits of one of them in mountaineering magazines. To his credit were difficult ascents of Cerro Torre and Fitzroy, the Paine Towers, and several big peaks in Peru and Alaska. This time he and his companion were going after Torre's slightly smaller neighbor, Aguja (meaning "needle") Standhardt, considered an even more difficult climb.

Controversy swirls about the first ascent of this slender granite fang. "I'm sure it's never been climbed," he insisted from a bench seat inside the disheveled hut. "At least not all the way." A rope's length from the summit is an overhang of ice known as the "mushroom," he explained. A group claims to have made it past the mushroom to the peak, but many climbers believe the overhang is where the group stopped.

All of this talk about climbing Standhardt would be purely academic if the weather didn't improve fast. Like the Brazilians, the American climbers had been stuck in the same place for twenty-one days, sitting out storms. They were determined to hold out one more week. "If things don't change for the better by then," the apparent leader said pessimistically, "we'll call it quits and do some sightseeing before returning to the States." Then, nodding toward his younger partner, he added, "This is Mark's first trip to South America. It's depressing to think that he might leave here without even having a chance to get on the rock."

Good sites were scarce on the cramped bench, so Judy and I were forced to pitch the tent near a spot the Americans called the "Italian Camp" because a large party of Italian climbers had stayed here a few weeks earlier. The former occupants might have been superb alpinists, but they knew nothing about no-trace camping. A stone fireplace they had constructed was full of partly burned plastic food wrappings. Nearby were mounds of leftover lima beans rotting on the ground. The trees, scant enough in this little alcove, were showing the strain of human abuse; many had been hacked for firewood or used as part of some shelter. Ten burlap bags full of garbage leaned against a hut, "waiting" for someone else to dispose of them. Even more insulting was the used toilet paper scattered about and the piles of exposed shit in the bushes.

"Makes you proud to be a human being," Judy said, while picking up some scattered tin cans. "May a condor crap on their heads."

▲

After dinner, we walked over to the edge of the escarpment and looked out over the glacier. To the west was the Andean honor guard we were hoping to see: Cerro Torre; Aguja Standhardt, named for a local rancher; Torre Egger, named for an Austrian climber killed during a descent in 1959; Cerro St. Exupery, in honor of the pioneer French aviator and writer; and Aguja Poincenot, named after a French climber who drowned in the Río Fitzroy. Naturally these peaks and the rest of the Cordillera chain that dominates the northern half of Los Glaciares park were wrapped in their characteristic wreath of clouds.

Finding a nook out of the wind, we discussed the logistics for the next leg of our journey. A bus was scheduled to leave Chalten, the Town of Tomorrow, at 3:00 P.M. the following day for the return trip to Calafate. After another unavoidable night in Calafate's municipal campground with its yapping dogs and noisy campers, we planned to spend a couple of days camped near the Perito Moreno Glacier, the centerpiece of Parque Nacional Los Glaciares. Fifty miles by road from Calafate, deep in the recesses of the Andes, this wall of stark blue-white ice is the only glacier in the park not in regression. It advances across a narrow section of Lago Argentino, forming a giant dam and plowing into the forest on the far western shore. Travelers we had met in Chile told us that Moreno was not to be missed, with columns of ice the size of twenty-story buildings crashing into the lake, creating floating icebergs that jostle for space at the glacier's three-mile-wide face. We were determined to get there, to see what lay beyond the next horizon.

Glacier
Grey

ARGENTINA

Torres del Paine
Cuernos del Paine
Lago Pehoe
Lago del Toro
Rio Serrano
Mt. Balmaceda
Seno Ultima Esperanza
Puerto Natales

Lago de
Grey

Rio
Gallegos

CHILE

Straits of Magellan

Punta
Arenas

ISLA
GRANDE
DE TIERRA
DEL FUEGO

ATLANTIC OCEAN

PACIFIC OCEAN

Cabo de Hornos

N

# 4.

# THE CIRCUITO MAGNIFICO (CHILE)

THE BUS PULLED UP to the Lago Pehoe hostería right on schedule.

"Next time, just a day pack," I vowed, grabbing hold of my unwieldy backpack as the driver unceremoniously dumped it from the roof rack onto the ground.

"Let's face it," Judy said, grimacing, struggling to shoulder her own pack. "It doesn't matter how long we're going to be gone, we always end up with ridiculously heavy loads. I think it's genetic."

Complaints about weight aside, it felt wonderful to be back in the boonies. After leaving Argentina's Los Glaciares National Park, we had spent a few days in Río Gallegos and Punta Arenas, waiting for transportation and stocking up on provisions. Now we were about to embark on another wilderness jaunt in the same park where we had launched our Klepper kayak the year before.

We hiked down the gravel road to the developed campground near Lago Pehoe. An attendant notified us that the price for camping had doubled and that a hot shower was now available from 8:00 A.M. to 2:00 P.M., but otherwise it was the same windswept place with the same spectacular view.

Across the lake, Paine Grande and the other peaks were turning pink and gold as the sun settled below the cordillera. Rising up from the slopes were dark green strands of southern beech, some of them tinted orange and yellow as the austral summer turned into fall. A condor flew above like a giant black moth drawn to the last flicker of light. With some melancholy, I reflected that this was our last planned trip to Patagonia; there was no telling when we'd be back.

Judy fixed dinner, which meant pouring boiling water in a plastic Ziploc bag, while I sat at the edge of the lake studying the map resting on my knee. The *circuito,* or circuit trail, around the Paine massif, would take us sixty miles along rivers, glaciers, backcountry lakes, and through a high mountain pass—areas in the park's vast interior that we had merely glimpsed from a distance or had missed altogether during our first trip by kayak. We'd be traveling clockwise around the range, starting near the north side of Lago Pehoe and exiting somewhere near the park entrance. We had been told that strong, lightly loaded backpackers could complete the trek in four days. I gave us three times that long.

▲

Our day began with a ninety-minute hike back up the deserted road toward the Lago Pehoe ranger station. We had to register with the authorities and pick up a backcountry permit. However, when we reached the log-cabin office, there was a sign on the door that read: OUT IN COUNTRY. WILL RETURN IN ONE HOUR. One hour from when?

The hour passed and still no one appeared, so we left a note specifying our intended route and started hiking toward Salto Grande, the thundering cascade between Lago Nordenskjold and Lago Pehoe. According to our brochure map, there was a footbridge here leading to the main trail between Grey Glacier and Paine Grande. What we didn't know, and what the ranger undoubtedly would have told us, was that the bridge had been washed away by a recent flood. A day hiker returning from the waterfall gave us the bad news.

Backtracking to the ranger station, we sat on the front stoop and discussed our options in light of this new development. We could either continue up the road to a trailhead near Lago Amarga (a minimum of a day-and-a-half hike back toward the park entrance) or we could begin the circuito far to the south, near park headquarters at the head of the Río Serrano. Either way meant a lengthy delay and much road hiking.

*Tent overlooking Lago Pehoe, with Paine Grande and other peaks rising in the distance.*

Lago Amarga was closer, so we headed in that direction. Almost immediately, a shiny new Volkswagen micro-bus came chugging up the hill behind us. I stuck out my thumb and to my amazement the VW stopped. Inside were a middle-aged couple and a young boy. The man rolled down his window and, in German, then Spanish, asked where we were headed. When I replied in Spanish, he laughed and said, "Americans. Get in. We'll take you there."

We turned off the main road toward the Lago Amarga guardería. The graded track undulated across dry, shortgrass steppes; perfect grazing ground for guanacos. The guanacos of Torres del Paine have grown accustomed to vehicles and hikers, unlike their counterparts outside parks, which, while usually protected, are subject to poaching. Without even trying, we spotted at least two hundred of them feeding along the roadside. By contrast, when Torres del Paine became a park in 1959, no guanacos were known to be in the area.

Eventually the Río Paine valley and the ranger station appeared through the front windshield. "I envy you," the woman said, as she helped unload our packs. "To go beyond the sierra sounds so exciting. Perhaps when our son is grown, we will do it too." We said our goodbyes, and Judy and I went off to find a ranger as they left for Punta Arenas.

After checking in with the ranger, who issued us backcountry permits, we crossed the Río Paine using a rickety suspension footbridge that swayed and creaked in the wind. The wetlands nearby were superb habitat for waterbirds, and from the bridge we observed buff-necked ibises, coots, southern lapwings, and swans. Huge flights of upland geese passed in front of the black mountainside.

The trail soon split. The right fork continued up a wooded, parklike valley as part of the circuito trail. A spur trail led toward the Paine Towers, the three jagged needles that lie north of the Paine Horns. Actually an old tractor road, it provided convenient access through the head-high brush and rolling ground. Jackrabbits, or hares, were everywhere. Hunger and the scarcity of people had made them tame. We were able to approach quite close before they loped away.

When we reached a small valley harboring a cluster of ranch buildings, we dropped our packs and got out binoculars. Near a small house a half-mile away we could see two orange tents and a couple of people—climbers perhaps—and some horses grazing in an open field. But the main thing that caught our attention were the Paine Towers looming overhead—five thousand feet of near-vertical granite rising from rolling grasslands. We scanned the pink and white monoliths, from the bare rock rubble at their bases to their sharp, sunlit peaks reaching into the sky.

A little bit of searching uncovered a pleasant campsite sheltered from the incessant west winds that swept over the sierra. There was a creek nearby to supply us with water. Birds were everywhere, enjoying the sunny summer day.

▲

A chilly rainstorm blew in during the night, but by the time we were packed the sun had returned. Under blue skies, with the mountains at their shining best, the temperature soon hit seventy degrees Fahrenheit. We stripped down to shorts and shirtsleeves, thankful for the breeze that helped dry off the sweat and keep away the flies.

Rather than return to the suspension bridge, where we were certain to pick up the main trail, I set the bezel on my compass and we bushwhacked across the flat, dusty ground toward the Río Paine valley somewhere to the northeast. Cattle trails wound through the scrub. Bashing through a dense thicket, we recoiled in fright when a large herd of bovines bellowed in alarm and stampeded in front of us. CONAF, the governmental agency that administers Chile's parks and reserves, is trying to eliminate grazing from Paine, but it is a touchy issue (as it is in several U.S. national parks) that can take years or generations to resolve. In the meantime, wildlife suffers. I saw neither guanacos nor rheas, two of the park's star attractions, in the areas where livestock was allowed to roam.

It wasn't until our first orange-painted stake, a park trailmarker, that Judy gave me credit for orienteering, going cross-country with map and compass. Really, though, there was no chance of becoming lost in this section; all we had to do was follow the Río Paine toward its source in the mountains. I put the compass back in my pocket.

The route snaked through scrubby beech forest and open meadows bright with daisies. The bushes were heavy with fat calafate berries; the seeps shimmered with yellow foxgloves. Mountains hemmed us in our left. Lingering snowfields on the summits contrasted with the charcoal-colored scree above treeline.

After a cold but not too deep stream crossing, Judy and I tied our wet running shoes to our packs and continued hiking in dry leather boots. A short time later, we came upon a barbed wire fence, a remnant of the days when the Río Paine valley was owned by private ranchers. On the other side of the fence was a brown stud bull the size

*Judy and an unfriendly bull gaze warily at one another, in the Río Paine valley.*

of a cape buffalo with the disposition to match. It huffed and pawed at the ground and lowered its horns in a most unfriendly manner.

Judy backed up slowly. Lions, tigers, and bears she doesn't mind, but stick a yapping dog or a ballsy cow in her path and she starts to hyperventilate.

"C'mon, he's only bluffing," I said.

She wasn't convinced. "Oh, really? Then you go first." We made a wide detour and skulked across the paddock where the beast couldn't see us.

This was the last bull or cow we saw during our hike. We made camp in a flowery little depression free of cow chips, cow tracks, and overgrazed vegetation. I sighed as I dipped my hot and sweaty feet in the rushing waters of a nearby stream, but Judy screeched as she plunged her whole body into the flow.

While Judy bathed, I went for a stroll, following the stream to the Río Paine about a hundred yards away. The river here was as wide as a four-lane road, swift and deep with numerous rapids and some minor drops. Families of geese paddled at the fringes of the current. It was a wonder how the goslings, looking like fluffy grey tennis balls, were strong enough to make headway against the river's powerful flow. But by following their honking parents, the flotillas safely hop-scotched from one eddy to the next.

Some time later, Judy came out to join me, binoculars in hand. "Is that really you?" I joked. Her hair was fluffy and combed; her clothes smelled fresh and clean. I wanted to give her a big hug, but I resisted. She was a new woman, but I was the same dirty old me.

▲

Another cloudless day greeted us at dawn. "Is this the park we were in last year?" I asked, stepping out of the tent in only my shorts and running shoes. When we showed slides of our first Paine trip to friends, they grew weary of our constant references to williwaws and driving rain. By contrast, the weather over the last three days had been more typical of southern Arizona in winter—not too hot, not too cold, with plenty of sunshine.

The trail continued past an abandoned cabin, a relic of the early 1900s, then was lost upon entering a large meadow. Walking through the grass was easy, interrupted only by us stopping often to birdwatch. A large flock of upland geese—the males white with black wings, the females a dark shade of brown—lifted off in alarm when we disturbed their feeding. A group of *bandurria*, or buff-necked ibis, took to the air. Their dramatically marked black and grey wings were unmistakable. A pair of big black and white lapwing plovers flew back and forth over our heads, the air ringing with their plaintive piping.

At the far end of the meadow we had a decision to make: Should we follow the faint path that led up the steep open ridge on our left, or stay in the valley where the trail *should* go? Judy thought we should climb. I opted for staying low. Someone once defined a good marriage as "two people who don't go crazy at the same time." Luckily, while I went crazy trying to find the trail in the brush-choked valley, Judy kept her cool and did not once say, "I told you so."

Finally, admitting I was wrong, we left the river drainage and struggled up the ridge—a task that would have left me breathless under normal circumstances, let alone with the load I was carting. Judy followed slowly behind me, hands on her shoulder straps, head down staring at her feet. The mountainside was dry and dusty, covered with a sparse growth of hardy shrubs and short brown grass. I was thirsty, but I wanted to ration the water I had left because I didn't know what lay ahead.

The view from the ridgetop told us what to expect. Nestled between a series of semiarid steppes was Lago Paine, out of which the Río Paine flowed. The lake was frothy with whitecaps. Nowhere was there a sign of a trail. Nowhere was there a sign of another human being. We hugged a narrow bench above the south shore, following a combination of cattle and horse trails that converged, diverged, and melted away into dead-ends. There were some narrow scree chutes to traverse, then came the old range fence in the middle of nowhere that the ranger had marked on our map. There was something significant about this fence, but what? The ranger's explanation in Spanish had eluded us, and the line on the map told us nothing about which way to go. Uncertain, we stopped.

Again I opted for staying low, which seemed the right decision, at least for the first hour. Halfway down along the lake, however, we suddenly had three new options to consider: We could cross a series of extremely steep scree chutes that plummeted onto the bouldery shoreline fifty feet below; we could climb three hundred feet of steep, loose rock to the next higher bench, where we hoped the hiking would be good; or we could turn back and forget the whole thing.

We chose Door Number Two.

The climb was a leg- and lung-buster. The slope was so steep and crumbly that to gain one foot meant scrambling perhaps two or three. Fortunately, I had assistance: A wall of rising wind literally pushed me up the mesa, an ally for once instead of a foe.

I reached the bench in about thirty minutes, ditched my pack, and slid back down to help Judy, who was still far below. Fierce gusts kept knocking her off her feet. I expected a fight when I offered to take her pack. Instead she grunted "Thanks" as she unfastened her waistbelt and rolled out of the shoulder straps.

Our climb paid off with a clearly defined foot trail where before there had been none. "Okay, I was wrong," I apologized, as we shuffled along the ridge. "We should have headed high right away, like you said."

Judy was in a generous mood. "I know," she replied.

We reached the end of the lake around six o'clock, and dropped back down to water level. In no time at all, the trail disappeared again in a jungle of chapparal brush and wind-flagged trees. In spite of the frustration I felt at that moment, I liked the fact that one of the best hikes in South America was only faintly marked and challenging to follow, rather than a no-brainer highway that typifies many of the overdeveloped national park trails in the United States.

At 7:00 P.M., footsore, hungry, and hot, we decided that finding the trail could wait until morning. We made camp at the edge of a grassy clearing. A green ribbon of evergreen and deciduous beech forest formed a windscreen behind us, and a waterfall-streaked mountain lay ahead.

After dinner, I went for a quick hike while Judy stayed behind and wrote postcards to friends. The trail had to be somewhere in this valley, I thought; better to find it now rather than stumble around in the morning. Besides, I felt obliged to make up for my earlier blunders.

I took off on an angle toward the sound of a stream. A half-hour search revealed nothing in the way of footpaths, but there were other things to see. A large brownish-grey owl had settled on a tree a short distance away, blending with the foliage until only its yellow eyes remained. The bird was easy to identify since it was the same species, *Bubo virginianus*, that I had seen hundreds of times across North America. Known as the *tucuquere* in Patagonia, the great-horned owl blinked and swiveled its head as I walked slowly toward its roost. I was less than twenty feet from the bird, and ready to snap its portrait, when suddenly the silence was shattered by a loud chattering. I looked up and saw a flock of more than a dozen austral parakeets perched on the bare branch of a tree. Their unexpected presence was too much for the owl. Without a flutter, it sprung into the air and glided into the dusky forest.

▲

The weather changed around midnight. One look outside the tent in the morning was all it took to declare this a rest day. Fresh snow blanketed the mountainsides below a heavy layer of grey scud. Pelting rain and gale-force winds would make for a very wet hike.

We had built a buffer of bad-weather days into our itinerary, so I actually welcomed the opportunity to catch up on my notes and rest my legs a bit. I had had arthroscopic surgery a few months earlier to repair torn cartilage in one knee, and it was starting to act up. After climbing that last scree slope the knee started clicking and now was producing a dull, throbbing pain.

"Nothing to worry about," I said, while I rummaged through the first-aid kit for a couple of aspirins.

"Good," Judy said matter-of-factly. "Because I can't carry you out."

The rain let up around midafternoon, but it was still cold and wet and too late to strike camp. We crawled out of the tent for another game of hide-and-seek with the trail. By now I was certain the path was on the mountainside, but where? My question was answered when I looked up and spotted two backpackers on the hillside about a hundred feet above us and a hundred yards away. Dressed in brightly colored raingear, definitely gringo in style, they passed in and out of the dripping shrubbery, moving quickly. They were on the trail!

I was just deciding whether to call out, when the guy in the lead suddenly looked down. He stopped, turned to say something to his companion, and pointed at us.

"¡Hola!" I shouted, waving my arm. "¿Hablas inglés?"

"You bet," the leader called back. "Where you from?"

Judy and I climbed quickly to meet them. The man in front introduced himself as Steve. Tall and athletic, he looked to be in his mid-thirties, but what was most distinctive about him was the yellow-and-black baseball cap on his head.

"Where'd you get the CAT hat?" I asked. Caterpillar Tractor Company had its world headquarters in Peoria, Illinois, about thirty miles from our home. Judy's father had retired from CAT, and her brother, aunt, and uncles still worked there.

It turned out that Steve and his friend were working for Caterpillar in Santiago, Chile, and had both lived in Peoria. Standing on the trail in a cold, gauzy mist, we laughed about meeting Peorians *here* and compared notes about our hikes. They, too, had taken the "low" route at the lake. "Thanks a lot!" Steve said good-naturedly. "I wanted to go high, but Paul insisted we follow your tracks. Good fun going up that scree slope, eh?"

"Yeah," Paul chimed in. "Thanks to the delay, we had a *real* interesting time last night. I've backpacked in the mountains of Colorado and Wyoming but last night's weather was the worst I've ever been in." Caught by darkness, they had been forced to set up camp on the open steppes above Lago Paine. Their tent was flattened when the storm rolled in.

"This morning was pure bedlam," Steve continued, his haggard, bewhiskered face proof of a sleepless night. "We threw all our wet gear into our packs and headed up the lake. Notice that we found the trail this time," he pointed out for his partner's benefit.

They were headed for a *refugio* to dry out. The park map indicated that a trailside hut, one of four along the *circuito*, was within a mile or so. As is the custom among travelers, we exchanged names and addresses, assuming that we would probably never see each other again. "If you have time, give me a call when you're in Santiago," Steve said as we shook hands in farewell. "We've got a spare bedroom, and while it may not sound good now, a swimming pool."

▲

A cold rain fell off and on during the night. It was a good morning to sleep late, but the parakeets thought otherwise. It was 5:00 A.M. when I first heard their sharp, squeaky chatter in the trees behind camp. Judy buried her head under a pile of clothes and drifted back asleep. Not me. I listened to parrot talk for the next two hours and not once understood what was said.

We hit the trail at nine, wearing rain pants and parkas against the blustery winds. Puddle-jumping aside, it was easy going now that we could pay more attention to the scenery than route-finding. Mountains boxed us in, with the Río Paine snaking down the center. The valley was mostly wooded, interspersed with marshy openings and verdant meadows. Crossing a small creek, we flushed a family of spectacled ducks; the adults performed a convincing "broken wing" act to lure us from their six tiny ducklings. Much more common than ducks were *becasinas*, or common snipes. It seemed every few yards one would zip out of the tuft-grass at our feet and zig-zag through the trees, like a jet fighter.

Some time after lunch, we reached the top of a small rise, and there was Lago Dickson sprawled out before us. Near its outlet we stopped to admire the small icebergs stranded on shore, remnants of the Dickson Glacier found along the margin of the lake's far end. I filled my canteen with iceberg drips, water that fell as snow hundreds or thousands of years ago. It was a slow and tedious process, but it was almost full when two backpackers approached us from the *refugio* in the distance. They were doing the circuito in the opposite direction and wanted information on Lago Amarga. After I cautioned them to follow the ridge above the lake, the taller of the two men asked how we had fared during the recent storm. I told him of our protected campsite at the forest's edge. "You were fortunate," he said in German-accented English. "We were in the mountains, near the pass. It was very windy, and the snow was as deep as our ankles. We couldn't find the trail for more than a day until the snow melted."

When I commented that we were meeting more Germans in Patagonia than any other nationality, the shorter hiker, an artist by profession, attempted to explain why. "Germany is a relatively rich but geographically small country; you can drive across it in a day. The desire to travel, to see the world, has always been important to us. Workers feel it is their right to have three months' paid holiday per year, and most businesses agree. No offense, but many Europeans find America's standard annual leave to be archaic." No offense was taken from this civil service employee, since I wholeheartedly agreed.

We parted company. They continued on to Lago Paine with their ton of vacation time; we headed toward the refugio, depressed that our time in South America was more than half over.

From the outside, the Lago Dickson refugio resembled a dumpy old herder's cabin, but inside it was clean, roomy, and vacant. There were two bedrooms and a kitchen area; the bedrooms even had doors. The windows were without glass, but faced away from the prevailing winds. Although it was only midafternoon, we decided to spend the night.

We were unpacking and about to brew up some tea when two hikers ambled in. Young and trim with a mop of black curly hair, the man was dressed in patched blue jeans, an olive-green field jacket, and black army boots that were falling apart. About the same age as her companion, the dark-haired woman was attired in tattered cotton sweatpants and sweatshirt and a leaky plastic raincoat. Burlap potato sacks covered their backpacks; a common practice among European trekkers, who use the sacks to protect the pack's contents.

The couple, Israelis, said that they, too, were heading to Lago Amarga. Like the Germans, they had been tentbound in the mountains during the snowstorm, but lacking a gas stove, and unable to make a fire, they went the last day and a half without eating since all their food had to be cooked. "I hope we get this fire going," the woman said, watching her companion try to ignite the wet wood. "We sure can use a hot meal."

While her friend puffed valiantly at the wisps of white smoke, the woman explained that they had been been in South America three months and still had about eight more months to go before their money ran out. "Many Israelis take a year off to travel after finishing their two years in the military," she said. "Which is what we are doing. South America is popular because things are cheap here, and it is a good place to hike and camp."

The cast-iron stove started to back up horribly, flooding the dining room with acrid smoke. I brought out my MSR camp stove and boiled up some water for us all.

That evening almost changed our opinions about refugios. A cold rain fell in great drenching sheets, hammering the corrugated roof of the old herder's hut. The harder it rained, the cozier we felt inside. Judy spread her sleeping bag on the wooden bunk and burrowed between the nylon covers. I turned off my headlamp, casting us into total darkness. Above the howl of the wind I could hear the Israeli couple, laughing softly in the adjoining room.

By midmorning, Judy and I were already a few miles from the refugio, hiking steadily uphill on a narrow trail nearly overgrown with dense thickets. Then we made a turn to the south, and suddenly we were in an extensive grove of *lengas* (high beech) and *coihue* (evergreen beech). The large old stand was ideal habitat for Magellanic woodpeckers, the "big carpenters" who require snags and older trees for food and nesting sites. I tried tapping on a couple of snags to attract their attention, and listened for their calls, which are rather raspy squawks, but all I heard was the loud scolding chatter of the little tree-creeper, known as the watchdog of the forest.

On our right was the quick and cold Río de los Perros, named after the herdsman's dogs that perished while trying to cross. The sight and the sound of water gurgling over rock brought a smile to my face. The forested nook reminded me of my first backpack trip as a college freshman. That simple overnight solo hike into the hills and hollows of the Missouri Ozarks changed the life of a city kid. It awakened a passion in me that still burns twenty-five years later. Now, in Patagonia, poking at wet, furry puma scat with my hiking stick, I couldn't have been happier.

Alternating hiking for one hour with ten-minute breaks, we pushed higher and deeper into a land of remoteness and rugged alpine terrain. We set up camp among a stand of dwarf beech, the last bit of cover before the trees succumbed altogether. A half-day's trek away was the pass, the crux of our trip.

Glistening black cliffs and hanging glaciers ringed the mountain amphitheater. The clatter of waterfalls reverberated off the encircling walls. Above and beyond the treeline, we found a little glacial lake that tinkled with ice floes. All around the lake the land looked as if giant bulldozers had been at work, pushing and shoving and scooping. Lichens, mosses, and other tundra plants helped soften the harsh contours.

We strung a nylon tarp between two trees, which kept us dry while we ate dinner in the rain. There was no sunset, only a steadily darkening dreariness. An icy fog snaked down the mountainsides, gathering around the lake, then enveloping our campsite. I checked the thermometer key-ring on my jacket: thirty-eight degrees. We had climbed several thousand feet since morning.

We were putting away the stove and securing our gear for the night when we heard a distant clomping from somewhere down the mountain.

"People?" Judy wondered, staring into the gloom.

"Maybe, but who'd be out hiking this late? You can barely see the trail."

Out of the fog they appeared: two men—our CAT backpacker friends.

"What are *you* doing here?" they shouted in surprise.

"Whaddya mean? What are *you* doing here?" I replied. "Kinda late to be on the trail, isn't it?"

Steve explained, as he and Paul joined us under the tarp. "We spent two nights at our last camp, the one near Lago Paine, after we met you, figuring we could make it here in a single long day. But we got a late start this morning; plus, it turned dark much earlier with the fog and all. For a while there, I didn't think we'd find the campsite. We certainly didn't expect to see you guys again so soon."

Our friends were wet, tired, and hungry. Paul put a sweater on under his rain jacket and briskly rubbed his hands together to warm them up. Steve emptied his pack on the ground and flashed his headlamp on a small pile of freeze-dried dinners.

"Paul, how's chili and beans sound?"

"Why not? We're among friends."

Judy and I watched in amazement as the two men shared the contents of the single aluminum pouch, and that's all. We didn't have the heart to tell them that our dinners consisted of one freeze-dried meal *apiece*, not to mention half a package of freeze-dried veggies, a generous dab of margarine, a chocolate bar, and a cup of instant soup.

"No wonder our packs always weigh a ton," Judy chuckled, while Steve and Paul found a spot to pitch their tent.

"Geez, Jude," I teased. "You eat more than both of those guys put together!"

"Yeah, and don't think I don't feel guilty."

▲

A hint of clear weather returned in the morning. The CAT guys were just waking when Judy and I shouldered our packs.

"Don't wait for us," Steve jested, poking his head out the tent. "We're probably going to be here awhile. Hope to see you later—if not on the trail, then in Peoria. We'll be back this year."

We climbed to the glacial moraine and skirted the edge of the iceberg lake. The forest thinned out, reduced to a few stragglers twisted and bent by the prevailing winds. Following a meltwater rivulet gushing out of a snowfield, we tromped over shale rock and sidled through patches of brush as we closed in on the mountain pass.

The trail faded away among the loose boulders and talus. We might have lost it completely if not for the orange markers painted on rocks. A couple of hours into our hike I stopped to check the park map. Without contour lines I couldn't be certain, but I guessed the pass to be at five thousand feet. We had a thousand feet higher to go.

We weren't exactly on top of the world, but you couldn't tell that from the view. Far below was the glacial lake and our last camp, and beyond were the deep blue valleys of distant mountains. Overlooking all was Paine Grande, the highest peak in the park, and the remnant of a batholith—a large body of intruded igneous rock thrust upward by tectonic forces millions of years ago. Dark clouds were torn apart as they scraped over the summit, a foreshadowing of surging winds across the divide.

I snapped a few pictures and was in the middle of changing film when a wet, sticky sleet began to blow in from the west. Further complicating things was the cold air being whipped off a large glacier to our right. The temperature instantly dropped, sending shivers down my sweat-dampened back. I closed the camera, stuck it in my fanny pack, and quickly joined Judy behind a boulder where she was slipping on raingear. We helped each other up. Then, heads down and hands in our parka pockets, we trudged on for the final push.

What little vegetation there had been gave way to a moonscape of pockmarked rocks and an occasional sheltered niche glazed with white moss and a thin crust of lichens. Our eyes teared and noses ran as we bucked the cold headwind. It was like pulling a loaded sled up the mountain, so hard was the invisible wall pressing against my chest. At times the wall would suddenly crumble and I would lurch forward with only a last-second jab of my hiking stick preventing a fall.

The closer we came to the pass the more the gale intensified; all its power was being funneled into the narrow rocky defile. If the wind speed was fifty miles per hour where I had changed film, it was at least a hundred up here. With Judy settling into her own pace behind me, I plowed ahead to see if I could punch through the notch. At least, that was the plan. A short walk from the crest, I was broadsided by a gust that thumped me to the ground. Stunned, and unable to regain my feet, I crawled behind an outcrop and waited for Judy, but she, too, was on her hands and knees.

We muscled to our feet. The wind was too strong to stand in, so we bent over double with our chins almost touching the rocky slope, linked elbows and charged ahead. The air currents sent us weaving and swaying like a pair of drunken sailors on a pitching deck. Judy grabbed me when I was about to fall. I did the same for her.

Somehow we reached the gap. "Stay there! I'll take your picture," I hollered, letting go of Judy's arm.

"No, don't let go ... " she screamed. Too late. She was knocked flat on her back. With her arms and legs clawing the air, and her backpack acting as a carapace, she looked like a big upturned beetle. I tried unsuccessfully to stifle a laugh.

"But it's a great picture," I argued, as she swore at me for thinking first of photographs.

Together we broke on through to the other side. Almost immediately the wind lost most of its fury; blue skies prevailed over ominous grey. Half walking, half sliding, we veered down the steep mountainside to a sheltered hollow and slouched behind a hedgerow stunted by the wind. Only then were we able to fully appreciate the scene before us.

A thick carpet of jumbled ice a mile wide and riddled with crevasses, Grey Glacier dominated the view. From this height we could peer down into its yawning fissures, as well as trace its course from the Patagonian ice cap to Lago Grey. Despite its impressive size, Grey Glacier is in full retreat, as are all the glaciers in the park. One glacier, for example, is known to have receded by as much as fifty-six feet a year for the last ninety years. If the trend continues, Grey and the rest will some day be just a memory. But sitting there, marveling at the glacier's enormity, we found it hard to believe that something so big could ever melt.

The trail plummeted downhill, *straight* downhill, with no switchbacks on a forty-five-degree slope. We had to thread our way through a contorted, grotesquely knotted forest covered with moss and ferns. Our top-heavy frame packs, though wonderful on most trails, were a nuisance here, constantly catching on low-hanging branches and forcing us off balance. We vaulted from tree to tree, grasping frantically for handholds as we skidded downward. Judy took a few hard falls and wrenched her elbow. I took a painful slide that bruised my tailbone.

About six o'clock, a couple of hours into our manic glissade, we were overtaken by Steve and Paul. They, too, had taken a beating at the pass. The sun was poised to drop behind the peaks; usable daylight would be going fast. We all agreed that it would be nice to find a campsite, but there had not been a single flat spot since the divide. A dirt ledge we would have normally dismissed as inadequate managed to hold both tents. Paul and I set up our stoves side by side while Judy and Steve went to fill up the water bottles.

"You know, the first thing I'm going to buy when I get out of here is a big, fat chocolate bar," Paul said, tearing open another one of their weight-watcher dinners. "I bet I've lost ten pounds on this hike."

"Here," I said guiltily. "Take this, and here's one for Steve." I handed him two Hershey chocolate bars, the big kind with almonds.

"Gee, thanks! You sure you can spare them?"

I patted our bulging food bag. "Yeah, I think we'll be all right."

▲

On the next day's hike, Judy and I emerged from the dark sloping forest into a level sunlit clearing the size of a football field. My first thought was that the area had been clear-cut, but a second glance revealed that a recent rockslide had caused the destruction. The opening was littered with bouldery debris, branches, and shattered tree trunks. The path was totally obliterated. Our progress was very slow. Slithering under and over the wreckage, it took an hour to traverse the obstacle course.

Hot and thirsty, we paused to rest at the finish gate, collapsing in the shade to kill the few remaining swigs in our water bottles. I pulled off my boots and socks and air-dried my sweaty, calloused feet. I was ready for a nice, well-maintained section of trail where I could walk upright instead of climb or crawl, but the pair of hikers that strolled by brought us some grim news.

Looking like they had just stepped out of an advertisement for trekking in the Swiss Alps, the woman could have passed for a young Britt Eckland in pleated shorts and knapsack, while her companion was a chisel-faced golden boy with perfect white teeth and a soccer player's physique. With a French accent, Britt told us of a good camp with water about thirty minutes away, and another an hour beyond that. The only catch was that we'd first have to cross a dangerous gorge. "The wind is terribly strong in there," she cautioned, brushing a strand of long blonde hair from her face. "You can easily slip and hurt yourself going down." Then, wincing at our packs, she added, "But for you, I think going up will be much worse."

When they mentioned they were planning to make it over the pass that day, I advised them to reconsider. It was already pushing three o'clock; they'd be lucky to make our bivouac ledge by nightfall. "Oh, but we are fast walkers," Golden Boy smiled, blinding me with those gleaming choppers. "We plan to complete the circuito in four days. Why, how long will it take you?"

"Oh, a little longer," I said. So what if this was our ninth day on the trail, and that we had four more to go before signing out at the park headquarters? We said goodbye to the couple and ambled down the path toward the notorious chasm. I sensed Judy was a little nervous. "How bad could the crossing be?" I tried to reassure her. "After all, if those two could make it, so can we."

My partner still harbored doubts. "Maybe, but did you see their packs? They were half the size of ours. And in case you didn't notice, that woman's legs were a full foot longer than mine."

I had to admit, I did notice those legs. And upon reaching the breezy ravine, I also fessed up that I, too, wasn't so sure about reaching the other side. To our left, the fifty-foot-deep gully merged into a water-streaked cliff; the other way was impenetrable forest and an even less appealing eroded pitch. The only possible descent was by means of a treacherous switchback trail that others had kick-stepped into the loose, powdery scree. One wrong move or a dislodged rock would mean a nasty tumble to the large jagged boulders lining the torrent at the bottom. What we needed was a climbing rope for a top belay, but all we had was twenty-five feet of flimsy parachute cord.

I shielded my eyes from the blowing gravel and sand and, taking one small step at a time, gingerly tottered down. The trick, I learned, was to blot out everything in my vision except the few inches in front of my feet. Before I knew it, I was at the bottom, yelling up to Judy that it was a piece of cake.

She soon joined me, and we rock-hopped across the mountain stream to face our final challenge—a test of strength and skill that deserved to be an American Gladiator event. A thin steel cable was anchored around a tree at the top of the precipice and dangled to the ground. We'd have to climb hand over hand up the wire rope, digging our feet into the almost vertical gravel wall.

At the top our arms felt like jelly, but there was consolation as we lay at the rim gasping for air. From here on, the route was mostly downhill with no real perils; this we knew from our visit the previous year. There would be a camp near enough to Grey Glacier so that on a windless night we'd be able to hear from our sleeping bags the huge booming thunder and sharp cracks caused by the compression and thawing of the ice. At the lower elevation, a network of backcountry trails would guide us through Magellanic forest and grassy plains. We'd be in some of the park's best wildlife habitat when we followed the Río Grey down to the administration center at the edge of Lago del Toro.

And if everything proceeded as planned, on our final night in Torres del Paine—the finale, really, of our wilderness travels in Patagonia—we would set up camp at the excellent campground by Lago Pehoe and gladly pay the six dollars. Only this time, when the attendant asked us if we wanted to take that wood-fire-heated shower, we wouldn't refuse.

# 5.

# In the Land of Lauca (Chile)

"THERE MUST BE a better way to spend a vacation," I mused, while prostrate inside the glaring tent. I had all the classic symptoms of mountain sickness and wasn't enjoying myself a bit. The breathlessness, queasiness, and loss of appetite were uncomfortable enough. But it was the steady, pounding hammer blows between my eyes that made me curse the *altiplano* (high plateau) and long for sea level nearly three miles below.

"*No te preocupes*" (Don't worry), I heard Hernán, the park ranger, tell Judy. "Lorenzo will feel better soon." He explained that *el soroche* (altitude sickness) is like a horrible hangover: The initial effects can be crippling, but it's really not that bad. "Most people feel better in two to three days," he assured her. "Then again, some do not become acclimatized at all, and die."

Hearing a moan from inside the tent, Hernán came over to see how I was doing. "Ah, very good!" he said cheerfully. "I see that you are awake." I peered out from under the bandana draped over my eyes. The short, stocky ranger was squatting near the front door, inches from my feet.

He had been pondering why I was suffering from el soroche while Judy had only a mild headache. "It is because you are so tall," he said, his eyes twinkling. "Your head is up in the clouds, where the atmosphere is thinner and harder to breathe."

▲

Earlier that week, el soroche had been far from my mind when Judy and I flew into Arica, a Pacific port city of 140,000 people about 1,270 miles north of Santiago, Chile, near the border with Peru. We had been traveling in Patagonia for two months and wanted to see a totally different part of Chile and the Andes before we returned home. Lauca National Park is one of the highest parks in the world and a jewel in the Chilean park system. A CONAF administrator we had met in Santiago told us that Lauca is one place not to be missed.

Arica, however, was another matter. Located in a harsh desert where an inch of rain per year is cause for celebration, Arica is a veritable oven by day and not much more tolerable by night. Haze blocked the view of the distant Andes; all we could see were the coastal mountains rising directly from the pounding surf. The relatively cool breeze off the ocean was the only respite from the hot and stifling city streets.

As usual upon arriving in a new town, we went hunting for a place to stay. All the hotels with air-conditioned rooms were full; many were booked solid for the next two weeks. The reason, according to the woman at the tourist office, was that Arica was a destination for landlocked Bolivians who were attracted not only by its swimming beaches but also by its status as a duty-free port. Another factor was that these were the final weeks of summer vacation for the kids.

After an hour or so of poking around, we finally found a vacancy at a low-budget hotel (six dollars for two) near the center of town. Our room, like all the others, had a single window that opened onto a narrow enclosed courtyard, thereby eliminating any chance of capturing the ocean breeze. To keep from suffocating, the drapes had to be pulled back, permitting anyone walking in the courtyard to peep in. We tried to avert our eyes as we padded to the communal bathroom, but we still saw a lot of sweaty people lying half-naked on their beds. And I'm sure they saw us. Modesty disappeared when the temperature inside our room reached a stuffy ninety-five degrees.

Because information on Lauca was scarce—pamphlets and brochures were not yet available—our next stop was at the regional CONAF office. There the administrator in charge of Lauca gave us a brief history of the area we soon would be visiting.

We learned that the park had been established in 1970, in part to protect the vicuña, a wild relative of the domesticated llama and alpaca, and in part to protect a portion of Chile's altiplano, a vast plateau between the western and eastern ranges of the Andes with an average elevation of thirteen thousand feet. When the Spanish arrived in South America, the distribution of vicuña extended from Ecuador to northern Argentina. As a result of unrestricted hunting for their pelts and wool—the world's finest—the vicuña nearly disappeared. In the 1960s, when biologists first took a wildlife census in Lauca, only about four hundred animals were found. Hunting was immediately banned. Now there are more than ten thousand vicuñas in the park. In 1981, to acknowledge Lauca's 460,000 acres of unique high-altitude ecosystem, UNESCO declared it a World Biospheric Reserve.

It was so comfortable in the air-conditioned office that we were in no hurry to leave. Fortunately, the administrator (who was a dead ringer for Charles Bronson) seemed willing to spend some time talking about birds with two tourists who couldn't stand the heat. Smiling modestly, he said he was the first biologist to study Lauca's flamingos. "Did you know that three of the world's six species of flamingos are found in or near Lauca National Park?" he asked.

One of the great things about traveling is that you learn something new every day.

▲

Although Lauca lies only one hundred miles east of Arica and is accessible by the main Chile–Bolivia road, it proved harder to reach than we had anticipated. We were warned that hitchhiking could take a week, that buses were infrequent and nearly always full, and that the ubiquitous taxis in town were not equipped to make the half-day journey to such heights. After a weekend of searching, we finally discovered a tour agency that would take us to the park, along with eight other tourists.

The day before leaving, with all our preparations out of the way, we decided to celebrate by going to a movie in the afternoon. The temperature was approaching the century mark in the shade, and the thought of sitting in an air-conditioned theater, no matter what the film, was very appealing.

The streets were like Coney Island on the Fourth of July as we jostled our way downtown. Roving bands of gypsies, the first we had seen in Chile, hassled shoppers and passersby. Two young women who couldn't have been over sixteen, wearing long flowery dresses and loose blouses with beads and gold chains around their necks, approached me and asked for money to buy milk for their hungry babies. "*No tengo dinero,*" I said, brushing them off. They sneered and laughed. A few minutes later a rag-tag gang of kids approached us, the same con artists we had seen panhandling up and down the streets. One of them had a small brown monkey on his shoulder and asked me if I wanted to buy it. When I told him, "No, get lost," he parroted my words in a hideous fashion and screeched maniacally as he turned away.

"What'd he say?" I asked Judy.

"I don't know, but I'm sure it wasn't 'Have a nice day.' "

We snacked on *empanadas* from an open-air cafe and sipped ice-cold drinks made from milk and fresh fruit (mango and banana were our favorites). More than the nearby ocean—which, to my taste, was too cold and full of jellyfish for a relaxing swim—it was the fruit drinks and inexpensive tasty food that made Arica passably livable.

At the movies, a triple feature was showing. First up was *Le Marginal*, a campy cop flick starring Jean-Paul Belmondo and some beautiful aspiring actress. Neither of us had heard of the French film, but the billboard outside claimed that critics in Europe loved it, and it did have Spanish subtitles. We paid our 150 pesos (about 75 cents) for the ticket and left the searing sun for the darkness of the old, boxy theater. The movie had already started. The serious young usher directed us to the balcony, and we hung onto the poor guy's arms in the total darkness.

About the time our eyes had finally adjusted, we realized we had made a mistake: there was no air conditioning in the theater, not even a fan to suck out the humid heat generated by three hundred or so warm bodies. My glasses fogged up. My face dripped into my popcorn. I wanted to leave in the worst way, but we were trapped in the middle of the row, far from the aisle.

A huge, overweight man sat behind me. His fat knees kept brushing the back of my head. Whenever a sexy scene came on the screen, which was often, he'd emit a piercing, ear-splitting whistle.

To our right, another latecomer came bumbling down the aisle, only he didn't have an usher with a penlight to guide him. Some wiseguy stuck out his foot and tripped him. The poor man went flying down the aisle and landed with a thud on his face. The commotion caused a rapid-fire ripple of catcalls, whistles, and raucous laughter. Soon the whole theater was convulsing, generating even more heat.

Before sunrise on the appointed day, we boarded the minibus for the trip up to the park. In the dim glow of the dome light, our fellow passengers introduced themselves: Eduardo and his two sisters were on school break from a university in Santiago; the three Argentine women were all professionals on their annual holiday; the Brazilian couple were on their honeymoon. Judy and I looked out of place with our bulging backpacks loaded with food and gear for ten days. The others in our group were unencumbered since they would be returning to Arica that evening.

During the first part of the drive, we coasted over a smooth tarmac road that sliced through the sun-scorched Atacama Desert, a region far drier than Death Valley or even the Sahara. Although extremely barren, it was not boring. On the steep, parched hills in the Lluta River valley were scattered geoglyphs, consisting of blackish volcanic rocks that showed up clearly against the tawny terrain. These immense stone designs, some more than 150 feet in length, depicted humans, vicuñas, dogs, eagles, and condors. Archaeologists believe they were made by a pre-Incan civilization a thousand years ago, possibly serving as primitive highway signs for nomadic wanderers.

In the *precordillera* (foothills of the mountain range) the blacktop gave out. In its place was a bumpy, dusty gravel road that followed part of the ancient Inca highway and wound ever higher into the cold and dry altiplano. Terraced slopes and occasional Inca fortifications were vivid reminders of this dominant group of South American Indians who occupied Peru, Bolivia, and much of northern Chile prior to the Spanish conquest.

Midway through our trip, we pulled over for breakfast at the Restaurante Arbolita, which was actually nothing more than a simple shrine and a lone spindly tree beside the road. Alexis, a thin, amiable man who never took off his aviator sunglasses and blue baseball cap, was our combination driver and guide. He explained that this informal truck stop was of great significance. The shrine was dedicated to Carmen, patron saint of *chóferes*, or truck drivers. In return for sprinkling water on the thirsty tree, Carmen was supposed to grant safe passage to the driver and his passengers. "Unfortunately, it does not always work that way," Alexis admitted, acknowledging the fact that we had already passed scores of crosses marking the sites of accidents. Nevertheless, we all felt better when he took a liter bottle of water and drained it over the base of the tree.

While dishing out coffee and ham-and-cheese sandwiches, Alexis gave a little speech about the ill effects of oxygen deprivation—not a bad idea, since from Arica to the park was a climb of nearly fifteen thousand feet in four hours. "Some of you may know about el soroche," he said, "some of you may not. In any case, to avoid becoming ill I'd like you to follow these simple precautions as we head higher into the mountains: number one, don't move quickly; number two, don't bend down and stand up fast; number three, don't tilt your head." He paused to catch his breath. "Any questions?" There were none. "Don't worry about it," he concluded. "El soroche is mostly psychological anyway."

A few miles farther on we entered a thick fog layer, climbing through it into extremely inhospitable, rocky terrain. The only vegetation growing here—and I was amazed that anything could grow at all—were man-sized candelabra cacti. I was reminded a little of the Sonoran Desert of southwest Arizona, except that desert was a rain forest compared to this lunar landscape.

We stopped at a canyon rim to take a break. Marking the spot was another little shrine, this one festooned with crosses constructed from license plates. According to Alexis, who had a miniature race-car helmet as a dashboard ornament, each license plate had come from a vehicle that had crashed on the road.

"Why so many accidents?" I asked naively. This shrine alone had fifteen plates, and we had seen others with even more.

Alexis shrugged his shoulders. "Many reasons," he said with an air of fatalism. "No brakes. Fall asleep. Flat tires." Then, tipping his head back and lifting an imaginary whisky bottle to his lips, he grinned and said, "This, too."

Alexis knew his job, but his idea of safe, responsible driving and what I viewed as safe, responsible driving were worlds apart. When the grades became steeper, his race car psyche took over; he pushed the poor minibus to the hilt on the downhills to build momentum for the next hill. We rebounded in and out of our seats as the vehicle jounced over the corrugated dirt road. With sheer precipices only a few feet to our left, a blowout or locked breaks would have meant the end. When my alarm became obvious to Alexis, he gleefully shouted not to worry, "Remember, my friend, Carmen is watching over us!"

Near Putre, a tiny town on the western outskirts of the park, there was a military installation that slowed him down. A big billboard informed us that it was illegal to take photographs for the next mile or so for national security reasons. The Brazilian was preparing to snap a picture of some soldiers who were guarding the front gate. "Please, put that away!" Alexis ordered, covering the camera with his hand. "They are very serious about this."

After we were well past the security zone, Alexis explained that the strong military presence in northern Chile was due to an uneasy border truce with neighboring Peru. "Peru never has forgotten that it lost territory to Chile during the War of 1892," Alexis said. "They are under the impression that they are merely loaning northern Chile to us, and when they decide it's time to ask for the loan back, they need only say so and take it." Momentarily distracted, Alexis swerved to miss a *campesino* (peasant) struggling uphill on a bicycle.

The thin air and long, tiring drive were having their effects. Several among us began to nod off. Soon, the Santiago girls and Judy and I were the only ones awake in the back; not because we weren't tired, but because we felt safer keeping a close eye on Alexis, who was starting to show signs of fatigue himself.

Despite the many hairpin turns and teeth-rattling jolts, we arrived intact on the high plains of the park. This was my first glimpse of the altiplano. Mile after mile of grassy rolling hills were framed by snowcapped peaks. Bands of caramel-colored vicuña sprinkled the open countryside. These graceful creatures are one of the few wild animals that can not only survive but flourish on the harsh grasslands of the high-altitude plateau. They are the smallest of the llamoids, considered by some biologists to be the ecological equivalents to the pronghorn antelope of North America's Great Plains. And like the antelope, their speed and stamina are astonishing. With necks stretched out and ears flattened, vicuñas can easily lope across the rough terrain in excess of thirty-five miles per hour. Some of the animals proved it when they kept pace with our vehicle racing along in third gear. After playing with us awhile, the vicuñas would break cover and disappear into the rocky wasteland.

We reached the park's east end by midafternoon. As we climbed a rocky shoulder, we caught our first sight of Lago Chungará. The same color as the deep blue sky and overshadowed by the snow-crowned 20,834-foot Parinacota volcano, Chungará is both figuratively and literally breathtaking. Four miles across and close to fifteen thousand feet above sea level, it is one of the world's highest lakes of its size.

Alexis parked in front of the CONAF facility, which contained an office and picnic area. This seemed to be a good site from which to explore the lake and its surroundings, especially since Judy and I would be the only tourists here once our companions left.

Everyone was wide awake and eager to pile outside, except Eduardo, who was still asleep on Judy's shoulder. "Eduardo, wake up," his sister whispered, giving her brother a gentle nudge. He groggily lifted his head and looked around. "Where are we?" "Where are we?" his other sister teased. "You've been sleeping. We've already eaten lunch and walked around the lake. Now it's time to go back."

Eduardo was crestfallen, until we all broke out laughing. "Very funny!" he snickered, flushed with embarrassment. "I knew you were joking. Very funny."

Box lunches appeared on the picnic tables. There was hot soup in China bowls, unidentified cuts of meat, potatoes and vegetables, bread and apples, and bottles of Coke—precisely the kinds of heavy, gaseous stuff not recommended when trying to avoid altitude sickness. Still, we were hungry, so we all sat down to eat, except for one of the Argentine women who wandered back to the minibus, saying she was feeling nauseous and lightheaded. Alexis was a little irritated. "She moved around too quickly and tilted her head. You can't say I didn't warn her." Saying that, he stuffed a hefty slab of meat into his mouth and washed it down with a half-liter of soda pop.

Suddenly, the cloudless sky turned dark and a wind-whipped rain began to fall. The rain turned to hail, punctuated by streaks of lightning. We had been hit by the deadly *viento blanco,* or "white wind," a notorious feature of the altiplano. Everyone ran for cover. Normally, Judy and I would have donned our foul-weather gear, but to save weight on this trip we had left all nonessentials in Arica. Our uncoated anoraks would have to suffice. For half an hour we were besieged by the sound of banging and rattling as we took cover from the hailstorm under the tin roof of a picnic shelter.

When the scouring storm had passed, Alexis rounded everyone up, saying they had a couple of other places to visit on the return ride. He handed our packs down from the roof rack and shook our hands. The Santiago siblings kissed us on the cheek, imploring us to go back to Arica with them, where we could sleep in a hotel. We tried to explain that we preferred our tent to the insufferably hot Arica hotel, but there was no time. Alexis was already in the driver's seat, revving up the oxygen-starved motor. With a grinding of gears, the microbus rattled down the road, leaving us standing by our packs, waving goodbye in the deserted parking lot.

We weren't alone for long. Hernán, the ranger in charge of Lauca's Chungará District, hustled us out of the rain and inside his *guardería,* a combination office and home. He introduced us to his dark-haired wife, who was sitting at a wooden table in a darkened corner. The pretty young woman smiled weakly at us, then went back to playing cards with an expressionless Indian-looking man who never once looked at us.

Hernán told us about a nearby little stream where we could find drinking water. Then, when the rain let up, he led us back outside to a spot in the picnic area where we could pitch our tent. The gravelly campsite was close by his *guardería*, squeezed between low rock walls designed as windbreaks and a cement-block outhouse under construction. A wilderness camp this wasn't, but it was late in the day, and it was convenient.

Hernán welcomed the opportunity to talk to visitors, even though we had a hard time communicating. While we unpacked our gear, which elicited admiring comments and a few embarrassing questions about how much certain items cost, he told us about life as a park ranger at the top of the world.

His closest neighbors, discounting the Chilean border guards at the frontier with Bolivia, were in the tiny Aymara Indian village of Parinacota, fifteen miles to the west. Another CONAF ranger was stationed there, but since neither rangers were equipped with vehicles, they rarely had contact except by radio.

For some reason, the subject of our ages came up. I told Hernán that Judy and I were thirty-six, even though we looked like twenty-six. Hernán thought that was funny and had me guess how old he was. "Thirty-five?" I said. He shook his head. "Forty?" I guessed again. Hernán laughed and patted me on the back. "You are comedian. I am only twenty-eight."

When I told him how fortunate he was to live and work in such a beautiful area, he beamed and replied that he, too, thought this was a wonderful place. "Unfortunately, my wife prefers the city," he said, frowning. "She is from Arica and says there is nothing to do up here. She is growing tired of playing cards."

Excusing himself for a moment, Hernán returned with his guest book, which he wanted us to sign. There were few entries, maybe one or two every other day. A quick glance through the back pages revealed that most of the visitors were from Europe, Chile, and nearby South American countries. I looked for a name from the United States and was surprised to find that George Schaller, the internationally famous zoologist-author, was here a few months before. He had been complimentary about the park in the comment section, noting how approachable the wildlife was, which indicated good protection. I told Hernán about Schaller, but he shrugged and said he didn't remember meeting him.

A funny thing began to happen to me about this time. I found myself repeating the same questions and being unable to understand the most rudimentary answers. And I began breathing too fast, my heart began thumping, and I felt a sudden onset of nausea.

"Rest, please," Hernán said, showing great concern. "If you need anything, stop in my office. Maybe you'll want to play cards later on."

He hurried off when rolling thunder and rain returned to the altiplano. The westerly wind had redoubled its force, and we faced another terrifying icy blast that whirled sharp, grey sand through the air. Huddled inside the tent, we recoiled from the sizzling flashes of passing lightning. As if that weren't enough, marble-sized hail battered the ripstop nylon. I peered through a chink in the entrance flap and saw that the brown, open moorlands were coated in white, and the brilliant hue of the lake had turned into a boiling mass of greys and blues. I burrowed deep into my sleeping bag and tried to ignore the viselike grip on my head.

Once the high country was in darkness and the air had cooled, an equilibrium was established and the wind abruptly stopped. Hernán crept out from his office to inspect our dome-shaped mountain tent. "Excellent!" he said, nodding appreciatively at the fact that it was still standing. "Too bad, though," he confessed. "I bet my wife your tent would blow down."

▲

The night was an eternity. The air was bitterly cold, and I was soon shivering. I tossed and turned, plagued with flulike aches and chills. My breathing was labored, and more than once I felt on the verge of vomiting. I swallowed a few aspirins and popped some Diamox tablets that a doctor friend had given me to combat altitude sickness, but nothing worked. The only sure cure for el soroche is to get back to lower elevations, where symptoms quickly disappear.

I waited for sunrise, hoping that by then my headache would be gone. The only thing I could do was rest and drink plenty of water. The downside to imbibing so much water, and mixing it with diuretic medicine, was that I had to get up a total of eleven times during the night. Judy groaned whenever I unzipped my sleeping bag and staggered out of the tent.

The plus side to my urinary dysfunction was that every time I crawled outside I was met by a shimmering cosmos. A sliver of moon hung in the west, and the luminous Milky Way wafted like the smoke from a distant fire across the ink-black sky. The stars burned so brightly I could make out the shapes of Lago Chungará and the cone-shaped volcanos across the gravel road. On the lake the waterbirds were noisy, a grating *kuk-kuk-kuk-kuk, kakakaka, ka-ha, ha-ha,* and various loud, complaining henlike cackles and croaks. Normally I would have appreciated such interesting bird calls, but in my present condition the squeaky chorus only added to my headache.

▲

Sunrise on Lago Chungará was a time of perfect clarity. The temperature at dawn was usually in the low twenties, rising to the mid-seventies later on. Out of the darkness, the plateau turned from purple to pink to a beige so unnaturally bright it hurt my eyes. This was typical weather during early March, the time of our visit. From January to mid-April is the altiplano's rainy season, also known as the Bolivian winter. This period is characterized by warm, sunny mornings, afternoon rains, and subfreezing nights. The remainder of the year is nearly always warm with sharp, clear skies, except from June to August, Lauca's true winter, when temperatures plummet and snow covers much of the ground.

Sunrise may have been a magical time, but I was still feeling miserable. I had absolutely no appetite. During my period of acclimatization, the simplest task, even bending down to tie my shoes, would leave me panting and with a throbbing headache. Judy, on the other hand, suffered little ill effect from el soroche save the usual shortness of breath and a mild headache. I envied and was repulsed by her ability to eat complete meals while I forced myself to drink more water. I was embarrassed at my feebleness, wallowing in my misery.

At 3:00 P.M., under the direct rays of the sun, the thermometer dangling from the ridgepole inside the tent registered ninety-five degrees Fahrenheit. Our nylon dome on the altiplano was as hot as the hotel room in Arica. Unbelievable. I considered escaping to the cool shade of Hernán's house, where Judy was meeting with some recent arrivals, but the mere thought of moving, let alone talking with other tourists, made me stay where I was.

It was then that Hernán decided to earn his pay. He and a helper resumed construction on the outhouse a few feet from my head. They slopped on concrete and pounded on a tin roof, chattering back and forth. I almost yelled for them to stop: Didn't they know someone was dying in here? But I thought better of it, and was glad I did because the task didn't last long. Hernán finished the work day by pushing his newlywed around in a wheelbarrow, both of them laughing.

▲

Within a couple of days I was up and on my feet just as Hernán had predicted. With a clear head, I was finally able to truly appreciate the beauty and diversity of this sky-high Chilean park.

Taking advantage of the fine, windless morning, Judy and I hiked east along the lake in the direction of Bolivia, whose border was only a few miles away. A crystalline sharpness peculiar to these elevations defined objects near and far. We stopped often to gaze over Chungará's glass-smooth waters and talked about bringing the Klepper here so we could explore the other side of the lake, especially near the base of the volcano. The idea was intriguing; paddling did sound more enjoyable than backpacking at these altitudes. We wouldn't have been the first boaters, though. Unlikely as it seems, the year before, Lago Chungará had become the site of the world's highest sailboat regatta when fourteen members of Arica's yacht club hauled their boats to the lake and raised their sails in the thin air.

The rarefied air would have been utterly quiet if it hadn't been for the chickenlike clucks of the *tagua gigante*, or giant coot. This slate-colored bird, nearly the size of a turkey, is the only coot with red bill, legs, and feet. The species is unique to the altiplano and abundant in Chungará. At any given time, we could usually spot a couple dozen of them skulking in the emergent vegetation near shore. They were preoccupied in the building of nests—bulky affairs consisting of huge floating platforms of matted vegetation. We walked down to the bank, where one nest had run aground. "This has to be the record-holder," I announced, measuring the weedy incubator with my size twelve boot. It was seven feet in diameter and probably could support an adult human being.

The lake draws many other birds as well. Ornithologists estimate that 435 species of birds inhabit or pass through Chile, and northern Chile has recorded more birds (237 species) than any other region. By the end of our hike, we had identified grebes, flamingos, gulls, cormorants, shorebirds, geese, and a variety of ducks. Adjacent to the lake, in the cold, grassy steppe-land or *puna* that clothes the high Andean slopes between twelve thousand feet and the snowline at 16,500 feet, we observed ground doves, sparrows, and many small birds feeding among forbs and clumps of spiky *ichu* grass. Rising on an up-current of air, a condor observed everything from far overhead.

It was perplexing that the vicuña could survive in this submarginal range, with such wide expanses of gravel and bare soil. When we stumbled upon a small herd while exploring a draw off the road, some of the animals moved restlessly away, but most seemed to wander aimlessly as they grazed, stopping only to stare. As they fed, they nipped off portions of plants, rather than ripping them from the soil the way domestic animals would have done. The vicuña's specialized, razor-sharp dentition helps it survive in spite of the habitat's limited resources. Cattle and sheep do not fare nearly so well on the puna.

The land and its living organisms seemed in balance, yet there existed the potential for great havoc. We had been told that Lago Chungará may some day be drained. An enormously costly aqueduct designed to pump water to Arica was already constructed, but wasn't operational yet due to ecological concerns about changing the level of the lake. There were also political considerations. Chungará is part of Bolivia's watershed as well as that of Chile, and its government wasn't keen about the lake being diverted to irrigate Chile's desert. So for the present, Lago Chungará and its giant coots, flamingos, and other wildlife were safe.

On the way back to camp, we were joined by Fortunado, a wiry, leather-skinned Bolivian man whom we had met earlier. His flatbed truck was broken down in front of the ranger office, and he was waiting for a friend to return from Arica with spare parts. Taking short, even steps and maintaining a steady pace, it seemed that he could keep going all day, although like us he must have felt warm because he removed his thin, brown poncho, folded it, and carried it over his shoulder.

Fortunado delighted in telling us something about his country when we mentioned we were thinking of visiting Bolivia the following year. Speaking a combination of Spanish and Quechua (an Indian language commonly spoken in Peru, Bolivia and Ecuador), he had the ability to be eloquent, even though we shared a limited vocabulary.

When I asked him why so many truckers like himself make the long, difficult journey to Arica, his answer was that "there is money to be made." The merchandise in Arica's Free Zone was not available in landlocked Bolivia, he explained. As soon as he delivered one shipment, he turned around to pick up another. "It is a rough road, very hard on vehicles and drivers. Our attitude is, I am leaving today; I may get where I'm going in three days, it may take ten." Fortunado kicked a stone out of the way and gave a soft, ironic chuckle. "For me, on this trip, it has been closer to ten."

We were all amazed at what we saw when the ranger station came into view. Fortunado's friend was just pulling up in a flatbed truck bulging with crates, boxes, and tractor tires, atop of which was chained a new Toyota four-by-four pickup truck. Fortunado shook our hands with gusto and said he must go. "Come visit my country. Go to Titicaca. It is even more beautiful than Chungará." We wished him luck, and he ran off to join his friend, who was out of the cab and waving a box of spare truck parts over his head.

▲

"No problem," was Hernán's reply during our final evening at Chungará, when I asked him about the chances of hitchhiking to Parinacota. During our five days at Chungará only a handful of lorries and cars had passed by, most headed into Bolivia, not the direction we wanted to go. When I brought this to Hernán's attention, he assured us that a truck would pass in the morning.

In hindsight, walking would have been faster. We waited in front of the park office from dawn until midafternoon before a truck finally rumbled by. Judy and I grabbed our backpacks, cried "¡Adiós!" to Hernán and his wife, and dashed to the road. The big tractor-trailer didn't slow up. Instead, all we got was a mouthful of dust. "Stay there!" Hernán yelled from his porch. "Another one will come." This time he was right. A big flatbed semitruck stopped to pick us up. We climbed into the open back, where a small group of campesinos already sat. We greeted them in Spanish, since we didn't know Quechua or Aymara. With subtle hand gestures, they motioned for us to join them on the folded tarp and spare tires that helped absorb the bumps.

It was difficult to talk above the noise, so I tied a red bandana over my nose and mouth to try and seal out the choking dust. I shot furtive glances at my fellow traveling companions, who avoided eye contact. The man closest to me was the oldest, with short grey hair and wrinkled leathery skin. His brown pants and white shirt were worn through, and on his feet were leather sandals soled with scraps from automobile tires—the same outfit worn by most of the campesino men we had seen on the altiplano. Next to him was a short, rotund woman, probably in her sixties, but her dry, brown face was timeless. She wore a traditional long woolen dress and bright sarape, and on her head was a small bowler-type hat that somehow resisted getting blown off. Across from me, hunched over out of the wind, was a younger man, also in traditional clothes. And next to him was another woman who cradled a baby girl in the pleats of her blanketlike dress. When Judy smiled at the baby, and the baby smiled back, the mother immediately covered the child's eyes with her hand.

The truck was able to maintain a speed of only fifteen miles per hour, but because of the beating we were taking in the open trailer, it felt like we were going much faster. For my part, this little hitchhike ranked as one of the more grueling road rides of my life. The campesinos, however, took the pounding in stride, not even wincing when we hit a series of bumps that sent us all bouncing.

In spite of the dust and jolts, there were some beautiful moments. At the west end of Lago Chungará, a flock of flamingos suddenly appeared overhead, flashing brilliant pink in the sun before veering off. Judy and I pointed skyward and nodded. The old man and woman smiled, ever so slightly, even though the sight of *parinas* (the Quechua word for flamingo) was no big deal for residents of the altiplano.

About an hour later, the eldest woman turned around and began to pound on the metal roof of the cab to get the driver's attention. I asked our fellow passengers if this was Parinacota, since there was nothing except desolate high plains wilderness as far as the eye could see. The old man nodded.

Everyone climbed down easily enough, except for the stocky woman. She tossed her net sack to the ground, which landed with a thud five feet below, then hesitated about taking the plunge herself. The driver honked his horn and yelled something that sounded impatient. Her companions had already scurried off, so I reached up and grabbed the old woman under her arms and helped ease her down. Without saying a word, she scooped up her sack and hit the trail, chasing after her friends who were by now far ahead.

"Let's not lose them," Judy and I said in unison, as we hurriedly hoisted our packs onto our backs. We hoped the campesinos would lead us to the centuries-old village of Parinacota a few miles away, hidden in a fold of the sweeping tabletop plateau.

Within a few minutes, though, they had ditched us. "It's no use," I wheezed. "We can't keep up." I was amazed at how fast these short-legged people, wearing sandals and toting heavy bags over their shoulders, could shuffle across the rough country.

"You think this is really the way to Parinacota?" Judy wondered, looking around at the barren wide-open spaces. "Shouldn't there be a road?"

I, too, was puzzled. Maybe we had misunderstood the old man. Maybe we were trailing them not to the village, but to somewhere else.

*The rustic isolation of the Village of Parinacota gives visitors the impression of having stumbled upon a long-lost Inca site.*

The anxiety persisted as we followed a confusing network of narrow paths in the general direction the campesinos had taken. Finally, forty-five minutes after leaving the road, we spotted the village about a mile away. It was smaller than we had expected; a cluster of buildings amid an expanse of high, open, rolling terrain. Large *bofedales* (sedge-meadow bogs) sprawled in front of the village; and a pair of perfectly symmetrical volcanoes called the Nevados de Payachatas loomed overhead. These perpetually snow-covered summits tower more than six thousand feet above the plateau and are visible for miles.

Up close, Parinacota (which means "lake of flamingos" in Quechua), resembled a long-lost Inca site. Scores of llamas and alpacas grazed peacefully right outside town and, because no trees grow on the altiplano, all the squat buildings were constructed of skillfully layered rock. As we strolled through the village, though, it soon became apparent that the twentieth century had arrived. A recently built park office, housing a refugio, a laboratory, and an interpretive display, stood in sharp contrast to the seventeenth-century church and windowless stone huts nearby. Outside the office, a horse was hitched alongside a new four-by-four compact pickup truck donated by the World Wildlife Fund.

We learned from Lorenzo, the ranger on duty, that at an elevation of 14,400 feet, Parinacota, like most of the isolated villages in the altiplano, is populated by Andinos, a short-statured, barrel-chested, dark-skinned people who have managed to keep their race relatively pure despite hundreds of years of outside intrusions. When Lauca was created, Parinacota suddenly became part of a world-renowned national park. "The Andinos are inseparable from the altiplano and, like the vicuñas, can be easily threatened," the ranger emphasized. "It is CONAF's commitment, our responsibility, to preserve their pastoral customs and lifestyles."

Lorenzo acknowledged that it is difficult to balance the old ways with the inevitable introduction of modern technology. An example of this was the generator that provided electricity to the village for a few hours every evening. "It's there," he said, "but most villagers don't use it since they own nothing that needs electricity."

Judy mentioned the mother covering her child's eyes during the ride over. He nodded. "They believe that having their picture taken, or even staring into an outsider's eyes, may steal away their soul. The Andinos are a proud people, as strong as the land in which they live. They do not ask much from the outside world except to be left alone."

There were no hotels or inns in Parinacota, and nowhere really to camp. The only public lodging was the refugio's four bunks. Lorenzo said that tourists like us could use them, provided visiting rangers or scientists didn't show up and bump us out of our beds. We decided to take that chance. After two months of tenting, the refugio, with its flush toilets, running water, gas stove, and electric lights, seemed luxurious.

▲

The next morning Judy and I were in the kitchen at first light. It was cold inside the unheated stone room, not much warmer than the freezing temperature outside.

By now I had regained my appetite and was trying to make up for lost meals. I had plenty of trail food still in my pack but the cheese, bread, and fruits I craved were not to be had. The Andinos subsist almost entirely on llama meat and *calapurca*, a concoction of fried corn, potatoes, and onions. Even if I had wanted to try some of the regional dishes, I would have been out of luck. There were no restaurants, markets, or grocery stores in Parinacota or elsewhere in the national park. Lorenzo had given us a sampling of llama steak, but during the remainder of our trip I resigned myself to the usual backpacker's fare of granola, gorp, and gluey minute rice.

We were sitting down to our second bowl of oatmeal when Lorenzo walked in. He had to prepare breakfast for some visiting scientists who would be here in a couple of hours. First, though, he made himself a cup of coffee and sat down with us for some conversation.

Lorenzo told us he was just filling in at Lauca, since the regular Parinacota ranger was out traveling with the scientists. Normally, he was the ranger at Isluga Volcano National Park, on the mountainous plateau to the south.

"Have you heard of Isluga?" he asked hopefully.

"Yes, indeed," I answered, adding that I hoped to visit there some day.

He seemed pleased. "Most people do not know of Isluga, it is so far off the main road. Also, the altiplano's thin air and isolation isn't for everyone." Even his wife and kids, he mentioned, prefer living at sea level.

Once every two weeks, he drove his motorcycle down to Arica for four days. The journey took ten hours, a very tiring and expensive ride. But even with inadequate pay, the separation from his family, and the fact that few tourists have discovered his park, he had no plans to leave or to change careers. "I enjoy living among the Andinos," he said, finishing his coffee. "They are even more traditional in Isluga than they are here. It took me a long time to get to know them, and I don't want to give that up."

Before we left to make room for the scientists, I gave Lorenzo some Smoky the Bear coins as presents for his kids. The tokens were emblazoned with Smoky's face and the pledge to fight forest fires. He broke into a wide grin. From a desk drawer he produced a decal of a cuddly, beaverlike rodent, the *coipú*, dressed in a firefighter's outfit complete with helmet and shovel. Out of the animal's mouth was the message, "El Bosque es Vida y Trabajo—Evitemos Los Incendios Forestales." The Forest Means Life and Jobs—Let's Prevent Forest Fires.

He gave us the decal. "It will remind you to come and visit me in Isluga some day."

▲

We quickly became enchanted with Parinacota, especially the surrounding countryside and the Andino way of life. Every morning, herders led their alpacas and llamas out to the bofedales. Every evening they herded the animals back to their rock corrals.

There are few domesticated animals more appealing than these

*Llamas and alpacas graze peacefully on the altiplano, in the shadow of a pair of perfectly symmetrical volcanoes called the Nevados de Payachatas.*

New World, humpless relatives of the camel, with their long necks and long ears, short tails, and gaily decorated ear tassles and collars. The smaller alpacas were the cutest. Most were pure brown, black, or white, but others were colored as if by a committee with black bands across their eyes, white bodies with brown tails, or all-brown bodies and two white legs. I couldn't resist taking photo after photo of them with the Nevados de Payachatas as a backdrop.

The boggy areas of the altiplano also serve as a magnet to much of the region's wildlife. Vicuña, smaller and sleeker than the alpaca, were common on the dry, grassy hillsides that fringed the bofedales. Enormous flocks of black-and-white Andean geese flew back and forth, mingling with flamingos, ducks, and a variety of shorebirds. This was the best place we had found for the glossy black puna ibis and the Andean avocet, which helped swell our bird checklist for the park to thirty-four species.

We searched the muddy edges of ponds and marshes for the tracks of pumas, but we had little hope of actually seeing the cat. In all his years of wildlife research, the chief administrator we had met in Arica had observed them only twice. "Ten years ago, pumas in the park used to prey heavily on llamas and alpacas," he had told us, "but now that there are so many vicuñas and birds, they rarely bother the domesticated animals."

The most memorable animal of all lived among volcanic boulder mounds scattered among the bogs. We were often startled by a sharp whistle, followed by an eruption of grey, rabbit-sized furry bodies leaping with great agility from rock to rock then disappearing in an instant. At other times, especially on rainless days, dozens of them would lazily bask in the hard, yellow light and would be easy to approach. These were mountain *vizcachas*, close relatives of the chinchilla and guinea pig, and members of the rodent family. One of the world's highest living mammals, they range throughout the Andes, where they form colonies of around eighty individuals that exploit natural shelters among the rocks as protection against the cold. With long fluffy tails, big tufted ears, and long drooping black whiskers, they looked like they could easily have hopped out of Alice's Wonderland.

While photographing a colony of vizcachas several miles outside the village, I stumbled upon something even more interesting at the top of a boulder-strewn slope: the roofless but still standing ruins of a tiny stone church. Near the arched doorway was a stone basin on a pedestal, and ringing the remains were several rock corrals, so old they appeared part of the earth.

We sat in the shade next to one of the walls and rested. It was definitely a "power spot." But whether the power came from the earth's geological properties or from my own psyche, I wasn't sure. I had felt it before when I visited the Acropolis late one evening, when no one else was there. It was the sensation of having one foot planted in the present, and one foot planted firmly somewhere else. In the Brooks Range of Alaska I had once come across a simple stone circle marking an ancient hunter's camp, and for an instant I thought I heard whispering voices. On Canada's Baffin Island, above the arctic circle, I passed the site of an old Thule village and discovered two small graves, one with a weathered skull inside. I sensed that the spirits of the Thules were still around. Now, I was at this centuries-old site, high on a bleak but beautiful South American plateau, with the Andinos' predecessors seeming to hover there.

Moving on, we passed through a lava field pocked by cinder cones. The mounds ranged in color from rust-red to tan, and on their stony slopes were the most extensive colonies of *llaretas* we had seen thus far. Odd members of the plant kingdom, these peculiar, bright green, mosslike growths vary from basketball-size to ten feet wide and three feet high. From a distance, they resemble a single, cushiony plant that softens the outlines of rocks on which they grow. But closer inspection reveals that they are thick and cement-hard, like coral. They are composed of thousands of tiny, fleshy leaves that produce miniature yellow flowers and globules of clear resin. Near to Parinacota, we had noticed that large patches of llaretas had been broken off and carted away. When I asked Lorenzo about this, he told me that the llareta is so woodlike and resinous that it makes an excellent fuel; and because they grow extremely slowly (a large plant may be several centuries old), the llareta is becoming extinct wherever it is left unprotected.

From atop the tallest cinder cone, we gazed out over a grand sweep of Chilean countryside. The mile-wide bofedal held thousands of animals—grazing, grunting, honking, and squawking, teeming with life. The cast of characters consisted primarily of llamas and alpacas and dense flocks of Andean geese, but mixed among the main players were groups of vicuñas and birds, from elegant flamingos to chunky, nondescript snipes.

We watched two alpacas—a shaggy brown male and a black and white female—engage in nonstop copulation for at least twenty minutes. Mounted on top, the male didn't want to break things off despite the female's best efforts to end the tryst. The female finally had had enough. I've heard of camels spitting, and this relative of the camel did just that. She swiveled her head around and let loose big gobs of spit that plastered her suitor in the eye.

"Don't get any ideas," I warned Judy when she laughed and looked in my direction.

▲

Our days in Parinacota raced by. In nearly two weeks we had merely scratched Lauca's surface. There were still hot springs, calderas, fumaroles, and mountains to explore. Plus, on the western outskirts of the park, at an elevation of twelve thousand feet, there were groves of *kenua* or Polylepis trees, almost the only trees in the cold, high Andes that provide food and cover for the rare and secretive *huemul*, or Andean deer. But all this would have to wait for another visit. My leave of absence was nearly over, and we soon needed to return to Arica. But getting out of the mountains wasn't going to be easy.

We forgot all about our impending departure during a long day of hiking around the Lagunas Cotacotani, a chain of lava-formed ponds that mirror the Payachatas on their jade-green waters. Upon returning to the village, we found a possible answer to our transportation dilemma parked in front of the antiquated church.

"A taxi, *here?*" Judy asked incredulously.

It had just arrived. Three unsmiling campesinos stepped out first from the tiny rear seat. They were followed by a tall, fair-skinned man with a short beard protecting his face from the biting winds and strong sunlight. He was dressed in green whipcord wool pants and a safari-type bush jacket and was toting a green internal frame backpack. In my role as the unofficial Parinacota welcoming committee, I ambled over and asked him where he was from.

"Arica," he replied, looking past me to scope out the village.

"Arica?" I echoed. "You're from Arica?"

There was a pause as his eyes settled back on mine. "Oh, you mean my nationality, don't you?" he laughed. "I'm English, of course."

In the meantime, the Andinos piled back into the taxi. They were headed for Visviri, an even smaller village farther up the plateau. When the driver returned from his business in town, Judy approached him about the possibility of taking us to Arica. After lengthy negotiations over the price for the one-way journey, he promised he would meet us in front of the church at eight o'clock the following morning.

As Jim, the Englishman, was new to the place, we guided him to the CONAF facility. We shared some of our freeze-dried shrimp creole dinner with him since he had brought only kippers and crackers. And he apologized profusely when we gave him a handful of tea bags, saying it was "inexcusable for an Englishman not to have packed a good supply of tea."

Before leaving London, Jim had written down ten objectives for his South American odyssey. Some of his goals were wildlife-related: to see a Magellanic woodpecker, some flamingos, some Magellanic penguins, some condors, and a puma. Other goals had to do with places: to see the Paine Towers and the altiplano; to visit Tierra del Fuego and Amazonia; and to take a combination of buses and trains from La Paz, Bolivia, to Caracas, Venezuela. "I've done everything I set out to do," he said, glancing at his pocket notebook. "Except I haven't been able to find that bloody puma. Maybe I'll be lucky and catch one in Lauca."

Jim related the difficulty he had encountered in attempting to reach Lauca from Arica. "I tried to find a tour agency that was coming up here, but none of them could find enough customers to justify the trip. I was all set to hitchhike, but then I met an Italian lad who said it took him three days to hitchhike, most of the time spent standing by the side of the road." Finally, after several days of futile searching, Jim found a taxi driver that would do it, for a considerable fee. "I think I ended up paying for the campesinos, but that's all right."

After eating, the three of us went for a hike behind the village to the crest of a gentle hill. A deep red-violet glow suffused the sky, making a silky backdrop for the first stars of the Andean night. The summits of the Payachatas were cloaked in dreary mist, but the rest of the slopes glistened pinkish in the setting sun.

"Will you look at that?" Jim exclaimed, pointing to a flock of flamingos settling down for the night in a nearby shallow pond. Jim said they looked like some graceful Chinese artwork, a dozen statuesque bodies connected to extremely long necks and legs.

The onset of darkness was accompanied by rapidly dropping temperatures. My toes and fingers were already feeling the bite. "What do you say we head back to the refugio for a cup of tea?" I suggested.

"Splendid idea," Jim agreed. "My treat."

▲

In the morning, the outside thermometer registered twenty degrees Fahrenheit, and we could hardly bear to peel ourselves from our sleeping bags. We were out in front of the church with our backpacks at 7:45, fifteen minutes early. An hour later, there was still no taxi.

We sat on a knoll overlooking the village, gradually warming up as the sun melted into our bodies. I felt almost as invisible as a vizcacha on a boulder as Parinacota woke up around us.

A mob of children bustled past us, pushing a homemade wheeled cart. They were healthy, round-faced little kids, shy around gringo strangers. They stopped and stared when they spotted us. We waved. They giggled and scampered off.

We watched in amusement the alpacas and llamas that were corralled within the circles of low rock walls. Most of the animals were docile, but some sparred with their cellmates, spitting and nipping at each others' faces. I knew practically nothing about llamoids, but guessed they were hungry and wanted to be led to pasture.

Around nine, a woman from the village came to fetch the bunch. Garbed in a red shawl and a long dress, and joined by two frisky dogs, she was easy to spot as she herded the string of four hundred or so animals to a bofedal a half a mile away. Once there, the alpacas and llamas got down to some serious grazing. Satisfied that everything was under control, the Andino woman lay on her stomach and sipped directly from a small stream running through the bog, then snuggled inside one of the small, three-sided rock shelters that were scattered about. Solitary groups of vicuñas meandered at the fringes of the domesticated herd, cropping the clumps of coarse, yellowing grasses and dwarf, ground-hugging plants as they went. Vicuñas sometimes mate with llamas and alpacas, but the herders and their dogs will usually keep them apart.

At eleven, Jim met us in the courtyard of the old church. Together we watched a pair of *picaflores de la puna*, or altiplano hummingbirds; two-inch darts of brilliant green busily tending a nest at the corner of the top eaves. Two nestlings nearly as large as their hovering parents protruded from the teacup-sized grassy bowl.

Also nesting within a few feet of the hummers were *pitios del norte*, large woodpeckers very similar to the North American flicker. The birds occupied a cavity in the rock wall, but the hummers buzzed them mercilessly, trying to drive them away. The Andean flicker was revered by the Incas. They believed the birds carried magic sticks in their bills that melted holes in rocks. Of course, the "magic sticks" were actually dried reeds or shafts of grass, and the "melted holes" were naturally occurring crevices in the rocks, the only nesting sites in the treeless world of the altiplano.

At one o'clock, thinking that we had been forgotten, I went for a walk by myself to a small marsh outside town that offered excellent photographic opportunities. Judy remained at the church, stubbornly keeping a lookout for the taxi while she sat in the shade and wrote. Jim had taken off for the Lagunas Cotacotani. We had wished him luck (I wasn't really that sincere) in his quest to see a puma.

The view from the one-lane bridge was of a special type of wilderness, a symbiotic blend of people and nature living in harmony. The nearby wetland was emerald green, a bucolic setting for grazing llamas and families of geese. Farther off, a soft, cloud-filtered light bathed the dry plateau. Above were the cold and misty Payachata peaks. I snapped a few pictures, knowing full well that film couldn't do justice to the beauty before my eyes.

I heard a car backfire in the distance and wondered if it was the taxi. No matter. My el soroche was gone and I was in no hurry to go. For the moment I was quite content just to sit and look at this farthest edge of civilization.

# 6.

# LAKE TITICACA—AN ANDEAN OASIS (BOLIVIA)

WE HAD ARRIVED at the faded little resort town of Copacabana just an hour earlier, but already the local Bolivianos were gathering to watch Judy and me begin our journey on Lake Titicaca. The men in their shapeless wool pants, drab suit jackets, and handknit helmetlike hats eyed us curiously as we assembled our folding canoe on the sandy beach. They had undoubtedly seen a lot of things in their lives, but it was not every day they'd see a boat materialize out of a duffle bag.

Feeling self-conscious, we snapped and pounded the boat together as swiftly as we could. Our efforts were hampered by lassitude and a buzzing in our heads. A mild case of el soroche was to be expected considering we were 12,600 feet above sea level, even higher than La Paz, Bolivia's sky-high capital, from where our trip had begun. We had been in the altiplano for a week, but were still not acclimatized to the effects of forty percent less air.

It took about thirty minutes to shape the jumble of pieces into a rigid sixteen-and-a-half-foot open canoe. The crowd pushed forward to examine this strange Norwegian-made craft. They touched the fabric hull and aluminum framework and passed around our

*Brightly colored dories, moored on Lake Titicaca, near the little resort town of Copacabana.*

break-apart plastic paddles and blaze-orange lifejackets. They murmured quietly among themselves, not in Spanish, but in Aymara, a living language of the Andean highlands that predates the Incas.

We stowed our camping kit (including a week's worth of food) into waterproof bags. Next we slipped into lifejackets, strapped on knee pads, and replaced our running shoes with wetsuit booties. Apparently it was a slow day in the religious shrine-filled town, because from up and down the beach came more of the curious. Dark-eyed children peeked through the crowd, joined by women wearing multilayered skirts, oversized shawls, and anachronistic-looking bowler hats tipped slightly off-center. Normally, I would have found this all very interesting, but now I wanted to get away from being the center of attention and move out of the glaring sun.

Figuring we were ready to depart, four robust fellows picked up the empty canoe and carried it to the water's edge. Judy and I chased after them lugging the far-heavier gear bags. I thanked the men for their help, but failed to convey the message that we weren't ready to depart: A strong onshore wind was blowing and the waves were starting to foam.

"What should we do?" Judy muttered, staring out at the vast, inland sea. "We can't camp here, not with all these people, and we can't haul all this stuff back to town."

With so many eager eyes upon us, I felt out of control. I didn't want to go because of the wind and waves, but with everyone waiting on the beach I didn't want to stay either.

We decided not to disappoint our audience. Hyperventilating from excitement and the rarefied air, we pushed the boat into the surf and jumped in. A wall of water caught us broadside. There was a moment when the canoe teetered and I thought we might take a swim, but Judy did a saving high-brace while I powered furiously ahead. Bouncing past the breakers, I glanced quickly back to shore. A contingent of local citizens stood abreast in the bright, high-altitude sunlight. They solemnly watched us glide across the lake, our destination Isla del Sol, the sacred Island of the Sun, mythical birthplace of the Incas.

Quartering into the waves, I began to relax. The boat was handling well, which was a relief since it had been a last-minute decision to bring it. Normally we would have chosen our Klepper kayak, but the Pak-Canoe's relative lightness (fifty pounds) and portability (one storage bag instead of two) made it a more appealing choice for this type of trip, where we had anticipated difficulty even reaching Lake Titicaca.

We skirted the shoreline as we wound slowly to the north. After months of planning and preparation we were finally paddling on the "highest navigable lake in the world," a title that dates back to 1872, when the first steamer to enter ferry service was carried up the Andes on mules, section by section, and reassembled on Titicaca's shore. I had seen photographs of Lake Titicaca and the surrounding country-side in old *National Geographics* and books, but pretty pictures of quaint villages, balsa rafts, smiling tourists, and hard-working residents didn't prepare me for the real thing.

Approximately 140 miles long by 70 miles wide, Titicaca forms part of the boundary between Bolivia and Peru. The lake is a silvery oasis in the scrub-covered highland. Fed by the melting snows of the Cordilleras Occidental and Real, in addition to the normally dependable summer rains, Titicaca is probably the deepest large lake in the world without an outlet to the sea. When Jacques Cousteau took his mini-submarine to the Island of the Sun, he discovered that Titicaca is a staggering fifteen hundred feet deep, proving once and for all that the lake is not "bottomless," as has long been rumored. Titicaca is central to the people who farm its shores. They believe that their white-bearded god Viracocha rose from the water's chilly depths to establish their culture.

Off to our right was the *puna*, a wide, open expanse of semi-desert, swept by high winds. In the month of September, which is the beginning of spring on the altiplano, the yellow puna, backed by the sterile white snow of the mountains and the deep blue sky, seemed empty. There was no sign of rain. The rocks were a rusty brown or a rich cuprous green. Hillside terraces, cultivated for many generations, had recently been hoed. Dry and dusty, they were ready for planting, waiting for the rains.

Harsh and bitterly cold when the sun doesn't shine (we heard that passing clouds can cause a temperature drop of thirty-two degrees in five minutes), the puna was even more intriguing because of its inhospitality. This contrast was exhibited in many of its plants.

In the wild, uncultivated pockets between the terraces were stony slopes covered in coarse ichu grass and a type of large bromeliad called the *puya raimondii*, identified by its sharp-pointed, tough, sword-shaped leaves. Confined to a few parts of the high Andes, the puya is thought to be a relic plant from the time when dinosaurs roamed the swampy, early Andean coast of South America. As the mountains were uplifted, the primitive puyas adapted to keep pace with climatic changes until they now survive at elevations of up to about thirteen thousand feet. The puya is said to live a hundred years and bloom only once before it dies. Its flower stalk is the world's tallest, up to thirty feet high. There were no giant puya plants in flower now, however; the only green came from scattered small groves of introduced eucalyptus trees.

We continued paddling until five o'clock, passing a sweeping pebble beach, then cutting across a mile-wide bay. On the other side of a dark grey promontory began a rough area of cliffs smacked by waves and with few places to land. We had gotten a late start and were in need of a campsite. Out of desperation, we headed for a tiny inlet with a gravel bench just above the waterline.

"Don't be surprised if we have company during the night," I said, noticing the fresh tracks on shore of cows, sheep, and sandals. Maybe it was a little paranoid, but we stashed all our loose stuff inside the tent and looped a bicycle cable lock from one of the tent poles to the canoe.

We were famished, having not eaten since departing La Paz on the bus that morning. Judy rustled up an appetizer using bread, avocados, and bananas—the last of our "city food." This suited me fine because our freeze-dried dinner was slow in cooking. Normally flaming like a blowtorch, the MSR stove was working at a fraction of its normal output: in part because of the thin air, and in part because impure automobile gasoline was the only fuel we could obtain in Bolivia. Thirsty as well as hungry, we filled our water bottles directly from the lake, hoping that the iodine tablets we added would kill off any nasty protozoa that might want to blossom in our intestines. The sun set precisely at seven. The sky gradually darkened, only to come alive again with stars. But the air was so clear that the stars seemed never to shimmer, shining steadily instead. One of the first constellations to appear was the Southern Cross, considered in these parts to be a celestial llama with her young, browsing the heavenly puna. This was followed by the Pleiades, Scorpio, and many others with names unknown. The only evidence of civilization I could see lay across the next bay, where a dozen or so lights low to the ground marked a small village.

After supper we went directly to bed so we could be up with the dawn. Outside our tent the world seemed to die. The great winds, so forceful during the day, left us in an eerie stillness.

▲

The quiet of the lake was quite a contrast to the noise of La Paz. With its million inhabitants of diverse ethnicity and customs, negotiating the city had been as interesting a challenge as charting our way through the altiplano backcountry.

Founded in 1548, a little more than a decade after the Spanish conquest of the Incas, La Paz is the cultural as well as the governmental seat of the nation. More hilly than San Francisco and with the traffic gridlock of New York City, it's a fascinating mixture of the new and old: a place of high-rise office buildings and exquisite sixteenth-century churches; of smartly dressed urbanites who look and behave like Europeans, and Andinos in native dress, minding the old ways, speaking Quechua more often than Spanish.

La Paz appears unexpectedly when driving in from El Alto airport, the world's highest commercial airport, situated at 13,400 feet above sea level. Suddenly the road pitches into a canyon as raw as a fresh wound, showing the city spread out in a bowl below, all watched over by snow-capped Mount Illimani in the distance. The valley is filled with lights and traffic; a modern city dropped here in the middle of an ancient land. Unlike most other large cities in the world, where the wealthy occupy the heights, the higher a Bolivian's social standing, the lower he lives in La Paz because of the altitude and temperature. Thus, the poorest peasants are the ones who must commute daily from the top of the encircling cliffs down to the city below.

The budget hotel where we stayed was wonderful. The price was reasonable, the employees were friendly, and the small coffee shop was a comfortable place to linger while writing postcards, meeting other travelers, or catching up on our notes. It also had a small travel agency where we booked bus transportation to Copacabana, located one hundred miles northwest of La Paz on a peninsula in Lake Titicaca.

Physically, I was in far better shape this trip than I had been when starting out in Lauca. Some of the credit was due to the Acetazolamide (Diamox) tablets I had started taking several days prior to leaving home. The prescription drug can be used as a treatment for acute mountain sickness, or prophylactically to speed up the acclimatization process by increasing arterial oxygen. Dosages have be started early to work effectively as a prevention; something I failed to consider when at altitude in northern Chile's altiplano.

Judy and I also drank *mate de coca*, a brew of the leaves of the coca plant, which is believed to prevent heart problems and headaches in high places; no restaurant in La Paz would be without it. Although cocaine is made from the coca leaf, in its tea form coca is not strong. It didn't affect me as much as a good, strong cup of Colombian coffee.

Dining in La Paz was always an adventure. During the few days we were there—in between visiting ice caves in the Andes and waiting for transport to Lake Titicaca—we sampled everything from *sopa de maní* (roasted peanut soup) to *pique a lo macho* (a casserole of fried beef, French fries, raw onions, and tomatoes). Frequently, what we ordered was not what appeared on our plates. At an open-air restaurant off the Prado, La Paz's main street, I asked for fish, the meal of the day, but ended up with a spaghetti and meat sauce. Was my Spanish that bad? Apparently so.

We walked miles through La Paz, struggling to catch our breath at the top of each hill. But one morning we took the easy way out and signed up for a half-day city bus tour. It was time well spent. Juan, our guide, showed us things in the city we might have otherwise missed; and we got a crash course on Bolivia—the poorest, highest, most isolated, and least developed of all the Latin American republics.

A friendly, opinionated guy in his mid-twenties, Juan was college educated and well informed about Bolivia's history and folklore. Whether walking down the busy streets or sitting in the microbus, Juan was always there explaining with a personal touch.

Juan on the Church: "Ninety-five per cent of Bolivians are Roman Catholic, the rest are Protestant and a few other religions. But of those ninety-five percent, only a few are 'real believers'. For example, when I am making lots of money, things are going well with my girlfriend, and my health is fine, I don't go to church. But when I'm broke, my girlfriend leaves me for my best friend, and I am sick, then I *run* to church!"

Juan on cocaine: "Bolivia's main cash crop is the coca leaf. Sixty percent of Bolivians chew the leaves. It gives you an energy rush and masks the sensations of hunger and pain. Bolivia is also the world's leading producer of cocaine, the refined extraction of the leaf. However, you won't see the white powder here unless you really look for it, and I suggest you don't. In Bolivia, the sentence is a flat twenty years no matter how much cocaine you're caught with. If you end up going to jail, I hope you're rich."

Juan on Chile: "Don't praise Chile while you are in Bolivia. Our two countries have been engaged in border disputes since the War of the Pacific in 1880. We want Chile to return the strip of land that connects our country to the sea. In exchange, they want mining rights here. Bolivians have never gotten over the devastating *enclaustromiento*, which left us without an outlet to the ocean. Even now, my government uses the issue as a rallying cry whenever it wants to unite the people behind a common cause."

Juan on Peru: "There's a saying about Peruvians: 'They are able to steal your socks without taking off your shoes.' I am very proud of Bolivians. We only know how to steal the shoes."

Judy and I had already visited some of the La Paz markets on our own, but Juan took us to a few that we had missed. Women occupied the sidewalks and corners, selling radios, cassettes, fruit, chewing gum, cigarettes, furniture, watches, pens, shoes, pots and pans, sweaters, and ponchos. Their babies, swaddled or crawling around, stayed close to their squatting mothers.

Off the larger streets were a maze of narrow alleyways that housed scores of stalls connected by burlap canopy archways. One long aisle sold nothing but fried fish from Lake Titicaca. The next one had big open burlap bags filled with grains and produce raised in the highlands: twenty varieties of corn; forty kinds of potatoes; and beans, squash, and peppers. And next to that was an aisle containing red, orange, and yellow tropical fruits and huge hampers of shiny green coca leaves imported from the lower provinces. We could tell instantly when we were approaching the *carne* aisle. Odiferous cuts of red meat hung from hooks on the ceiling. Behind the counters were dead and live turkeys, chickens, and guinea pigs. Not a pet here, guinea pig cooked whole on a spit is a basic food in the altiplano, reportedly tasting a bit like—what else?—chicken.

Then there was La Paz's *Mercado de Brujas*, or Witches' Market, where dreams come true the old-fashioned way—through the spirits.

Need help finding a wife? Need a new truck? Need to have your new house blessed? Everything is possible on this narrow street indistinguishable from most others in La Paz. Run by the market's dozen or so witches, the curbside stalls offer everything from incense, minerals, and herbs to multicolored candies, mysterious potions, small stone images of Pacha Mama (Earth Mother), and necromantic llama fetuses (to be buried in the foundations of new houses in good-luck ceremonies). It's a one-stop shopping center for Aymaras, whose belief in otherworldly powers has provided comfort during centuries of living with drought and floods, famine and disease, and conquistadors and their descendants.

"How about it?" I asked Judy, pointing at the figurine. "Might as well pick one up as long as we're here. Only costs a dollar." I was considering buying a palm-sized stone amulet showing a man and a woman hugging. The witch explained that you put it in your house if your marriage is on the rocks.

"Sure, why not?" Judy agreed, as the witch watched us intently. "It's cheaper than going to a marriage counselor!"

▲

Upon waking, we found a perfect morning for our second day on Lake Titicaca. We were on the water at dawn, taking advantage of the early calm. Hoarfrost covered our gear, but it disappeared quickly when the sun crested the mountains.

There was another bay and a series of headlands to cross before reaching the strait that divided the mainland from the Island of the Sun. I kept a weather-eye to the east, in the direction of the looming, cloud-covered Cordillera Real. Between Mount Illampu (20,932 feet) to the north and Mount Illimani (21,195 feet) to the south, the Cordillera Real *averages* over eighteen thousand feet in height for more than one hundred miles, making it one of the most impressive collections of mountains in the Andes, if not the world. The katabatic, or downhill winds, careening off the high inland peaks have a fearful reputation: dead calms can suddenly switch to williwaws; twenty-knot headwinds can flip 180 degrees in a few minutes; eight-foot waves on Lake Titicaca are not uncommon. Our canoe, designed for whitewater as well as flatwater, could handle a wide range of conditions, but nothing that insane.

The rocky shoreline was backed by a treeless landscape, offering little safety if the cold air from the slopes rushed in. The best anchorages were already claimed. At the head of nearly each cove

*Many miles from the terraced slopes of Isla del Sol, the snowy mountains of the Cordillera Real rise white and glistening above the intense blue of Lake Titicaca.*

was a cluster of low, chocolate-colored adobe houses. Although we would have undoubtedly been welcome, or at least tolerated, in these isolated farming communities, we ourselves were too shy to intrude into their midst. We liked meeting individuals, but not thrusting ourselves into the center of a group.

Before making the mile-long crossing to Isla del Sol, we stopped at a lonely gravel beach snuggled against a high open bluff. I climbed the nearby ridge to stretch my cramped legs while Judy rummaged through the food bag. The view from above emphasized Titicaca's size: cold, deep blue water as far as my eyes could see. With a surface area of more than thirty-six hundred square miles, it is South America's second largest lake, after Venezuela's Lake Maracaibo.

The lake is its own weather-maker. Its size and more or less constant temperature of fifty-two degrees Fahrenheit moderate the immediate climate, permitting a longer growing season than in other parts of the altiplano. Principal crops adapted to the relatively benign countryside include potatoes, barley, fava beans, quinoa and *oca* (types of grains), usually hand cultivated with digging sticks and hoes. After harvest, the stalks are eaten by llamas, alpacas, sheep, and cattle, which in turn are sources of meat, wool, and leather. A small commercial rainbow trout fishery—introduced in 1939 by foreign aquaculturists in order to improve the protein content in the diet of the local people—also provides food for the table and money for store-bought goods.

Fishermen, farmers, raft makers, and villagers normally lead peaceful lives beside Titicaca's waters, but there is growing concern about how long this peaceful existence can last. Recent studies show that the puna surrounding Lake Titicaca was once forest and grassland. However, a rapidly expanding population has already hopelessly overgrazed and depleted the poor soils on its shores. Bolivia has a population of about 6.5 million, seventy percent of whom live on the altiplano, making it one of the world's highest heavily populated regions. Still, from my vantage point above the lake, it looked as if life here hadn't yet reached the twentieth century. The high plain, desolate and enormous, stretched far away—a difficult country, both for its people and visitors.

And yet, no matter how deserted the lakeshore appeared, we could almost always find someone up on the hillside, silently and impassively watching our every move. This morning was no exception. After I joined Judy for a snack on the beach, two men showed up on the ridgetop and came jogging down the stony slope to meet us. The older one carried a cloth sack in each hand; the other an empty plastic bucket. Their reaction to us was to be repeated at almost every stop we would make in the ensuing days: After a brief exchange of greetings, they knelt beside the boat, examining, marveling, touching everything.

Conversation was difficult; Spanish was a hesitant second language for both of us. Through sign language and a few mutually understood words, I offered to take the men for a short paddle. They laughed and politely refused. "She is a real beast," the older man remarked, nodding toward the lake. They thought we should be in a motorboat and offered to send their friend to pick us up—for a small fee. We never got the idea across that we enjoyed traveling by canoe and weren't heading to a particular destination.

We were preparing to depart when the younger man, smacking his lips a little, asked if we had any sweets. The sudden request caught us by surprise. Judy took out a plastic bag of assorted hard candies that we had brought from home. The older man shyly took a lemon drop and said *gracias* as he popped it in his mouth. With an awkward giggle, the younger man smoothly snatched the bag from Judy's hand and put it in his back pocket. I sensed he was waiting for us to react, but we didn't know *how* to react. Was it worth making a scene over fifty cents' worth of candy? The older man seemed embarrassed by his companion's manners. He picked up his cloth sacks and wished us good luck. The younger man nodded goodbye.

Closely spaced waves and a stiff north wind made crossing the Strait of Yampupata more difficult than we had anticipated. Halfway across we entertained the idea of turning back, but we couldn't face returning defeated to our acquaintances on shore. We were committed to push on. Staying low in the canoe to increase stability, we paddled hard into the rollers.

Every time we rode atop the waves, I could glimpse a small, low island to our right about four miles offshore. This was Isla de la Luna, the Island of the Moon. Much smaller than Isla del Sol, with only a few dozen shepherds residing there, Luna nevertheless looms large in Inca mythology. The island was devoted to worship of the moon goddess, Mama Occlo. Legend also has it that it was the place where Viracocha commanded the moon to rise into the sky. On the island are the ruins of an Inca temple and a palace for the Chosen Women. Originally we had considered paddling there, but we now deemed the open water crossing too risky. Then, too, the clerk at the tourist office in La Paz wasn't absolutely certain, but she had heard that the island was closed to travelers because it serves as a prison for Bolivian political prisoners.

We pulled behind a wave-washed islet to take a rest and get rid of the couple of gallons of water that had sloshed into the boat. I glanced ahead to Isla del Sol. It seemed so peaceful, surrounded by clear aquamarine water. It was known to early inhabitants as *Titicaca*, or "Rock of the Puma," the name that was eventually given to the entire lake. I panned my binoculars across the shoreline and, in a sheltered bay, saw a flock of ducks, cormorants, and Andean gulls. The Andean gulls are the only gull to frequent the high Andes and are easy to recognize with their jet-black heads and wingtips and white bodies. "It'd be nice if there was a Flightless Titicaca Grebe among them," I said. But we never spotted this species unique to Lake Titicaca.

Refreshed by the short break, another burst of paddle-power brought us to a sloping shingle beach on the island. Like the pilgrims who travel here to pay homage to the birthplace of Manco Capac and his sister/wife Mama Occlo—the original ancestors of the Incas—we felt privileged and relieved to finally set foot on Isla del Sol.

I had found only bits and pieces of information about the enigmatic island, which is steeped in superstition and myth. The earliest reference dated back to the early 1600s, when the Inca chronicler Garcilaso de la Vega wrote:

"The Incas say that on this (Titicaca) Island, the Sun placed his two children, male and female, when he sent them down to instruct the barbarous people who dwelt on the Earth. … They say that after the deluge, the rays of the Sun were seen on this island, and over the great lake, before they appeared in any other part. With (this) and similar legends the Incas made the Indians believe that they were children of the Sun."

The island still occupies a very sacred place in present-day Aymaran and Quechuan folklore. Isla del Sol has also captured the imagination of several well-known adventurers and researchers. Tristan Jones, who crossed South America in his sailing cutter, *Sea Dart*, spent more than eight months navigating the lake, making the Island of the Sun one of his ports of call. The resulting story was chronicled in his incredible (and I do mean *unbelievable*) book, *The Incredible Voyage*. A recent map of the island honors Jones by naming a narrow rock outcrop, "Sea Dart Point."

Jacques Cousteau's expedition had a more scientific bent. He focused on investigating the stories told by Titicaca's fishermen of being able to touch the roofs of sunken palaces when the lake waters had fallen during long dry spells. Despite the danger inherent in a high-altitude plunge, the divers bravely descended into the depths of the lake near the Island of the Sun. They discovered a number of embankments and paved paths and a sort of giant puzzle composed of finely cut blocks set with great precision in the lake bed. Was this a checkerboard of wharves reserved for vessels of state that were used to carry important men to the sacred island? Or did funeral boats pull in here, carrying the mummies of dignitaries to some necropolis long since drowned by the waters of the lake? Archeologists are still seeking answers to these questions.

In my portable library, I had with me a *National Geographic* article by Loren McIntyre, a writer who has devoted his life to studying and photographing South America. While exploring almost every inlet and island of Lake Titicaca in a homemade cabin cruiser, he commented that the Island of the Sun's "sprawling crags rise out of the lake like the spine and limbs of a gargantuan sea monster frozen by some magic spell." As long as it stayed frozen, the island, seven miles long and indented by several bays and coves, was just the right size to be circumnavigated by us in our canoe.

Hugging the east shore, we soon noticed that we were being followed by a young woman walking along on one of the numerous trails that link the houses and fields of the countryside. Her skin was the color of light mahogany; her hair was braided into two long plaits

*A Bolivian woman in traditional dress, on the shore of Isla del Sol, watches the author take a campesino out for a canoe ride on Lake Titicaca.*

that were joined by a tuft of black wool. Wearing a shawl and a brightly colored, many-layered skirt, she was a spot of brilliance in an otherwise drab landscape. We waved from our canoe. She stood straight and gave us a winsome smile, but when we drew nearer she disappeared down a path without looking back.

A little later, we came upon a two-story mud-brick building perched on a small knoll above the lake. This was the Incas' Temple of the Sun. According to legend, the temple was built and attended by virgins, and only the most select people from all corners of the empire were taken to live there. Intricately positioned rock steps led directly into the water, where elegant, efficient *balsas* (distinctive gondolalike canoes made of dried and bundled *totora* reeds) may have docked many centuries ago. The temple had six rooms; each dark, quiet, and cool, insulated by mortarless masonry several feet thick. Framed by one of the trapezoid windows and doorways was Mount Illampu, perpetually snow-covered and revered by the Incas.

Before we had had a chance to visit the next ruins, we were hailed by two young men tending a flock of sheep. They spoke a patois of half-Spanish, half-Aymara, so we could only partly understand them. Mostly in sign language, we told them of our desire to paddle around the island and how much we enjoyed the lake. I invited them out for a canoe ride. They laughed and goaded each other into doing it. While Judy watched from shore, they took turns in the bow seat. I gave them a brief primer on how to paddle, but I don't think they were listening. Instead of easy, rhythmic strokes, they thrashed the water as if they were beating a rug. When we returned to shore, they asked if they could borrow the boat. Judy shook her head. "It's too dangerous," she said, pointing to the waves offshore. They then asked me if I would take them somewhere, but I couldn't understand where. "Sorry, I can't leave my wife," I mumbled, pointing to my scapegoat. Disappointed, they sat down on the beach and played melancholy songs on their squared-off wooden flutes.

Leaving the shepherds to their sheep, we continued up the east shore, intent on visiting the *Fuente del Inca*, or the Inca's Fountain. I had read that the fountain was nestled in a cleft in the hillside and was adorned with terraced gardens and a set of spring-fed baths, providing convenient drinking water.

Within twenty minutes we were there. The spot was marked by a small wooden pier where several dories bobbed at their moorings. The skiffs were painted in shades of blue and white, with curious names in big black letters across their prows. Some names, such as *Cruzero de Amor*, were Spanish; others, such as *Malku*, meaning condor, were Aymaran; a few were even in familiar English, *Rambo III*, *Bruce Lee*, *Rocky IV*, and *The Microman*. A couple of young boys sat in the shade of some eucalyptus trees, observing us with interest.

"I bet this is where those guys wanted to take the canoe," I said. "Imagine the 'splash' they would have made with their friends." Not one to appreciate puns, Judy groaned and rolled her eyes.

In the same cove was another pier where a motor launch, actually a hydrofoil, was docked. The boat belonged to one of the tour agencies that conducts day trips on the lake—the type of outings that usually attract those short on time and long on pesos. Embarking from La Paz before dawn, the tours include a private bus to the port of Huatajata, where you board a hydrofoil for a visit to the Island of the Sun—before having lunch at Copacabana, and then returning to La Paz in time for a late dinner.

As we approached the landing, I watched a dozen or so tourists trudge up the stone steps to the Inca Fountain. A few minutes later, I watched the same gathering trundle down. I glanced at my wristwatch: their total time at the fabled site had been just fifteen minutes, and now their leader was announcing that they had to go.

These islanders knew their tourists. A few of the more enterprising natives made a last-ditch effort to hawk their wares as the camera-toting group reboarded the boat. One brown-eyed girl, about ten years old and dressed in traditional clothes, stood next to a couple of bored white llamas, animals the conquistadors first thought of as a new variety of sheep. "*¡Fotografía! Fotografía!*" she chanted like a hotdog vendor at a baseball game. When one of the tourists snapped a few pics, the girl played her master stroke, her one word of English: "Mo-ney!" she demanded, thrusting out her open hand. The tourist handed her a couple of coins and hurried away to the boat.

The hydrofoil eased out of the harbor and, with engines wide open and hull raised to clear the water, skimmed across the strait toward Copacabana. If the tourists were lucky, the boat's arrival would coincide with a major fiesta, when the otherwise sleepy little town springs to life. On several days throughout the year, Indians from both the Peruvian and Bolivian shores and islands of Lake Titicaca show up and perform traditional dances, accompanied by music, drinking, and feasting. The festivities would be difficult to enjoy, however, in the fifteen minutes allotted.

We wanted to see the Inca Fountain at the top of the hill, but decided to postpone our visit until after we had rounded the island. We would arrange to be there early in the morning, before the tour boats and their entourage arrived.

Moving on, we passed small groupings of houses—too few to be called villages—all tucked away in coves. The coves looked snug and protected, but what we wanted was a deserted strip of shoreline free from inquisitive eyes. We found a narrow, pebbly beach, backed by a steep bluff covered with sweet smelling *koa* (incense) brush. The only way someone could see us was by standing directly above us or offshore in a boat.

Although it was late afternoon, the sky was still bright and there was bound to be good light for a few more hours. I set about securing the canoe to the beach while Judy trekked shoreward with our camping kit. "Lucky to find an uninhabited spot!" she said gleefully; however, camp hadn't been set up for more than a minute when visitors arrived.

A pair of young shepherds, attired in tee shirts, patched over blue jeans, and "Drink Coca-Cola" baseball caps, worked their way down a cliffside path we hadn't noticed. Of course, they were perplexed and intrigued by our canoe. They talked and joked between themselves as they inspected it from bow to stern.

Weary from the sun, the thin air, and people in general, Judy and I plastered ourselves against a rock wall with its thin sliver of shade. I could have easily gone to sleep—the glare off the beach and the lapping of waves had a soothing, hypnotic effect—but I forced myself to stay awake in case the boys thought of taking the boat for an unescorted ride.

"Well," Judy asked two hours later, "what else can we do for amusement? As long as they're here, it's a shame not to be interacting." We had talked with the boys as much as our limited vocabulary and conversational skills would allow. We had entertained them by reading Aymaran words from our small dictionary. We had showed them maps and photographs. But for the last half hour they had been sitting by the boat, staring at it, staring at us, waiting for our next move.

Finally, the smaller boy got up and started ambling down the beach. We smiled and waved. "¡Adiós!" Judy called out. A few minutes later, just as the second visitor got up to leave, the first little boy returned. He held his hands out to Judy, showing her a fistful of smooth beige stones with brown lines forming concentric circles on them. "They're beautiful!" Judy exclaimed. "Every rock has a 'sun' design on it."

The little boy was obviously familiar with the ways of gringos. After seeming genuinely pleased that Judy liked the rocks so much, he asked if we had anything for him. As a matter of fact, we did have some Smoky the Bear balloons and other such trinkets, but we didn't like handing them out directly to children who asked. We preferred to give them to an adult when we had had some special encounter with the family or child. This kid was a charmer, however, and had given us a gift first, so we gave him a few balloons and buttons and said goodbye.

But not for long. He was soon back with more rocks, asking for more gifts. We stood firm in refusing because we didn't think it was a good idea to present ourselves as a couple of *Yanqui* Santa Clauses, but it was very tempting to pay him off to leave. He finally put the rocks down and made a third exit. We were just beginning a self-evaluation on how we might have mishandled this cross-cultural exchange when he appeared again—with more rocks. "*No más, no más,*" we pleaded. "We have no more gifts. Much pleasure in meeting you. Goodbye!"

The night was blissfully quiet, until around midnight when we were awakened by thunderclaps and lightning bolts splitting the sky. We had been lulled into a false sense of security by the constant clear weather of the previous few days; now a violent deluge swept across the lake, sending huge combers smashing against the shore. We quickly got dressed and crawled outside into the wind and rain and the blackest sky I can remember. Spray off the lake shot high enough to drench the tent. In the gloom we carted the boat and camp to a lumpy mattress of rocks abutting the cliff, where we hoped the waves wouldn't drown us.

"One thing's for certain," I said, when we were back in the tent, weary and soaking wet. "We've got to get off this beach in the morning."

▲

Orion, my favorite constellation, was a welcome sight when I opened my eyes in the predawn hours. The storm had passed. The lake was silvery calm. We broke camp and were in the canoe as the sun inched above the eastern cordillera.

This was supposed to be the day we rounded the north end of the island. But upon noticing a couple of tiny, uninhabited islets ahead (they were not marked on our map), we decided to make an early camp. "It'll be nice to lie low for a while, all alone," Judy said. I agreed.

Our island hideaway was about a mile offshore of Isla del Sol and several miles from the mainland. It was a wonderful sanctuary, a grass-covered outcropping with only a single awkward place to land the canoe. I fantasized about being the first person to ever set foot here, but a short hike over the rocky mound revealed that half the island was sculptured with a pattern of semicircular, antiquated retaining walls supporting plots of arable earth. We marveled at the amount of back-breaking labor that had gone into creating a few acres of cropland. Who was responsible for the construction? How long ago was it built? Why was such intense cultivation necessary? Once again, the Incas and their predecessors left us with more questions than answers.

▲

A strong nor'wester blew in early the next morning, ushering in rain and strong winds. Paddling was out of the question, but we didn't mind. On the contrary, we welcomed the opportunity to stay put another day. We had enough food, abundant drinking water, a decent camp, some interesting books, and were both feeling fit. What could be better than our own little island on Lake Titicaca, steeped in the ghosts of an Incan past?

After the rain sped away, the sky turned as clear as a polished lens. I climbed the grassy knoll above camp and from my aerie surveyed our world. Breaking rollers raced across the lake; big white horses that I would be hesitant to ride even in our seaworthy Klepper. The Island of the Moon glowed like a pinspot of gold. And, far away, the snowy mountains of the Cordillera Real rose white and glistening above the intense blue of the lake. It was easy to understand why the Aymaras held this place in such high regard. Even I could almost see Viracocha surface from the deep to create the sun, moon, and stars along with the Andean world.

I returned to camp to find Judy already preparing breakfast. With the storm came a drop in temperature, which we faced with the help of hot chocolate and oatmeal.

We saw no people, no boats, no airplanes during our internment: only noisy wrens; chestnut-collared sparrows; ducks with blue bills and white faces; a black-and-white-tailed hawk; swallows chasing down invisible insects; and plain brown hummingbirds, some eight inches long, the size of a swift— by far the largest species I have ever seen. We stationed ourselves near a cluster of bell-shaped flowers growing on a rock face. Soon the air all around us was filled with hovering and darting giant hummers, their wings beating so fast we could hear the vibrations. It is no surprise that Incan sorcerers thought hummingbirds were invested with magical properties. More species of hummingbird live on the chilly slopes of the Andes than any other family of birds; over half of the flowering plants of the puna are pollinated by these iridescent little jewels.

It was the most agreeable of days, but we were somewhat disconcerted late in the afternoon when the wind showed no sign of abating. Distant lightning strikes and rumbling thunder told of more storms over the lake. We dove for cover when one of the squalls roared over the island, pelting us with hail, rain, and sleet, and finally enshrouding us in fog.

Throwing my sleeping bag over me, I listened with growing anxiety to the pounding surf and to the wind buffeting the tent. Nagging "what ifs" swirled through my head. What if the winds continued unabated for days, a week? What if the canoe broke free of its tie-downs, stranding us here? I even went so far as to ask Judy if she thought she could swim to the Island of the Sun. Certainly, with no subcutaneous fat, *I* could not have made it. "Maybe I could get there," she replied thoughtfully. "But if I did, it wouldn't do *you* any good."

As things turned out, Judy couldn't have swum the length of a swimming pool. While filling water bottles from the lake, she slipped on some loose boulders and wrenched a muscle in her back. "What kind of painkillers do we have?" she moaned, hobbling back to camp, where I sat working on the recalcitrant stove. She was stooped over like a little old lady. I dumped the contents of the first-aid kit in my lap. The strongest pharmaceutical we had was Tylenol with codeine. "I'll take one now and another in four hours," she croaked, crawling into her sleeping bag.

I patted her shoulder solicitously, but I wasn't overly concerned. I had witnessed a number of her Chevy Chase pratfalls in the four years we had been married, not to mention the nine years we had known each other before then; no matter how serious the spill, she was always fine by morning. Still, in my role as first responder, I would have been remiss not to mention that there could be a problem if a rescue was necessary.

"It's nothing, really," I said. "Something I read in some mountaineering magazine is all."

"What do you mean?" Judy asked.

"Well, if you must know, these two climbers were on a high peak in the Andes, either in Bolivia or Peru, I forget which. Anyway, one of them fell and was badly injured. He needed to be evacuated. His friend made it down to the nearest village and offered the Andinos money to help in the evacuation. They refused. The climber was desperate. He offered them more money, telling them how his friend was suffering and might die. They still refused."

"Yeah? So finish the story," Judy ordered.

"The climber couldn't get the campesinos to help him. The Indians are so accustomed to suffering and sacrifice that they accept it as part of their everyday life. What's the big deal when a stranger, especially a gringo stranger, is in trouble?"

"Mmmm." Judy was losing interest as her painkiller kicked in. "What happened?"

"Oh, he died and his body was left in the mountains."

Judy sat up and swallowed another pill. "Thank you, Mister Rogers, for that happy bedtime story," she muttered, before falling immediately asleep.

▲

I awoke with a start. I nudged my sleeping companion. "Wake up. Listen!" I urged.

"I don't hear anything," she mumbled.

"Exactly. The wind has died. We should get an early start," I said, flashing my headlamp beam in her face. "How's your back? You gonna be all right?"

As I predicted, she was feeling much better. She uttered a few token moans to elicit sympathy, but assured me that she could paddle. We launched the canoe at sunrise, cruising over roily, dark green waters as we rounded the island's north and west sides. Our only stop the entire morning was at Pilko Caima, Isla del Sol's primary ruin. On the shore nearby, a set of Incan steps leads up from the boat landing site to a trail that follows an ancient route to the sacred rock where the Incan creation legend began. The stone palaces of the Incan kings have fallen, but Aymarans still sacrifice unblemished white llamas here to ensure a good harvest, just as they did in the days of the lost empire.

At one o'clock we pulled into a long, crescent-shaped bay. The beach and rocky hillside looked forsaken, but by now we knew better. Within minutes a parade of islanders was wandering past us on a lakeside trail.

First to appear were three small, elderly women. On their backs were enormous bundles of bromeliad trunks, the woody puya stumps used as a substitute for firewood. The heavy ungainly loads helped account for the women's bent-over gait. They grunted a perfunctory "*Kamisaki*" (hello) without lifting their heads as they trudged past.

Judy and I carried our snack to a large boulder and tried to blend in, which is difficult to do when twenty sheep, seven cows, and two donkeys led by a couple of girls virtually surround you. The livestock grazed on the vegetation at the water's edge while the girls washed clothes in the lake.

We were about to shove off when a grandfatherly Aymaran turned up with five round-faced boys in tow. The youngsters, who all looked the same age but claimed to be brothers, were fascinated with the canoe, touching, examining, and sitting in it. Finally, the old man stepped forward. He was earnest-looking and very solemn. His forehead was broad, his nose hawklike, his cheekbones angular, and his leathery skin creased and furrowed. He saved me the embarrassment of not knowing the correct greeting by offering me his hand. I tried to explain what we were doing and how much we liked Titicaca, but I'm certain my explanation in pidgin Spanish was more confusing than enlightening. It didn't matter. He nodded goodbye and the boys ran after him, laughing and skipping stones on the lake.

Later that afternoon we congratulated ourselves on our circum-navigation of Isla del Sol. The following day, we would visit the Fountain of the Incas and re-cross the strait. Once on the mainland, we'd take our time paddling back to Copacabana; back to hotels, buses, and jet airplanes—back to another world.

# 7.

# Lost Worlds and Limitless Horizons (Venezuela)

WE HAD BEEN in Venezuela less than twenty-four hours—hard to believe as we watched a paca, a two-foot-long rodent with a short tail and several rows of white spots along its flanks, devour banana peels in the cloud forest outside the refugio. Judy and I were with our guides from Mérida, a university city of about 130,000 inhabitants that lies on the northern border of Sierra Nevada National Park. From the United States we had arranged to travel with guides in the relatively accessible Andes in the far west of Venezuela; later, we would accompany them to the Guyana Highlands, a remote corner of southeastern Venezuela near the border with Brazil and Guyana.

Our two affable *Venezolano* guides could not have been more appealing. Henrí was of Indian descent: slight and dark with smooth skin, shiny straight black hair, and a dazzling smile. He was quiet and gentle and had an air of mystery about him. José was the opposite: tall and thin with fair skin and short brown hair. He was also more gregarious, and possessed a repertoire of jokes which he was very good at delivering in English. Both were university students who loved to spend time in the mountains on their own and got paid to do it during their school breaks.

Judy and I had not been prepared to be hiking and camping this early in the journey. We had been under the impression that we would be taking a mountain bike tour from inn to inn through quaint Andean villages. Upon our arrival in Mérida, however, the outfitter said he expected we would want to backpack and so that's what he had arranged. We didn't protest. A day of mountain biking would be squeezed in later on, and the revised itinerary *did* sound intriguing: four days hiking from about 5,400 to 15,600 feet, in habitat ranging from subtropical rain forests to clammy, dripping cloud forests to open alpine meadows near perpetually snowcapped peaks; then trekking down a rough mountain road to a remote village where we would spend two nights. Our return would be via mule to a gondola-type cable car that would take us back down the cordillera into Mérida. A lot of variety in a short time.

This was the first time we had ever been on our own trip with guides. They carried the food and tents; we were responsible for our personal gear. I appreciated my lightened pack during the climb but, more than that, I was happy to be with people from the area who knew the trail and could tell us stories about the place. Both men had participated in various rescues and body searches and were more familiar with the mountainous 470,000-acre park than the rangers stationed there.

Unfortunately, Henrí and José were carrying incredibly heavy packs, and I began to feel badly about their discomfort. Especially Henrí's. Despite his well-tuned body, he got slower and slower during our second day so that we rarely saw him. When we stopped to rest and he eventually caught up, he was dripping with sweat and had a look of agony on his face, which he tried to soften with a smile. José acted as if he hardly noticed; if anything, he seemed a little embarrassed at his friend's weakness. Judy and I expressed concern, but the chief guide was stoic. "No," he assured us. "The pack is not heavy; it just does not fit him well." We left it at that, concluding that they enjoyed the hardship; that it was part of what they expected when they were outdoors—to be wet, cold, and challenged by the experience.

As we climbed higher, overhanging vegetation pressed in from both sides of the trail, creating a mountainside tunnel of greenery. September was the tail end of the rainy season and the forest was lush. Orchids and bromeliads hung from tall trees; on the ground was a fantastic array of ferns, philodendrons, and mosses. Shrubs festooned with red, yellow, blue, and purple blossoms were every-where, attracting tough little hummingbirds. Flocks of parakeets argued from the treetops. And the songs of other birds we could not see filled the air. The only thing missing from the picture was mammals; except for the paca, we hadn't seen any at all. José explained that although the park harbors typical northern Andean fauna—including spectacled bears, tapirs, pumas, jaguars, deer, coatimundis, and even monkeys—the populations are low and the animals difficult to observe. I was glad I left my heavy 300mm telephoto lens at home; the 80–200 zoom would easily suffice.

By two o'clock, having climbed steadily since nine that morning, Judy and I had to insist that we take a lunch break. If I were a guide, I would have been trying to get rid of food all day. It was obvious they were carrying far more than we could eat in the next few days. And what a *strange* assortment. I joked about them carrying watermelons, but as it turned out they *were* carrying huge papayas and bags of oranges, along with big bottles of ketchup, jars of mayonnaise, hot dogs, and other heavyweight foods. Right then I realized that our young guides may have been competent mountaineers, but they knew little about meal planning. "Oh, well," I thought. "As long as *they're* carrying it and not me."

During the afternoon, I tried to get a clear answer about when and where José planned to stop for the night. But he responded vaguely. The path took us across the sheer face of a cliff on a rickety plank secured by steel bars, then across a mountain torrent where earlier in the year a backpacker had drowned when he slipped while jumping across the narrow gorge. José and others had searched the chasm for nearly a week, but the hiker's body was never recovered.

"Not a comforting story for a tired, almost forty-year-old accustomed to the sedentary life of your basic paper-pusher," Judy mumbled when it was her turn to cross. She might have been miffed about this much-too-long day of hiking had not José—wise beyond his years in this matter—known exactly what to say: "You and Larry are very strong. Many people I take want to turn back. You are not like most Americans."

Funny, but we took this latter comment as a compliment, though at the same time were offended by the implication of what Americans are like. Still, we thought, if so many people had trouble on this day, why didn't José modify his plans? But Judy and I didn't verbalize our thoughts: God forbid he should decide we *were* like most Americans.

The trees grew shorter as we climbed up the mountainside. An elfin oak forest came and went, merging into the *páramo*, a vegetative zone of dense grasses and low-growing plants that thrive in the high humidity and altitude of the northern Andes. Clear, cold tarns, tinted blue and glacial in origin, lay tucked into the shoulders of the rugged mountains at elevations starting at ten thousand feet.

My ability to appreciate the special area was limited by the gathering dark mists, which were followed by heavy sleet. Plus, for the first time, I realized that I was feeling ill. We must have been between eleven and twelve thousand feet when Judy stopped to ask how I was doing. I confessed I had the beginnings of a headache and that my legs were loaded with lactic acid. "Seems that my old friend, el soroche, is with me again," I moaned. As I fell behind, gasping for breath and creeping along, Judy would stop to wait for me on little ridges or rocky outcroppings. From here she watched my progress and, at the same time, tracked José's route as he disappeared into the lowering fog.

At about seven-thirty, the three of us arrived at a refugio owned by the park and maintained by a climbing club. The small metal hut came as a welcome surprise, as I had thought we would be setting up tents. By then it was black outside and a blizzard was raging. Henrí had been falling farther behind and had not been seen for hours. He could be lost or dead. José decided to go look for him, but first Judy loaned him her rain jacket. He was still wearing shorts and a light windbreaker. And his running shoes were waterlogged. "His feet must be absolutely freezing," Judy commiserated after José left on his rescue mission.

About fifteen minutes later, they both returned. Henrí was in a hypothermic state, his body shaking uncontrollably. "I'm sorry," he stuttered, crunching up in a ball on the muddy dirt floor. We sat in the dark among the detritus from previous hikers, maneuvering to find spaces between the drips from the roof.

I suggested that I get the stove going since José was busy finding a dry change of clothes, and meanwhile we all needed something hot to drink. José was adamant that I not operate the stove. I assured him that I owned one just like it and had used it hundreds of times. He would not relent. I didn't know what to think. I could not decide if it was an insult to him for me to help, or if he felt so responsible for the equipment he could not allow me to touch it. There were some tense moments as I sat muttering under my breath about the situation. Judy hissed at me to relax.

Finally, José got the stove going and concocted a meal of watery soup and lemonade. They certainly didn't lighten their packs with that menu. An odd choice, I thought, but it was just what we needed—hot liquid.

*Our final camp among the granite peaks of the Sierra Nevada was a rocky ledge on the side of a ridge. José figured we were at an elevation of about 14,000 feet.*

We all settled into sleeping bags immediately after dinner, using the tents as overbags. Outside the howling and blowing snow continued. It had been a memorable second day.

▲

In the morning it was calm but the sky remained a scuddy grey. Slushy snow blanketed the ground. The twin peaks Humboldt (16,215 feet) and Bompland (16,021 feet), plus La Concha (16,143 feet), were obscured by swirling tendrils of dense, cool fog. Below the billowing clouds were the snouts of milky-colored glaciers, and beneath every snowfield was a waterfall that streamed down the wrinkles of the mountains. The scene was beautiful, right out of a Sierra Club calendar. Only after running around, taking this picture and that, did I realize that although I was breathless, my soroche was gone.

The hike that day was shorter, about five hours, with less climbing. We eventually made it over the divide and began a gradual descent among the boulders and granite peaks of the Sierra Nevada. Our next camp was a rocky ledge on the side of the ridge. José figured we were somewhere around fourteen thousand feet. Westward loomed vast mountains in Colombia, one hundred miles away and nearly hidden by mist. Below us stretched Venezuela's verdant lowlands, now pocked with fleecy clouds.

Arriving relatively early at camp was a treat. We had the site to ourselves and quickly cleared some ground to pitch the tents. There was time to read, write, and just relax before being served a dinner of tomatoes neatly stuffed with tuna salad, accompanied by sliced cantaloupe and fresh pineapple. Again, a strange choice, but it was appetizing.

That night Judy and I were awakened by the sound of voices. Henrí and José were talking and laughing, and the volume kept escalating. Judy finally decided she had to say something ... "*¡Más tranquilo, por favor!*"

"You say something, Judy?" asked José. She repeated her request. He went into paroxysms of giggling.

"You can just say 'shut up!'" he said, laughing.

Later, we learned that they both had been unable to sleep because they were so cold—their sleeping bags were paper thin. To pass the night they began telling stories and jokes, and apparently thoroughly entertained themselves.

▲

The camping portion of our trek ended the next day. We climbed down and then up a steep snow-covered precipice and emerged over the edge to see an observation area loaded with people. A sign announced that we had arrived at Pico Espejo cable car station, elevation 15,634 feet.

It was a surprise to Judy and me to have been so close to this mountaintop development when hiking that morning we had felt so isolated. The summit may look formidable, but even a novice can make it up and back in a day thanks to the *teleférico*. Starting at Mérida, eight miles away in a straight line, the cable runs to Pico Espejo, the fourth and final station on the world's longest and highest cable-car ride.

Several trails lead off into the mountains from the lofty station. It is also the jumping-off point for the climb to 16,411-foot Pico Bolivar, the highest point in Venezuela. José, who had climbed the major peak several times, said that on the crest of the mountain was a bronze bust of Simon Bolivar, the Venezuelan-born warrior-politician who freed most of northern South America from Spanish rule. "Every town in Venezuela has a plaza named after him," José stated. "Bolivar is to us what George Washington is to you."

We enjoyed having hot chocolate and munchies in the coffee shop and watching the other tourists. Some of them, having ascended 10,500 feet in an hour and a half, were suffering from the effects of the oxygen-poor air. Others were dressed for the shirtsleeve weather down below and were shivering outside in the freezing mist.

After taking the cable car to the next lower station, our guides left some of the gear and our leftover food with an acquaintance of theirs. We wouldn't be needing the stuff where we were going. Our goal was the mountain village of Los Nevados, a five-hour downhill hike from the Loma Redonda station. According to José, a small inn there served food, and we would be sleeping in a guest house.

"No more heavy pack," I said to Henrí, as he ditched the soggy tent and climbing rope. He rubbed his shoulders in mock pain and grinned. "*Sí*. Now I go very fast; no more last."

A trip to Los Nevados used to be something of an adventure before the cable car system was completed in the late 1950s. "It was a three-day mule ride from Mérida over the cordillera," explained José, as we tramped down the well-used path. "Now an occasional four-wheel-drive vehicle makes it in." José said that electricity and a better road were to come the following December, and that the village was already being wired for street lights. Our sensitive young guide was sorry to see the centuries-old pattern of Andean life transformed. "The serenity of isolation will soon be gone," he mused. "Civilization moves closer every day."

I, too, was glad to visit Los Nevados before the electricity arrived. But so were a lot of other people: Los Nevados, it seemed, was a popular destination. We were accompanied on the trail by about a hundred Venezuelans and a few international visitors. It was a school holiday and everyone was in a festive mood: walking, riding mules, running, laughing, and singing. The trail was rough and rocky, with very steep sections cutting through the open páramo. Across the valley, we could see the semiarid terraced and cultivated mountainsides, and we passed little farms hidden behind a profusion of scrub and blooming vines. As it turned out, this was one of the "bike trails" we would have taken. "Right," Judy observed when José pointed this out. "Good thing a trek was planned, because I would've had to dump the bike and walk anyway."

She was in high spirits when Los Nevados finally came into view, clinging to the angular hillside below us. I knew she was thinking of the inn, a delicious Andino meal, and a cozy room. Well, it was almost like that. The tiny village had been so overrun with tourists that the guest houses were almost full. The resourceful José did come up with a clean and simple room with two sets of bunkbeds for the four of us, and we were overjoyed to have that.

José told us about some of the other trips he'd led to Los Nevados that hadn't gone so well. "One couple came prepared for their hike with a suitcase and street shoes," he chuckled, stretching out on the uppermost bed. "By the time they reached the village, they were nearly crippled and one of the man's arms was longer than the other." Another time, according to José, a hiker burst into tears when she saw her spartan accommodations for the night, and had a fit when she learned that the inn served only corn mush and potato soup.

In the hour before sunset, I sat at the cramped table by the wooden-grilled window and tried to write my notes. But it was impossible. My eyes kept leaving the page and turning to the wonderful view outside: small, square houses with their white-washed adobe walls and tile roofs; the white-and-blue church built in 1912; the rugged, creased mountains cloaked in newly plowed fields, stitched together with rows of flickering poplars; and the Río Nuestra Señora canyon, where we planned to hike the next day.

I could also see wide-eyed, rosy-cheeked children walking along the road. Looking as young as six, they walked seriously through town or across the fields, one with a scythe over his shoulder, others leading mules or smaller children. I wondered what they thought of us, or of the children from Mérida, who showed up just to spend a few days looking around their town.

▲

As a new adventure in travel, we arranged for mules to take us back to the cable-car station. Only Judy and I would be riding. José had returned to Mérida the previous day to get started on preparations for our journey to the Guyana Highlands; and Henrí, I surmised, was too dignified and proud to climb on a mule when he was perfectly capable of returning under his own steam.

The muleteer, a moustachioed mountain man wearing a handwoven poncho and a wide-brimmed hat, showed up early in the morning in front of the inn. He hitched to a post the seven mules that would carry Judy and me, two French couples, and himself; in addition, there was another couple of animals for baggage. The mule driver told me that the animals made this trip every day. I tried not to be too sentimental as I looked at the one loaded with our backpacks and saw its open sore. I felt very badly for it, and for the driver as well, when he told me he was sick. Coughing into a dirty bandana, he said that at the station he would pick up other tourists or supplies for the village that arrive via the cable car.

"Heeeeah! Heeeeeeah!" sang the driver, prodding the reluctant mule team with the crack of a short-handled whip. We started off uphill with great views of the rumpled valley, passing a steep mountainside field of green wheat with red gladiolas scattered throughout. As we got higher the vegetation changed dramatically, becoming more open and uncultivated. Purple, yellow, and pink were the dominant colors along the road, with gentians, geraniums, alpine heather, avens, and a host of other tundra plants in bloom.

As a rule, vegetation on the páramo grows close to the ground. An exception is the giant *espeletia*, a member of the daisy family, and the most characteristic plant of the moist high country. When fully developed, the espeletia can reach treelike dimensions—twenty feet in height—but most are about as tall as a man. The plant's thick central stems and rosettes of furry leaves have given rise to its Spanish name, *frailejón* (tall friar). In the mist, I suppose their brooding silhouettes did resemble clerics in contemplative meditation.

The few country folk we met along the way were shy and aloof. Dressed in Andean browns and greys and toting burlap bags over their shoulders, they moved to the side of the trail as our mule train passed. I could just imagine what they said among themselves about the crazy gringos. Judy told me that I looked ridiculous on my mule, with my long legs almost dragging the ground. She, of course, could not see herself in her loud red jacket on a mule named Oscar perpetually in last place.

For hours I listened to the French guy on a white mule yell, "*¡Mula, mula, mula!*" as he prodded his steed to quicken the pace. The mule totally ignored the bore, but in its own way did seem to enjoy jockeying for position with the other animals. I was constantly amazed at how sure-footed the beasts were as they negotiated the precipitous, uneven path without injuring themselves or us. This easily qualified as my longest-ever trail ride. I could see and feel my mule's chest heaving in and out and feel its strength waning as it stopped to rest, the same way I'd had to stop while hiking up the mountain. "Poor thing. What a life," I thought, as I concluded that for uphill travel mule power is the way to go.

After four hours, the large white cross at the cable-car station loomed into view. A silent competition began among the riders to see who could reach it first. The positions of the mules changed back and forth. We were eyeing other riders like bumper car drivers in an amusement park. I gave my mule a final kick and it stopped in its tracks, unwilling to go a step farther. In the final stretch, Judy's Oscar plodded ahead. She raised her hands in exultation, "*¡Gané! Gané!*" ("I won! I won!") she yelled. The losers clapped, and we dismounted without saying goodbye to our trusty steeds and headed for the cable car.

▲

A few days later, we regrouped and began a different phase of our travels in Venezuela. This time we were heading south from Ciudad Bolivar across the Gran Sabana—a region of hills, rivers, grasslands, and forest, stretching almost to the border with Brazil. Like Patagonia, the Gran Sabana has a unique character that has attracted and fascinated explorers and adventurers for centuries. In this remote and lightly settled area are found the geological features known as *tepuis*. These massive steep-sided mesas rise dramatically above the rolling savanna floor and have been called everything from "islands in the sky" to "landlocked Galapagos."

More than a hundred *tepuis*—a Pemón Indian word for a table mountain or plateau—are scattered over an area of some two hundred thousand square miles, mainly in southeastern Venezuela. Because of their high, perpendicular walls and inaccessible locations, fewer than half of the tepuis have been explored. One of those that is well-known, if only because of the sightseeing planes and helicopters that constantly buzz its escarpment, is Auyan-tepui—home to Angel Falls, the world's highest waterfall. Fifteen times taller than Niagara, this spectacular cascade plunges more than thirty-two hundred feet. Mount Roraima, the tepui where we were headed, had no such claim to fame, but its 9,094-foot-high summit was accessible and offered plenty of exploration for us.

Our group now consisted of José, and a new "leader," Gonzalo, an older (late twenties) guide with extensive outdoor experience. We were also joined by Michael, a Czechoslovakian-born Canadian, our fellow "tourist."

Judy, Michael, and I were comfortable in the back of the Toyota Land Cruiser as it climbed out of the forested valley of the Caroní River and crossed the shrubland and grasses in the hot afternoon sun. There were few developments along the road, and for refreshment we sipped milk directly from the coconuts Gonzalo had brought. It was languid and decadent, and we thought it was great, especially after hearing stories of the slow and tedious bus ride that other travelers had made to reach our destination.

Our most frequent stops were at military checkpoints, which seemed unduly close together. Gonzalo shrugged. It was no big deal, he thought; but he did say he had been quite surprised that when he had traveled in Canada he had never been stopped. We were obliged to get out of the vehicle a few times so that it could be searched and to hand over our passports while we waited. No matter how ordinary it may have been to Gonzalo, it always made me nervous, especially looking in the faces of what appeared to be very young kids toting automatic rifles. Michael, having grown up in a totalitarian state, hated the checkpoints more than the rest of us. Gonzalo assured us that it was rare to have to bribe someone, and he thought that because we (Michael, Judy, and I) looked suitably middle-aged and middle class, we would not be hassled. And we weren't. Once a sentry barked at José to put on his shirt (he was driving without it), and another time we had to dig for quarters because a guard liked to collect them; but otherwise all was routine.

The road down to Santa Elena—a tiny community located in the extreme southeastern corner of Venezuela edging the Amazon Basin—had recently been paved which meant that we could get to our embarkation point in one day instead of several. But we were aware of the effects that the road would have on the area: more cars, more settlers, more tourists, more garbage, more deforestation, more pressures on what had been very isolated ecosystems and indigenous populations.

Mining, especially for diamonds and gold, has been going on for a long time in the region, and the two towns we passed through, El Dorado and "Km 88" (the eighty-eighth kilometer from El Dorado), had the distinctive feel of frontier settlements populated primarily by rough-looking men. Later, I met two university professors from Caracas (both women) who had been sightseeing in the Guyana Highlands on their own. They told me that in one mining center they had been refused entry into the only restaurant-and-bar in town because they couldn't prove they were "disease-free." The powers-that-be assumed that all unescorted women were prostitutes, and the government-issued card was required.

At Km 88 the climb got steeper. Shifting to low gear, we passed through dense rain forests and cloud forests to the summit of *La Escalera* (the Ladder), as this higher part of the road to the Gran Sabana is called. There, at nearly five thousand feet above sea level, the open savanna suddenly appeared. Moreover, on the horizon to the west we glimpsed our first tepui. We were all excited, even Gonzalo, who was the only one among us who had been here before. The bearded, shaggy-haired guide pulled over to the side of the road and snapped a picture with his Nikon.

The tepuis are remnants of a vast sandstone plateau that was laid down hundreds of millions of years ago. Through a combination of tectonic uplift, which created fissures and fractures in the plateau, and subsequent erosion, the tepuis took on their present-day form; mere fragments of the original sandstone formation. An identical process has occurred in many regions of the Colorado Plateau in the American southwest.

The first account of a European sighting a tepui is that of Sir Walter Raleigh, the English explorer, better known for his attempt to establish the Virginia Colony during the reign of Queen Elizabeth I. Raleigh traveled through the Empire of Guyana in the late 1500s in search of El Dorado, the legendary treasure city of South America. He went on to describe a crystal mountain, appearing as a white church tower with a river falling over its side. The way to it, he said, was impassable and inhabited by hostile tribes.

Raleigh would not have seen Roraima, nor did he discover El Dorado, but this did not deter other fortune hunters from prowling the area during the centuries that followed. It wasn't until 1838, however, that Roraima itself was visited and described by a European. This time the exploration was not fueled by reports of gold or diamonds, but by border disputes between Venezuela and the colony of British Guyana. As Venezuelan outposts stealthily crept eastward, Britain decided to explore this contentious region. On behalf of the British Geographical Society, German-born explorer and scientist Robert Schomburgk led an expedition to Roraima's base, proving that stories about the existence of the magnificent mountain were more than myth.

Although he himself never reached the top of Roraima, Schomburgk's writings inspired others to continue exploring the remote area. The influx of outsiders gave rise to a mystical premonition among the Amerindians who dwelt about the tepui's base. The churning rain clouds and frequent electrical storms above the massif were said to herald the approach of more white men. The powerful torrents of water that crashed down and over the cliffsides was the veil with which the "woman-mountain" hid her face against strangers.

Tragedy did, indeed, follow. It is said that the souls of Amerindians wander Roraima's summit, victims of a charismatic leader, Awakaipu, who in the mid-1800s promised his tribesmen riches and power equal to the white man's if they were obedient and loyal to him. One night Awakaipu revealed that the Great Spirit would grant his followers white skins if they would kill each other. Then, he explained, their souls would be released to ascend to the top of Roraima. In two days time they would be resurrected, and the treasure and knowledge of the white men would be theirs. Awakaipu proceeded to kill a bystander and drink his blood. The gathering of faithful erupted into pandemonium and four hundred men, women, and children were killed. As days passed and no resurrected tribesmen returned, the followers remaining in camp realized that the promises of Awakaipu were not to be granted. He was clubbed to death by an angry mob.

Mount Roraima's crown remained known only to those wandering spirits and to the mountain's endemic flora and fauna for several more decades, although there were ongoing efforts to reach its summit. Finally, in 1884, a British botanist named Everard Im Thurn, along with two companions, became the first known human beings to stand atop the plateau. They spent just a single afternoon exploring their hard-won prize, but they had opened a pathway that enabled numerous scientific expeditions to follow. Their route up—by a "very wearisome and difficult though at no point dangerous" ledge—is nowadays used frequently, since it is the only access that does not require technical climbing.

Interest was high in studying an area so isolated and peculiar. After attending a lecture given by Im Thurn in England, novelist Arthur Conan Doyle of Sherlock Holmes fame became smitten with the idea of a South American plateau unchanged for millions of years. In 1912, he published *The Lost World*, the classic science fiction story of an expedition to a flat-topped mountain inhabited by dinosaurs and prehistoric plants. In reality, no one visiting Roraima has ever found evidence of primordial creatures. Still, the terrain is so labyrinthian and difficult that very little of its forty-four square miles has been explored. The Amerindians know why: The great spirit Makunaima protects the mountain and does not want white men on the sacred summit.

▲

After our first long day on the road, we pulled over at dusk and set up camp under a *maloka*, a steep-sided thatched roof shelter still used throughout the Gran Sabana. Gonzalo warned us to watch for the spiders that are said to be common in the *moriche* palm thatch. The arachnid's bite causes brutal pain and a dangerous fever that can be fatal to those with a severe allergic reaction. We saw none of the spiders, but the instant the breeze died we were visited by hordes of biting sand flies called *puripuri*, or simply *la plaga* (the plague). We abandoned the maloka and set up our tents instead.

Late the next morning we left the highway. Following jeep tracks, we drove cross-country to the Pemón Indian village of Peraitepui on the approach to Roraima. Here we would leave the vehicle and begin our hike.

The village was small, consisting of several wattle-and-daub huts. Most of the dwellings had pleasant-looking thatched roofs, although some were newly covered with tin. A few concrete buildings were under construction. Gonzalo found two brothers who were to act as porters and guides for the trip to Roraima. He told us that it was expected by the villagers that guides would be employed, and the "mayor" who registered hikers tried to encourage it. But if people refused, or said they could not pay, they were usually allowed to hike anyway. I appreciated the fact that we were with Venezuelans who understood the etiquette of the area, and glad I did not have to agonize about whether I was doing the right or the wrong thing.

Living the outdoor life of farmers and hunters, the Pemóns are remarkably strong. The brothers took off on the two-track trail toward Roraima at an astonishing pace, considering their loads must have equaled their own weight. They carried some of the communal gear and much of the food, stored in bright yellow bags strapped to small handmade frames of wood and string. We, on the other hand, toted only our sleeping bags and personal items in complicated backpacks of aluminum alloys, plastic buckles, padded waist belts, and nylon threads.

The day was windy, sunny, and warm. There was precious little shade and few shadows; the earth seemed as hard as iron. The route took us through wild and lonely country, with a few refreshing creeks to cross, meadows of waist-high yellow grass, and patches of burnt-over savanna. On the hillsides around us were the charred remains of a forest, and we could see the smoke of other fires in the distance. There is some controversy about whether the treeless areas of the Gran Sabana have always been open or are the result of indiscriminate burning. I hoped the purple haze that seemed to go on forever wasn't actually air pollution.

Many of our questions about the area were answered by Gonzalo's friend, Gabriel, a botanist who was accompanying us on our hike. He was working for a power company that was committed to studying the flora and fauna of the Caroní River basin to ensure that the company's hydroelectric developments have minimal impact on the ecosystem, including the native human populations.

Brimming with enthusiasm, Gabriel pointed out to us the special vegetation we were passing along the way, spouting a confusing flood of both Indian and Latin names for each plant. His knowledge was extensive, not only of the names, but also of the natural history of each plant, its uses, and its habitat. Although he was diligently studying English from a textbook he had brought with him, and trying to converse in English with José, he was too embarrassed at first to practice with us. A few hours of hearing me drone on in Spanish at my preschool level, however, soon made him realize that he could appear no more foolish than me, and he charmed us with his heavily accented speech.

Although his primary job was to complete plant surveys, Gabriel was also responsible for educating the residents of the area about conservation practices. One of his ongoing chores was to talk to the Pemóns about the intentional setting of grass fires, which they employ freely as a means of finding game, of making their paths easier, and especially of getting rid of deadly snakes.

"Snakes, you say?" Michael said, suddenly popping out of his hiker's stupor.

"Snakes?" Judy echoed, suddenly watching where she stepped.

We then were told agonizing accounts of people being bitten by venomous species such as the bushmaster, the fer-de-lance, and the cascabel. The bushmaster is supposed to be the worst. It will stalk a man, often raising up part of its ten-foot length like a periscope above the vegetation to spy out its prey. After hearing that, we all jockeyed for position in the middle of the group.

We occasionally came upon the Pemón brothers sitting behind a rock or a bush waiting for us to catch up, but they would rarely acknowledge us and did not seem to be the least bit interested in who we were or why we were there. José, a keen and inquisitive person, did his best to draw the Indians out and was particularly thoughtful about offering them snacks and checking on their welfare. They slowly responded to his warmth and gave him bits and pieces of information that he passed on to us.

This was José's first trip to the Gran Sabana, and he was ebullient to be in an area with so many excitingly new and exotic things. A master of conversation, he never seemed to run out of things to say as he switched back and forth between Spanish and English. Gonzalo, pretending to be exasperated with his partner, dubbed him La Boca, "the Mouth." But I enjoyed José's youthful zeal. I thought about how I would have felt to visit the American West at the turn of the century. To José, who had never been more than a few hundred miles from Mérida, the Gran Sabana was the untamed Great Plains.

Roraima loomed directly ahead of us, appearing alternately blue, green, or pink in the distance, depending on the shifting sunlight. Its changing face suckered me into taking picture after picture of the hulking silhouette. Next to Roraima was the slightly smaller Cuquenan-tepui. Much more difficult to access, what is known about it has been discovered by those explorers who reached it by helicopter. Gonzalo looked longingly at the escarpment with its marvelous blocks of columnar stones. An accomplished mountain-eer (he was currently trying to figure out a way to finance a Venezuelan Mount Everest team), he mentioned that he would like to be among the first to climb Cuquenan. "However, the expedition would be very expensive," he said glumly, "and I am only a bee-keeper, not a rich man."

In the afternoon, several other backpackers, a tour group from the United States, straggled past us on their way back to the village. We nodded to each other and said hello. Their bedraggled appearance made me wonder about the difficulty of the climb ahead, but none of them would admit they were as worn out as they looked.

It was nearing sunset when we decided to make camp along the forested banks of the Cuquenan River which, with the Caroní River, forms part of the southern boundary of the vast Canaima National Park. Created in 1962, the park encompasses twelve thousand square miles, about the size of four Yellowstones. Gabriel mentioned that there was only one ranger guarding the entire park at the present time. I didn't have the heart to tell him that the ten-square-mile state wildlife area where I work has three full-time employees.

The Cuquenan is often called the Devil River because of its fearsome flash floods. This evening it was only a foot deep with a gentle current. Everyone except Gonzalo and I waded easily across and began setting up camp; we stayed on the opposite shore taking pictures and chatting with a lone Englishman, Eddy, who had been abandoned by his porter.

After about twenty minutes, we wished Eddy well and continued on our way. None of those in camp were paying any attention as we began crossing the rocky ford until suddenly, when we were in midstream, I noticed the porters running along the river from the upstream direction, pointing and yelling.

"Gonzalo!" I shouted. "What's wrong?" He looked up, as confused as I was.

At that instant José appeared on the far bank, frantically waving at us. "Hurry, hurry!" he screamed. "The river is rising! Quick! The river is rising!"

I could not believe what he was saying, as the river was below my knees. But within a few seconds the icy water was gushing over my knees and foaming past my waist. I struggled to move my feet as Gonzalo and I hung onto each other for support, certain that at any moment both of us would topple over and be swept downstream.

Picking their way across the treacherous slippery boulders, the Pemóns waded into the swollen river, one holding on to the other, to offer a long branch for us to grab. Gonzalo reached it just as I was about to stumble. I grabbed onto Gonzalo. Then José was there, a marvel of balance, pulling on the tops of our backpacks to drag us onto a wave-washed boulder.

Giddy from our rescue, Gonzalo and I dried out and tried to reconstruct what had happened. Judy said that she had been watching us cross and thought we had stupidly picked a deeper route; she hadn't realized that the water was rising. Luckily the Pemóns were more observant. They had noticed the increased volume of the river upstream and were aware that afternoon rains around the tepuis, the source of the Cuquenan, were causing a flash flood. The place where we crossed was now an impassable series of sweeping rapids and cascades.

That night the two brothers left to go sleep at their own camp somewhere hidden from our view. Earlier, I had tried to thank them for possibly saving my life, but they had expressed no emotion at my gratitude. José told us that they were worried about *Canaima*, an evil spirit that they felt was lurking about our camp. Their gloom and foreboding were accompanied by silver and neon lightning flashes to the north and the hissing of the Devil River. I didn't sleep well, wondering what Canaima had in store.

▲

Apparently Canaima had no plans for us that night. We awoke to sunshine and a much lower, benign river. Roraima gleamed golden in the morning light. A few thin, wispy waterfalls streamed over its side. It looked like an impregnable fortress in the distance as we prepared for our ascent.

Robert Schomburgk, who in 1838 may have camped at this very spot after a heavy rain, had this to write: "Before sunrise and for half an hour after, Roraima was beautifully clear, and we saw it in all its grandeur ... its steep sides are as perpendicular as if erected with a plumb line. I can ill-describe the magnificence of these mountains with their thundering and foaming cataracts."

Fortunately, the Pemóns were feeling much better. They were already packed and waiting at the edge of our camp, even though we still hadn't had breakfast. Once or twice I saw Ramón, the older of the brothers, staring up at the flat-topped massif, his face as blank as the granite he was sitting on. Depending on the source, I knew that Roraima in the Pemón language means "singing of waterfalls" or "Mother of Raging Torrents" or "Great, Ever-Fruitful Mother of Streams." Maybe Ramón was wondering if Mother was going to be kind to him.

Breakfast consisted of yogurt, granola, and Gonzalo's own honey made in the mountains of Mérida. "Honey makes you strong!" Gonzalo seriously avowed, right before he coughed into his handkerchief. (He had started the trip feeling ill and seemed to be going downhill, although he still maintained an impressive reservoir of strength and good humor.) José, however, granted his friend no sympathy. He reached over and patted Gonzalo's stomach, round and pronounced, compared to José's, which was flat and taut. "Gonzalo, you like your honey too much!" he observed. "You will be too fat to climb Everest." Gonzalo did not smile. He nodded solemnly and shrugged.

By noon we had reached the base of the plateau, where the plant community abruptly changed. A lush growth surrounded the bottom and continued up the steep sides. In the days of the early explorers the growth would have been thicker. In order to merely reach the base, let alone bushwhack their way to the top, I imagined their expeditions must have been huge. At the base of the mountain on the Guyana side is El Dorado Swamp, a place of green slime and snakes. In 1973, a British expedition slogged through the swamp in order to find a route to Roraima's summit from the Guyana side. They succeeded, but reportedly voted the climb as one of the most grueling and uncomfortable of their careers.

The route led upward at a demanding incline under a vaulted green ceiling. Draped in jungly vines, the trail wound around boulders and over twisting roots, across loose scree slopes, and under waterfalls. Water gushed out from cracks and holes in the wall, making the path so slippery that several times we could only advance on all fours. Occasionally, open vistas showed us the cliffs rising a sheer half-mile above or the view over the savannah back toward the village; but usually we were surrounded by thick vegetation leading directly into the clouds.

The last bit of scree under the overhanging wall was called the Devil's Trail, and the porters were very suspicious of the place: Maybe this was where Canaima would strike, by delivering a rock fall. I stayed

*Judy works her way up a damp, rocky trail on the side of Mount Roraima.*

close to Judy, thinking that maybe Canaima would be kind to a woman.

Sometime in late afternoon we reached the surface of the plateau, at about eighty-five hundred feet. The sight at the threshold was one of the wildest I have ever seen, resembling a lunar landscape; strange and alien, harsh and naked. The mesa's bleak and jagged surface was crisscrossed with deep fissures and bizarre rock formations. Pools of placid water stood between boulders, and in depressions on top of the slippery rocks were boggy morasses.

There was not one square yard of flat surface. We tried not to walk in the pools, mostly to avoid disturbing the plants, but it was impossible to always pick a route that allowed us to hop from rock to rock. Then there were the small black toads, less than an inch long, with enormous eyes and yellow bellies. Hundreds of the strange creatures covered the rocks. They were difficult to see, and we had to concentrate to avoid stepping on them. The toads cannot hop or swim. When handled or frightened, they would curl up into a ball and roll down the rocks. Gabriel giggled as he pointed them out and amused himself by holding them gently in his hand. "Larry," he called, drawing me over for another lesson in biology. "*Oreophrynella quelchii*, discovered 1894."

Our guides led us to a dry nook scalloped out of jumbled, blocky boulders. The split-level balcony provided room for two tents, as well as ledges on which the guides planned to sleep. Gonzalo called the campsite *el hotelito*, or "little hotel." In truth, it was your basic cave, but at least it would help shield us from wind and rain. The only evidence of wildlife using this lair was the tiny pelletlike droppings of a small rodent, the only endemic mammal on the summit of Roraima.

Judy and I were exhilarated by our successful ascent. But our very agreeable companion, Michael, was feeling dejected and embarrassed. The steep climb had gotten the best of the fifty-year-old. Worse yet, the youthful and vigorous José had insisted on carrying all of his gear. Of course, Michael had protested, but both Gonzalo and José said it would be "good practice" to carry a bigger load. Uh huh. They absolutely could not allow Michael to remain at the mountain base (which he had suggested), and they were so determined for him to get to the top that he could not resist their encouragement.

"Yes," Michael said, helping Judy and me to pitch our tent. Yes, he was certainly glad he had not stayed behind and missed the strange beauty of this place. But he did regret becoming part of the folklore of the guides. "Remember that crazy Czech-Canadian?" he could imagine them reminiscing for the benefit of their next group of hikers. "How did we end up with *that* guy?"

We tried to cajole ("Hey! At least you brought a backpack instead of a suitcase!") and console him by pointing out that José did not seem the least affected by his extra load. Michael began to feel better, as he watched the Mouth laugh and joke nonstop through dinner, and late into the night we heard José and the others singing in beautiful, soft voices that drifted out over the tepui. More than anything, I wished I could have accompanied them, but I was sure that my voice would really have enraged Canaima. Dejected, I went back to reading my book.

▲

We spent the entire next day exploring the fog-shrouded table-top, gaping at the surrealistic stone sculptures that created a giant fantasy land. They were shaped like Mesozoic creatures, giant insects, toadstools I could sit under, dwarf elephants, apples of rock chewed down to their cores, castellated ramparts and Roman pillars, all grown stiff for eternity, all blackened by algae and fungi that grow on the gritty sandstone.

Occasionally we traversed boot-sucking quagmires, where we stopped to examine tubelike pitcher plants and sticky, ruby-colored sundews—carnivorous species well adapted to the acidic and nutrient-poor soil. In the fissures between the rocks grew sunken gardens of mosses and lichens; most, if not all of which exist only on Roraima's summit. The tepuis have been called "natural laboratories" for studying the adaptation of species to harsh environments. Of an estimated ten thousand plant species thought to exist in this isolated ecosystem, half are unique to the tepui region.

Prior to starting our climb, Gonzalo and José had suggested we change our clothes in order to assure that we did not bring in seeds or spores of plants not native to Roraima's summit. Unfortunately, we had no other clothes. Strangely enough, in light of their suggestion, neither did they. How long, we wondered, would Roraima remain such a lonely outpost of life—an "island in time"?

According to the guides, the Venezuelan government has considered banning tourism in much of the region to protect the tepuis. As an alternative, they might allow Roraima to remain open—to "sacrifice" it, so to speak—and allow only scientific visits to the other tepuis. Before we left Peraitepui, word had gotten around about a pile of garbage left atop Roraima by a previous group. Our camp at el hotelito was relatively clean, but if you walked in the wrong direction, you found yourself in a huge "cat box" area littered with human excrement and toilet paper.

"Maybe we have to do what was done high up on Mount McKinley," Gonzalo suggested, as disgusted as we were with the unsightly mess. "Maybe we need a portable toilet up here." Something to consider, but I'm not sure how the spirits would take it.

Later in the morning, we set out for *El Valle de los Cristales*, "the valley of the crystals," which was only discovered in 1976. Because of the difficult terrain, it was an all-day hike to get there and it looked like misty weather would accompany us most of the way.

Ramón was still with us, although his brother had returned to the village earlier. He remained expressionless and aloof, usually hiking far ahead, maintaining just enough contact not to lose us. Whenever we took breaks, he would go sit by himself. I wondered if he knew how much we depended on him. The unfamiliar, mazelike world wreaked havoc with my internal compass. I tried to keep my bearings but soon acknowledged that I was in constant danger of losing my way.

Finally Ramón indicated that the valley was just ahead. We quietly entered the narrow defile and as we did the ghostly swathes of fog began to lift and a beam of sunlight bore down on us. The canyon floor was transformed into a frozen river, shimmering with translucent white and pink quartz crystals scattered about the ground. Even José was speechless. I looked over at Ramón for a clue; surely he must feel the mystical power of the place. Perched on a rock by himself, our perspicacious guide was busily cleaning his fingernails.

Next we came upon an enormous sinkhole in the rock surface, roughly one hundred feet in diameter and thirty feet deep. At the bottom of the hole was a pool of water, dark and fathomless. Gabriel and José inched their way down into the cavelike entrance to go for a swim, screaming in shock when they dove into the numbingly cold water. José, the ham, asked if he did it again would I please take his picture.

The crystals, the limpid pool, the eerie gargoyle formations, the reappearance of the fog—all added to the mystique of the place. But it was an intrusion of civilization that appeared the most strange here: the three-sided monument marking the geographical junction of Venezuela, Brazil, and Guyana. The Guyana portion of the plaque had been stolen, a political act indicating that the boundaries are still a bone of contention between the countries.

▲

The next morning was clear and bitterly cold. I sat alone, not far from the edge of the plateau, watching the sun strike the furrowed walls of the nearby Cuquenan tepui. A silvery waterfall, swollen by last night's rain, plunged thousands of feet down its tremendous side into the surrounding lime green forest. I also saw Ramón emerge molelike from his own camp among the rocks. He shook out something—clothes or blankets, I wasn't sure—then walked to the brink of the tepui and gazed toward the horizon. Was he thinking of home, or just admiring the view, or forecasting the weather? I would never know.

He came over to el hotelito not long after I returned. Squatting on his haunches near the cook area, he tried on Gonzalo's North Face Gore-Tex jacket and began admiring the MSR backpacking stove. He had never seen one so little, he told José, which was a positively animated conversation for Ramón. José explained how it worked and let him use it. I think Ramón was impressed.

Later, José said he intended to give Ramón his pocket knife, and that Ramón really liked Judy's running shoes, which would be nice for his wife. "A budding equipment freak," I thought with some regret. We were apparently not very interesting, but he did like our *things*. Well, what did I expect? That he should ask me what books I've read lately? It was very arrogant of me to begrudge his interest in our high-tech goods, to think that I could benefit from cross-cultural experiences while fearing, in a patronizing way, that he would automatically be harmed.

▲

Descending the tepui was brutal on the knees and physically more difficult than the ascent. Wet weather made everything slippery. We hung onto limbs and roots as we did our best to minimize our impact on the muddy path. Even so, we all ended up caked with a heavy cementlike layer of goo.

As we passed several German hikers on their way up, rolls of thunder broke over us, accompanied by huge bursts of lightning sounding like giant guns. It started to rain much harder, the beginnings of a torrential downpour. Ramón began to tremble. He told José that Roraima was "crying" because she did not like so many people being on her. (This was certainly an emotional mountain. Now, if I could just get across the Cuquenan River ... )

As we reached the base and traversed the open plains, the sky exploded. Electricity sizzled overhead. We shuddered and cowered but there was no cover. I could just imagine the headline in the Caracas daily: "Canaima 3; Gringos 0."

We half-laughed, half-screamed, while racing to catch up with Ramón. The mud on the trail turned into slippery soup; and in several places I had to help Judy cross what had been a dusty trail, now knee-deep in milk-white runnels. When the deluge lifted about an hour later, Roraima glistened with waterfalls where none had been before. The top of the tepui was one big catchment area with walls running along the rim.

The return to the village seemed to drag on forever. I could see it on the horizon but it never got closer. Miles and miles of the same miserably hot country. During rest breaks, I scanned the wide plains and steep rounded hills, hoping to see deer, puma, a giant anteater, *anything*; but all I saw besides insects was a pair of circling hawks.

For the first time since we'd met, I noticed José begin to flag. And I thought I knew why: He was wearing heavy mountaineering boots that Michael had given him, but they were too big; huge blisters were developing. The problem arose when José gave his running shoes to Ramón. Ramón's plastic sneakers had been in a terrible state of disrepair but he had gone up the tepui in them just fine. Ramón, however, told José that if he returned to the village in his tattered shoes he would be embarrassed. Apparently it was some point of honor for a Pemón guide to have decent shoes when returning.

José's thoughtfulness seemed typical of the Venezuelans we had gotten to know. Judy commented that she had never met so many appealing men. "More appealing than your typical wildlife biologist from Illinois?" I asked. "No comparison," was her reply.

When we finally reached the village, we were welcomed by the mayor, who had prepared *kichiri* for us, a red fermented brew made from manioc and potatoes. A smiling boy about four years old came running up to us carrying a flat hard slab of bread also made from manioc; its diameter almost equal to the child's height. I think José and Gonzalo would have liked to enjoy the afternoon in the village, sipping the kichiri, but we still had more of Venezuela to see.

After a few hours of jouncing across the savannah, wondering if Gonzalo really knew the right track to follow, we reached the highway and stopped for a cold beer in the nearest town to toast our trip. Three gringos got off a bus that pulled up and, upon spotting us, headed our way. They wanted to climb Roraima and asked for information on hitchhiking to Peraitepui. Possible, we told them, but not likely. On both the drive in and out we had seen no other vehicles. They were undaunted. We smiled knowingly as they walked away in their white shorts and sandals.

# 8.

# Ten Degrees North of the Equator (Costa Rica)

THE VAN SPED ACROSS the Pan American Highway, heading west out of San José. We had left Costa Rica's congested capital city at sunrise, and it felt good to be in the open countryside. Beyond the windows streamed a montage of heated plains and rolling hills. The pastured landscape was checkered with small rural villages where we stopped to purchase local tropical fruits—everything from papayas to pineapples to big juicy melons. The Costa Rican people, or *ticos*, as they call themselves, are accustomed to all kinds of foreigners doing all kinds of things. Even so, our trailer loaded with brightly colored sea kayaks was a definite attention-getter the farther we went from the city.

Our destination was Palo Verde National Park, situated in the fork between the Ríos Tempisque and Bebedero, about one hundred miles from San José. According to our plan, we'd take three days to float the placid Bebedero to the Gulf of Nicoya, passing through seasonally dry forest, mangrove swamps, and saltwater marshes. The remainder of our week-long outfitted trip would take us to a completely different area near the mouth of the gulf, where we'd find virgin jungle, palm-fringed sandy beaches, and coral reefs under the waters of a crystal-clear Pacific Ocean. The itinerary billed the trip as a "sea kayaking adventure in a tropical paradise."

This type of laid-back, low-adrenaline paddling tour was a departure for our self-assured, genuinely friendly, thirty-one-year-old guide. As co-owner of a successful Costa Rican company that specialized in whitewater rafting and kayaking excursions, Rafael was more at home leading helmeted clients through Class IV rapids—a natural choice in a water-rich, mountainous country, with perhaps more runnable rivers per square mile than any other nation in the world. But Rafael was a shrewd businessman and a serious dreamer. He was convinced that Costa Rica, the "rich coast," with almost one thousand miles of ocean shoreline graced with diverse vegetation and wildlife, unspoiled beaches, and secluded bays, could become just as popular for nature-oriented sea kayakers as it already was for high-thrills river runners. Our group, most of us with more disposable income than time, represented the "new breed" of ecotourists that he was trying to lure.

The drive to the park took five hours, time for Judy and me to become acquainted with our fellow travelers; we had met each other only briefly at a pretrip meeting the night before. There was Lois, a bookstore manager, well into middle age, who had the figure and energy of a woman much younger. Her husband, Hi, was a bear of a man with scruffy grey hair and a salt-and-pepper beard, not the type you'd think would hold a top-level administrative post in the U.S. National Park Service. Herb, their long-time friend and traveling companion, was a retired chemical engineer from San Franciso. Tall and trim, I guessed Herb to be in his early fifties, which delighted him since he was sixty-five. Rod was an expatriate Englishman living in British Columbia. And then there was Drew, a middle-aged California criminal lawyer, who I'm sure had quite an edge in the court room—well, so he told us—but, physically, he was soft and round.

While the rest of us had varying degrees of experience in the wilderness, Drew had absolutely none. Staying in shape for Drew meant the occasional bike ride on the weekend. And research? Going to Costa Rica had been a last-minute decision, he said. "Until a few days ago, I was all set to fly to Thailand." All set? On the way out of town we stopped so he could buy a toothbrush and other toiletries.

We veered off the Pan American Highway onto a series of confusing dirt roads that twisted through crackling ranchland and fields of sugar cane. There were no signs suggesting that a national park lay ahead. "Few tourists come to Palo Verde," Rafael explained between bites of just-picked melon. "There are few trails, almost no development. Plus, as you can see, it is rather difficult to get here." That was fine with me. This trip, plus another Judy and I had planned on our own, would give us the opportunity to visit some of Costa Rica's wilder areas, from glistening beaches to windswept high peaks.

▲

Costa Rica is a bright beacon in Latin America, blessed with political stability and natural beauty. Although located between Nicaragua and Panama, its neutrality and strong democratic tradition have insulated it from regional conflicts.

After El Salvador and Belize, Costa Rica is the smallest nation in Central America, averaging only 150 miles across and 200 miles long. Yet this compact country's location as a land bridge between the Americas has created an environment with a remarkable diversity of life-forms. The list of flora and fauna is truly staggering: about 850 species of birds; 15,000 species of moths; 1,500 species of orchids; 2,000 species of trees; more butterfly species than the entire continent of Africa; more than 350 species of reptiles and amphibians; and more than 230 species of mammals. Unique species, some not even named yet, occupy every niche of the country.

While most countries seem to be encouraging unrestrained exploitation of their natural resources, an amazing 25 percent of Costa Rica's territory has been set aside in one of the world's best systems of reserves and national parks. The protected areas include lowland tropical rain forest, high-altitude cloud forest, *páramo* up to 12,600 feet in elevation, both Caribbean and Pacific beaches, inland river systems, and dry thorn scrub forest—all this in a country slightly smaller than West Virginia.

▲

The checkerboard of small farms finally vanished, replaced by dense scrubby woods. In January, in the middle of the dry season, some of the trees were leafless, waiting for rains the way northern trees wait for spring.

Ten miles past the village of Bebedero, Álvaro, the assistant guide, stopped the van and got out to open a crude wooden gate. "Welcome to Palo Verde National Park," he announced, turning around with a big smile on his face. "A naturalist's paradise!"

A few minutes later, we pulled up at an old wooden building that looked like it had been a ranch house in better days. This was the park headquarters, staffed by a couple of rangers who didn't object to a solitary lifestyle. In a small clearing across the road was the official campground, our home for the night. As far as we could tell, we were the only visitors to this fifteen-thousand-acre national park, provided we didn't count the green iguana, a big fellow, three feet long with spiny ridges on his back, who had staked out his territory on a log near the picnic table.

At lunchtime, the guides prepared an alfresco buffet of fresh fruit, avocado, and cheeses. Afterward, Rafael asked if any of us wanted to go for a hike up La Catalina, a small but not insignificant limestone plateau that overlooks the region.

Hi wasn't too keen on the idea. But when he saw Drew accept the challenge, he sucked in his gut, laced up his running shoes, and muttered, "I suppose there'll be time later for an afternoon siesta."

The narrow path meandered through a junglelike growth of tall deciduous trees with scattered stands of giant bamboo. A very characteristic shrub in the area was the *palo verde*, or horsebean, a green tree from which the park takes its name. In spite of the lushness of vegetation, the forest had a relatively clear undergrowth, making it easy to observe the resident wildlife.

We hadn't been on the trail five minutes when we crossed paths with a troop of white-faced, or capuchin, monkeys playing in the trees and snacking on leaves and unripe fruit near a small waterhole. With their pink faces and white "cowls," they were unmistakable. When we moved closer, the monkeys shrieked in alarm and rushed off, swinging from precarious branches like trapeze artists. The traditional organ grinder's monkey, capuchins are known to be exceptionally intelligent. A few of the streetwise apes, who knew perfectly well that we were no threat to them, pelted us with sticks and whatever else they could find.

Judy and I, along with Hi and Lois, lagged behind to see what else might be attracted to the sun-dappled forest spring. We sat down on the broad trunk of a fallen tree and scanned the surrounding vegetation. Maybe we were lucky, but the next quarter-hour seemed to be scripted by "Wild Kingdom." A pair of collared peccaries, piglike animals with razor-sharp tusks, trotted into view. Weighing forty to fifty pounds, the omnivorous, dark grey porkers snuffled and rooted for fruit, insects, or anything else edible in their path. Shortly thereafter, a whitetail deer appeared out of the shadows. The small doe headed directly for the waterhole, stopping often in midstride to cock her ears and test the motionless air with her sensitive nose. She took a few quick sips from the spring and suddenly bounded off, spooked by the loud shuffling of three coatimundis, raccoonlike animals with short legs, long whiffly snouts, and very long tails they carry erect. The coatis slurped up some water then casually made their way through the brush toward the campground.

It was dead calm and hot, at least ninety degrees, with the humidity to match as we hurried to catch our companions. We were about two-thirds of the way up the plateau when we came upon Drew, sitting off to the side of the trail in the meager shade of a thorn tree. He was sweating profusely and red in the face. "You got any water with you?" he pleaded. I pulled out a full liter bottle. "Terrific! I forgot to bring a canteen."

Breathing hard, we finally emerged from the treeline onto an outcropping covered in tall grass. One of the payoffs was a refreshing breeze; the other was a panoramic view of the entire park. To the south, between low, rounded hills, I could see the glassy Río Bebedero as it looped its way toward the Gulf of Nicoya, sparkling blue on the horizon. Westward were large marshy areas and a mosaic of lakes; home to a wide variety and number of both resident and migratory waterbirds.

The sky was hazy, which is common to afternoons here, being so close to the Pacific Ocean. "Too bad," Rafael said, wrapping his tee shirt around his head to ward off the sun. "On a clear day we'd be able to see Lake Nicaragua, the largest lake in Central America, seventy-five miles to the north."

Upon returning to camp, Lois, Judy and I—the "birders" of our group—roamed the adjacent woods and grassy fields in the hour before dinner. Bright green parrots squawked and squabbled in the treetops. A rowdy gang of parakeets whirred overhead, their loud chattering audible long after they had flown off. Magpie jays, long-tailed manakins, black-hooded antshrikes, rufous-backed antwrens, tropical kingbirds, scarlet-rumped tanagers, and more, endlessly more, were a challenge to identify, which was not surprising as nearly every species was a new and wonderful addition to our life checklists.

Every birding field trip has one sighting that is more memorable than the rest. Ours showed up while we hiked the dirt road back to camp. In a tinder dry savanna, a hundred yards to our left, was a large, big-beaked stork. "No doubt about it," Lois said, matching the living bird with the color plate in the guide. It was a jabiru stork, an endangered species which nests in the forested areas of Palo Verde

National Park. The stork stopped feeding and cocked its head to one side, peering at us as if to say, "Okay, now you've seen me. Satisfied?"

▲

A deep-throated whoop like an Indian war cry woke me from a sweltering, sticky sleep. Off in the distance came another cry that reverberated through the forest. The vocalization could only be made by a howler monkey, or *mono congo*, as it's called by the locals. The largest of the American monkeys, this was one animal I had to see.

I pushed the light button on my watch: It was just past five, the sun would be up soon. Stifling a yawn, I threw on my clothes and slipped out of the tent, whispering to Judy that I was going to the waterhole. "Okay," she mumbled without opening her eyes.

I tiptoed quietly through the slumbering camp and hurried across the dirt road. It was quickly becoming light. No slow, lingering sunrises here—not in a country that lies just ten degrees north of the Equator.

Weird shapes and primeval sounds filled the gloomy understory as creatures of the night gave way to those of the day. A faraway booming, a cross between seals barking and lions growling, sent cold chills down my back. If I didn't know better I might have thought the forest was haunted.

I picked my way up the path, my eyes slowly adjusting to the green world. Suddenly there was a crash in the bushes, and I was nearly eyeball-to-eyeball with an enormous monkey. It looked like a small bear with a prehensile tail; its chestnut-colored body and black limbs cinched the identification. I had found my howler, or maybe it had found me. The animal bounced through a web of vines and joined about ten others of its kind lounging in the forest canopy. Some were nibbling large yellow-blossomed flowers from the tips of branches; others were hanging motionless, like huge toys. Except for occasional earthward glances, the troop totally ignored me. Mellow monkeys, I thought, howling their hearts out.

When I returned to camp, the group was already queuing up for an all-you-can-eat breakfast of ham, pancakes, *gallo pinto* (rice and beans cooked together), fresh fruit, home-made pastries, and Costa Rican coffee. "Don't be shy," chef Álvaro laughed. "You'll hurt my feelings if you don't eat it all." We did, too, in an effort to fortify ourselves for our first day on the water.

A flurry of activity followed the morning meal. After breaking camp, we unloaded the boats at the put-in, sorted through gear, and tried out different-sized paddles and fitted sprayskirts. The two married couples got stuck in tandem kayaks; the rest were outfitted in the smaller, more maneuverable singles.

Rafael gave a brief lecture on paddling technique and closed with some advice on minor hazards we might face, such as sunburn, dehydration, upstream eddies, overhanging tree limbs, and plants and animals that bite, sting, or prick. "It's always a good idea to watch where you put your hands and feet when climbing out on shore," he said. "There's not much that can hurt you, but this is a wilderness, you know."

Rafael squirmed into his red plastic Chinook, signalling the trip was about to begin. We obediently followed Mother Duck down the Río Bebedero toward the ocean. Trailing far behind, almost out of sight, was the *panga*, a motorized supply and safety boat that carried all the baggage, camping gear, drinking water, and food. Chino, the very young third staff member, was the skipper of the rowboat-looking craft. The last we saw of smiling Chino he was standing on the panga's rear seat to peer over the mound of gear.

The river was flat with a steady current dictated by tidal changes downstream. At first glance, the scene reminded me of the Suwannee, the Neches, the Satilla, or any of a number of rivers I have paddled in the southern United States. But looking closer, the narrow green corridor was made up of different vegetation, and, although the turkey vultures were familiar, other area inhabitants—from monkeys to butterflies—were not of the Deep South.

The dry tropical forest crowding the banks harbored birds of every size and color. Noisy chirps, whoops, and whistles told of many more birds concealed in the shrubs, ferns, and tops of trees draped with hanging plants. Pulling alongside Rafael, I mentioned that the Bebedero beat the Everglades for wildlife watching. "I'm glad you think so," he said. "I've been thinking of advertising in *Audubon* magazine."

The place was indeed extraordinary, but how much longer Palo Verde and other Costa Rica parks and reserves can stay this way is open to question. The sad fact is that even in environmentally conscious Costa Rica, deforestation is occurring at a rapid pace. Where its forests are not protected, they are disappearing at the rate of 140,000 acres a year, and many species are being destroyed with them. I needed only to gaze to my left, to the unprotected east bank, to be reminded of our penchant for consumption. A thin veneer of trees lined the shore; beyond that, the jungle had been cleared and replaced by sun-scorched pasture, bananas, and barbed wire. By contrast, to my right, within the national park's boundaries, the forest was a tumult of vegetation—dark, dense, and green, and full of monkeys, parrots, butterflies, and snakes.

The Costa Rican dilemma is economic: a crushing foreign debt. The country's main exports are coffee, bananas, and beef, and those markets fluctuate. Costa Rica must import petroleum and technology, and the costs of its far-reaching social programs have given the society and the economy an unpleasant jolt. Although Costa Rica has set aside some thirty-five reserves and national parks, the nation lacks the funding to enforce the regulations against illegal hunting and tree felling. Tropical forest researchers warn that if current trends continue, within ten years logging companies will have cut all of Costa Rica's unprotected virgin timber. Eyes will then turn toward the parks, and local interest in their survival will be crucial.

Many people in Costa Rica realize that the disappearance of their forests signifies a loss much greater in value than the money gained from their destruction. What some would like to import is more tourists to birdwatch, run rivers, hike, skin dive, study sea turtles, and bring in dollars. Tourism as a business can provide a strong economic alternative to destructive short-term exploitation of natural resources. But there's a flip side to ecotourism: problems in terms of ecological degradation, the same phenomenon we have in the United States of loving our parks to death. There are certain natural areas in Costa Rica that are now simply too crowded. Trails erode, rivers and coral reefs become polluted, litter falls where once only leaves did, and animals may change their behavior or simply disappear. Local communities may prosper when their backyards become the stuff of postcards, but they can also suffer when whimsy makes other destinations more popular, or when traditional cultural patterns are altered for the sake of tourists. The goal for thoughtful planners is to find ways for people to travel with minimal negative impact on the wild areas they visit, to travel with conscience and caution into the commercialism of nature.

▲

Chino motored past us in midafternoon on his way to set up camp farther downstream. The skiff looked as if it were riding dangerously low in the water. Worse, a chop was beginning to form on the river from upstream winds.

We paddled directly under a troop of howlers. Our beamy, stable kayak made an ideal platform for photography. I craned my neck until it ached and focused the telephoto on the largest monkey overhead; a shaggy, charcoal-colored primate about the size of a small child. Perched on a bough that drooped over the river, the animal gazed down at me with inquisitive dark brown eyes. But that wasn't all. The big adult male had testicles the size of ostrich eggs; furthermore, they were connected to his groin by threadlike cords that couldn't possibly support the ballsy weight.

"Take the picture already!" Judy implored. "We're drifting into a log." I did. Too late. Tired of the commotion, the overendowed monkey made a free-fall leap of about twenty feet, caught a vine just above the ground, and effortlessly scrambled up another tree where it wasn't about to be disturbed. I marveled at the acrobatics but couldn't help feeling a sympathetic ache between my legs.

Rafael and Rod were about a quarter-mile in front of Judy and me, lazily paddling and talking. The rest of the kayak train was a good distance to the rear, with Álvaro the caboose. A short time later, however, I noticed that something odd was happening ahead. Rafael was out of his boat and in the river near shore. Rod was turning circles in his kayak like a water bug out of control.

We quickly closed the gap, curious about what was going on. There was trouble. Rafael was bent over in belly-deep water, bailing madly with a plastic bucket. Rod, towing Rafael's kayak behind his own, was spinning around trying to pick up flotsam floating downstream. Pacing the bank, Chino had lost his smile; in fact, he looked as though he was about to cry. All this because the panga was sitting on the bottom of the river with only its gunwales showing.

Rafael called for help. I put my paddle down, slithered overboard, and breast-stroked to the sunken boat. "Here!" Rafael shouted, tossing me a thick rope. "Tie this to a tree and come back and help me bail." I took the line and swam to shore, but when I stood in the shallows, I immediately sank up to my thighs in quickmud. Slightly panicky, I tried pumping my knees. The more I struggled, the deeper I went. Fortunately, Chino, himself covered with black ooze, was there to lend a helping hand; he grabbed the rope and vanished into the forest.

It took an hour of mucking around to get the boat floating again. Amazingly, damage was minimal. The two-burner gas stove was lost, and a bit of food, but everyone's gear was retrieved. We all took the accident in stride, and even laughed about it, except for Herb. Muttering things like "I told them the boat was overloaded" and "My clothes better not be wet," he was the only one who never offered to help.

*Álvaro and his watercraft, on the muddy banks of the Río Bebedero.*

We made an early camp near the scene of the mishap, the first possible campsite we had seen all afternoon. As luck would have it, the tide was out, *way out*—a steep, slimy ten-foot bank lay between us and dry ground. We formed a human chain to unload the panga. Álvaro, his tee shirt and straw hat slick with mud, shook his head as the wet baggage was hauled out. "I can't explain. I can't explain," he ribbed Chino. "Last year *I* was the panga driver and nothing like this happened to me." Poor Chino, normally so bubbly, held his head low in shame. But then Álvaro said something in Spanish that made Chino laugh, and before long he was his usual jovial self.

Dapper Herb remained in his kayak during the work detail and was thus the only one among us who wasn't streaked with mud when we gathered on shore. He admonished Rafael for overloading the panga and stated his case that two skiffs were needed. Maybe it was true, but no one liked listening to a backseat panga driver, especially one wearing a clean white tee shirt and spotless Patagonia shorts.

The temperature was in the high eighties and humid. After setting up the tents, we did the best we could to clean up. Swimming in the silty, brackish river was refreshing, but climbing back up the bank covered us with mud again. And the fresh water was strictly for drinking, so we all remained on the grimy side. We plopped down in collapsible chairs and read, napped, and wrote postcards. I had a feeling more than a few of us wanted to ask Herb how he stayed so untarnished.

Later, as the sun set over the forest, Judy and I slid back down the bank and took the double kayak out for a predinner spin. A half-mile away was the meeting of waters where the Bebedero joins the much larger Río Tempisque, near the head of the Nicoya Peninsula. We poked along in back eddies and nudged up against impenetrable thickets of mangrove trees. This type of swamp, where the trees are supported by scores of branchlike prop roots that extend into the water, was not quite land and not quite water. But it was a beautiful evening and interesting things were afoot. Among the prop roots, we watched hermit crabs scuttle out of our way. Birds were everywhere, perched in the mangroves or streaming back and forth to nighttime sanctuaries. We spotted a tiger heron, a night heron, then a rare boat-billed heron, which patiently posed as I snapped its photograph. There were also assorted cormorants, anhingas, roseate spoonbills, vultures, ospreys, egrets, ibises, and ducks. A ringed kingfisher splashed into the water near our boat, reappearing with a small quicksilver fish wiggling in its beak.

The sky turned pink, baby blue, and orange in the western sky, signaling that it was time to return to camp, where the guides were putting the finishing touches on dinner. True professionals, they were proving that we could swamp the skiff, lose the stove, get caked in mud, and still eat well. We dined on fresh tomato salad, tortillas stuffed with beans, and Rafael's pièce de résistance: spicy jungle chicken. This was great stuff by any account, but it went down even smoother when accompanied by cold Costa Rican beers.

Sipping our *cervezas*, we sat around comparing notes, stargazing, watching bats swoop over the river. Herons squawked in the inky darkness. A few mosquitoes buzzed our ears. Dry lightning flickered on the horizon. Finally, about nine o'clock, most of us said goodnight and went to our tents.

The night was still warm. I lay atop my sleeping bag, wishing for a breeze. If anything, the humidity in the tent increased. I noted the day's events in my journal then clicked off my flashlight and closed my eyes. Judy was already asleep. I heard an animal prowling around in the dry leaves at the edge of the forest. For a moment, my heart beat quicker. What if it was a jaguar, the uncontested lord of the Neotropics? But it was probably only an iguana or an opossum. Nevertheless, I made a mental note to check the area for spoor in the morning.

I heard snoring; a steady, monotonous rasp. It was coming from either Hi, Drew, or Rod, or maybe Lois. I made another mental note that in the future we should pitch our tent farther from the others. More disturbing than the snoring was the high-pitched hum of mosquitoes. Then I started to feel bites on my skin. I checked around the tent with my flashlight beam and saw that it was swarming with gnat-sized flies, what the locals called *borujas*. They were entering in droves through the mosquito netting. By now Judy was as busy as I was, cursing and scratching. We doused ourselves with insect repellent. We jammed our clothes against the screened roof. Finally, we wrapped ourselves in a cotton sheet and suffocated while still being bitten.

At first light, our sleepy-eyed group huddled around the coffee pot trying to outdo one another with hellish tales of the long, hot, and insect-intense night. Hi and Lois showed us their welts to prove how miserable they'd been. Drew had mummified himself in a rain poncho and spent the night lying in a pool of rancid sweat. Poor Rod hadn't slept a wink. Not only did the *borujas* eat him alive, he also had to put up with Drew, the mystery snorer. Everyone suffered, clients and guides alike, except for Herb; somehow his tent was the only one in camp with no-see-um netting. Looking well-rested and quite pleased with himself, he smugly announced he hadn't suffered a single bite.

The good news, said Rafael as we finished breakfast, was that we didn't have to break camp. "We'll spend the day exploring the estuaries—birding, clamming, eating good food; partaking in what we ticos call *pura vida*, the pure life."

It sounded like a nice day, but he forgot to mention we'd be spending the night in the same place; same tents, same bugs.

▲

To the relief of everyone, especially Chino, the river was calm when we left our river camp of two nights. Our flotilla of kayaks and low-riding panga left the Río Bebedero for the Río Tempisque and floated south to its confluence with the sea. An hour later we glided into a sleepy fishing village where a forty-foot catamaran was waiting. Rafael had charted the *Banana Express* to take us to the mouth of the Gulf of Nicoya for phase two of our trip.

Our entire outfit, including a new supply of provisions from the van, was transferred to the catamaran. Baggage was stowed in the two parallel hulls. Our kayaks were stacked on deck. By ten-thirty we were ready to embark. We all crowded aboard, eager to reach the clear blue sea. All except Drew, that is. He was returning to San José. "Nothing personal, you guys," he said, as he saw us off. "But that's enough jungle adventure for me. Right now a shower and a clean, soft bed without *borujas* is what I need."

I found an out-of-the-way spot behind the mast and watched the boat's crew haul in lines and crank up the outboard. The skipper was a tough-talking, fortyish blonde named Linda. Obviously not too concerned about the correlation between UV exposure and melanoma, she wore a bikini that left little to the imagination. Besides giving her a great tan, long-term exposure to the sun had given her skin a distinct, leathery look.

Right away I pegged Daniel, the first (and only) mate, as a shady character. Swiss-born, gaunt, and also deeply tanned, with sun-bleached, shoulder-length hair and a gold earring, he was high strung. Every other word that spewed out of his mouth was "fucking." I figured he definitely had some other business going here as well, because a first-rate sailor he wasn't.

A few minutes after leaving, we got stuck on a mudbar exposed at low tide. Linda said something to Daniel. Not one to be second-guessed, he responded with an outburst of profanity. A brief council took place between Linda, Daniel, and Rafael. The upshot of the meeting was that Daniel and our three guides jumped into the waist-deep water and pushed while Linda gunned the motor. The boat slowly broke free. A minute later we were stuck again. Two more times this maneuver was employed before we reached deeper water. But that wasn't the end of our turmoil. While fighting tidal currents and wind, the catamaran's motor sputtered and died. Daniel threw his arms in the air and vented his blasphemy. Linda tried to ignore her first mate by sucking down a cold beer. Fortunately, ever-cool Rafael was there to sort things out. He offered Linda the use of his outboard that was clamped onto the trailing panga.

After an hour or so of chugging down the gulf, we finally caught the winds and hoisted the sails. It was exhilarating to shut off the motor and listen to the boat slice through the water. We made steady progress but had a long way to go. The Gulf of Nicoya thrusts some forty miles inland. Its waters separate the long, tall mountains of the mainland, which form the nation's spine, from the smaller mountains of the Nicoya Peninsula. Our destination was a tropical island resort at the far end of the peninsula.

We sailed past lunch and on through the afternoon. Darkness fell over the gulf. "Just a little farther," we were told. "We'll be there soon." I didn't care. I was enjoying the night cruise, the tangy air. The bioluminescence was better than any I had ever seen. Metallic blue flashes erupted off the bow, green, neonlike waves shimmered off the stern. And if I needed a break, I could always lie on my back and gaze up at a hypnotic star-studded sky.

A shout woke me from a catnap. It was nine o'clock, more than ten hours on our water taxi. "Where are we?" I asked Judy.

"I think we're here," she replied tiredly. "Wherever that is."

Staring ahead into the murk, I could see the faint outline of a small, dimly lit wharf. Farther inland, festively colored lightbulbs were strung between tall poles, even though Christmas was a month past. A Gloria Estefan tune wafted over the water, accompanied by the off-key howls and barks of some obnoxious dogs.

"Welcome to Costa Rica's 'Fantasy Island'!" Linda announced as Daniel brought the boat in.

"Looks more like Gilligan's Island," Herb muttered under his breath.

We snuggled up against a double-masted wooden ketch that Linda said was seventy-seven feet long. A beefy, bare-chested guy met us at the gangplank. There was no "hello." Instead, he drunkenly cursed Linda for being late. She shrugged it off and led us up a pathway to a circular palm-thatched bar and dining area. Johnny, the bartender, asked if we wanted something to drink before dinner. "Beer, coke, booze. You name it, I've got it," he said.

I was totally disoriented. One minute I'm sailing across the peaceful, dark sea, the next I'm on some angst-ridden tropical island. After a quick-fix dinner of rice and squid sauce, we went to our campsite: a sand volleyball court next to a scum-covered swimming pool. Looming over the court were palm trees festooned with cannonball-size coconuts. Trusting the odds, we crawled in the tents and fell asleep to the hum of a generator, a shouting match at the bar, and a pack of barking dogs howling to calypso music.

▲

A troop of howlers greeted the dawn with their terrifying roars, which drove the dogs hysterical. In turn, the dogs made sure no human being on the island was going to sleep past 6:00 A.M.

I wrote in my journal for a while, gratefully noting the absence of biting bugs, then made the big push to exit the tent. Herb was the only one up and about. He looked as fastidious as ever in his powder-blue shorts, white socks and sandals, and clean white shirt—unlike the rest of us who from the first day had assumed the appearance of shipwrecked castaways.

Promised showers were nowhere to be found, and there were murmurings of mutiny among our ranks, but all was forgiven when daylight revealed an island far different than the dark and depressing one first encountered at night. After a breakfast of freshly-squeezed orange juice, French toast, sweet rolls, and coffee, Rafael and crew went to work on the gear and boats. The rest of us took an island tour with Linda's daughter, who was a very capable guide for a ten-year-old.

Starting at the native-style bungalows tucked away in the quiet interior, she showed us baby monkeys, baby deer, parrots, and a tame coatimundi. We learned that the island's natural assets include one hundred acres of dry tropical rain forest, four beaches, and softly swaying palm trees. One of the beaches was brimming with fascinating tidal pools; another was carpeted with seashells. A short walk into the forest led to a cemetery with weathered wooden crosses dating from the last century. And across a narrow channel was a rocky islet, bristling with cordon cactus that served as nesting platforms for scores of brown pelicans and magnificent frigatebirds—huge black birds with long grey bills and tapered wings spreading a full seven feet. On the way back to camp, our guide said that if we extended our stay she would take us lobster hunting and snorkeling in the clear, blue water. "Maybe some other time," I said. And I meant it.

When we returned, the kayaks, cleaned of mud, were waiting for us on the beach, and the panga—a newer and larger one borrowed from Linda—was loaded with fresh provisions and gear.

It felt terrific to sit in a kayak again, to stretch out muscles and skim across the waves under our own power. The ocean changed from green to blue, depending on the depth, and was clear and bathwater warm—a welcome contrast to the silty Bebedero. We hopscotched from one clean sandy beach to another, breezing past island bird refuges and coves inhabited by people living in simple huts. "Fishermen," Álvaro said as we drifted offshore. "You see? They are setting the day's catch out to dry."

The fishermen sell their catch in Puntarenas, the nation's major seaport, located across the gulf on the mainland. It seemed strange that a city of forty thousand lay only ten miles away, when here we were paddling by thatched huts, islets screeching with birds, and a green unbroken forest that plunged down to meet the sea.

▲

The next morning we were on the water at eight-thirty, cruising leisurely toward our final camp. The plan was to spend two nights on a deserted, jungle-backed beach near the border of Curú National Wildlife Reserve. We paused for lunch at a broad, fine sandy beach flanked by rows of coconut palms and broad-leafed hardwoods that spread up the hillsides. Afterward, while everyone went for a swim, I went for a short hike into the forest; or, more accurately, I *tried* to walk into the forest. The heavy undergrowth gave me a new concept of "short distances." Blanketed in a steamy white mist, the dense jungle closed in around me. It was a greenhouse. The air was hot, heavy, and silent but for the humming of insects (big beetles of bright metallic colors, wasps and bees of many kinds, centipedes, leaf-cutting ants, army ants, leaf and stick insects) and the calls of birds (orioles and trogons, parrots and hummingbirds, woodpeckers and turkey-sized chachalacas). In a quiet lagoon surrounded by jungle vegetation I thought I saw a big boa coiled on shore, but binoculars revealed the "snake" to be just a shoot of a strangler fig.

My error reinforced the fact that I had much to learn about tropical rain forest ecology, but there wasn't much time. Our coastal trip was quickly grinding to an end and we had only a week-and-a-half left in-country. With Judy, I intended to learn more about the jungle and Costa Rica's other ecosystems, by visiting Chirripó National Park, home of the nation's highest peak at 12,580 feet, and protecting 124,000 acres and five life zones. Our steep, two-day climb to the summit would take us through rain forest, oak cloud forest, highland swamps with tree ferns and dwarf bamboo, the páramo, and finally alpine terrain. Maybe, just maybe, we would see the resplendent quetzal, universally recognized as the most beautiful bird in the Americas.

Chirripó would come later, however, and when we were on our own—no guides. Now, I was bedazzled by the emerald forest all around, yet, as always, a part of my mind continued to think about where I would go next.

While we clients were enjoying ourselves, Rafael and Chino were hard at work. They were returning to the island resort to pick up our old panga. The one Rafael borrowed from Linda had developed a serious leak; Chino had to bail constantly to keep the water out. Álvaro waxed philosophic about his boss's mission: "Better to have a small panga that floats than a big one that sinks."

Since we didn't know how long Rafael and Chino would be gone, we resumed paddling down the Nicoya Peninsula, with Álvaro taking the lead. The warm ocean breeze and gentle surf left us free to concentrate more on the scenery than boat handling. In the foreground were golden sandy beaches, rocky headlands, wave-washed islets, and dark, dripping cliffs. A vast green sea of vegetation loomed in the background. I could feel the hypnotic sway of the waves, the

*The Gulf of Nicoya thrusts some forty miles inland. Its waters separate the long, tall mountains of Costa Rica's mainland that form the nation's spine from the smaller mountains of the Nicoya Peninsula.*

wind, the sun rising and setting, and I could see how people get lost in the tropics, unable to return to their temperate worlds.

Squadrons of pelicans and brown boobies winged over our boats, diving into the waves after fish. Nearer shore, an osprey dragged a fish out of the water and was struggling to get airborne when it was suddenly swarmed, headed off, and buffeted by a half-dozen magnificent frigatebirds until it finally dropped its catch. Then, one of the frigatebirds, also called man-o'-war birds—an apt name for a pirate who sails the air with speed and skill to rob other seabirds—seized the morsel, and the others turned on it until it, too, was forced to let it go.

Judy's shout brought me out of my trance. A sea turtle was floating just below the surface! The dark shape submerged as I streaked near, but I arrived in time to notice that its carapace was about four feet across—a *big* turtle. According to Álvaro, it was probably a leatherback or Pacific Ridley; two species that nest on several of Costa Rica's Pacific beaches. "They are officially protected," he said. "But everyone knows that fishermen still catch them."

As the day grew hotter, things seemed to quiet on down. When we reached our campsite around two-thirty, the first priority was a plunge into the refreshing water. After that, we joined Rafael and Chino, who had arrived earlier with the replacement panga. Siesta time. We retreated into the shade under the palm trees and zonked out, occasionally reaching for a slice of juicy pineapple and watermelon.

Our idleness didn't last long, however, in such an idyllic location. First, along with Rod and Lois, Judy and I hiked through the magnificent undisturbed jungle towering behind camp. It was the stuff of Tarzan movies, with climbing vines, lianas, epiphytes, bromeliads, orchids, ferns, and great trees muscling their way skyward, blocking the sun from the forest floor. Under our feet, the organic mat was littered with fallen leaves, branches, and tree trunks in various stages of decomposition. Nutrients are absorbed so quickly by living things in a healthy rain forest that a fallen leaf can be recycled in a week.

A few hundred yards from the beach, we stumbled upon a huge ceiba tree, its leafy crown large enough to shade a couple of average-sized suburban houses. Dwelling in its maze of branches was a troop of howlers, comprising maybe two dozen monkeys in all. The monkeys seemed agitated at first but soon settled down, lazy as humans in the withering heat. A doting mother clutched a tiny, big-eyed baby to her body. A big male hung straight down from his prehensile tail to get at some leaves, which he picked with his hands.

We might have gone farther, and probably would have gotten lost, if it weren't for our promise to Rafael that we would return for "happy hour." Getting together for freshly popped popcorn and tamarind juice and wine had become a late afternoon tradition. Besides, we had another paddle scheduled for the magical hour before sundown.

We left camp around five and headed toward an estuary nearly a mile to the north. I was back in the double with Judy. Álvaro teamed up with Herb in the other tandem. Rod paddled solo. Cruising the coastline was easy, even with a stiff breeze and roily sea. The problem was the breaking surf in front of the river's mouth. The waves, torn apart by rip currents, beat wildly against white sand.

Our flotilla reassembled several hundred yards offshore. Álvaro volunteered to go first with Herb. Herb, in the bow, didn't say a word. Cinching up his sprayskirt, Álvaro instructed us to look for an upright paddle signal once they were through the combers. "This means we are okay," he said, "and also for you to follow."

Paddling with deep, even strokes, they punched through the hissing whitecaps and disappeared in the waves. After what seemed like a very long time, we finally saw them emerge on shore. But there was no paddle signal. It appeared as if they were dragging a flooded boat out of the water.

The three of us shouted back and forth, speculating about what might have happened and whether we should follow them. Suddenly, Rod yelled, "Hold on! I see the signal." Sure enough, Álvaro was on shore, waving his paddle, telling us to come ahead. Rod went next. Judy and I followed. We raced in on the back of a long roller-coaster curl. Before we knew it, we were through the breakers and into the tranquil river's mouth.

Álvaro and Herb ran up to greet us. They were soaked, and Herb was upset. "See that?" he said to Álvaro with a scowl, pointing to us as we came paddling in. "Now that's how a beach landing is supposed to be done!" Álvaro was unimpressed. "Oh, well," he shrugged. "It's all part of the trip."

The light was fading. We regrouped and nosed up the sluggish mangrove-lined river. Fortunately, the tide was flooding, providing us with ample water to paddle. Even so, the channel narrowed quickly, and soon there was barely enough room to turn around. It was a less-than-hospitable place: dark, humid, putrid-smelling; horrible with *borujas*, I was sure. But about a quarter mile and untold meanders in, we came upon a small clearing hewed out of the mangroves—the last place I had expected to see human habitation. Two half-sunk rowboats were tied to shore. Near a dilapidated shanty was a large mound of old conch shells. No one was around, but I think eyes were watching us.

The sun set. The mangrove tunnel turned grey in the dusk. The flat *quok* call of a night heron rang out; frogs and toads began to peep and trill. We wiggled the boats around and retraced our route to an uneventful exit. The high tide had washed out the surf, there were no boat-mauling waves this time. Silhouetted against the purple sky, long lines of pelicans flapped and sailed inches above the water as both they and we returned to our evening roosts.

▲

We had one full backcountry day remaining. Judy and I and some of the others decided to spend the morning circumnavigating a pair of small deserted islands directly offshore. Later, we would join the rest of our group and pay a visit to the Curú National Wildlife Reserve, a half-hour paddle to the south.

The paddle around Islas Tortugas was a sea kayaker's dream, replete with sea stacks, sea caves, seabirds, and sheer cliffs. We beached the boats at a secluded rocky inlet on Isla Alcatraz, accessible only to small amphibious craft like ours. From here, decked out with masks, fins, and snorkels, we floated away the morning with the warm sun at our backs and the coral reef underneath.

The soft white sandy bottom reflected the light so that it shimmered all around us. I swayed with the movements of the sea, which also gave rhythm to the sea fans and gorgonians beneath me. Staying close to the hard coral were the reef tenants; living jewels that glistened in the soft blue light as they paraded by in bizarre, kaleidoscopic dots and stripes. There were blue tangs, sergeant majors, wrasses, trumpetfish, triggerfish, boxfish, butterflyfish, jacks, and silversides. Parrotfish nibbled daintily on outstretched branches of coral, while angelfish drew near the strange visitors. My eyes searched out the crevasses and gullies, all curtained and draped with sponges and algae—red and purple, blue and green. Affixed to the bottom were spiny urchins and bristleworms. The sea's gifts were everywhere.

We waded ashore after an hour or two, tired but enthusiastic. This was definitely *pura vida*, I said with satisfaction. But sunburned and salty, Lois was still fantasizing about that elusive freshwater shower. "You want a shower?" Rafael asked, out of the blue. "Follow me."

As we paddled back to the mainland, Rafael explained that on his way to meeting us on Isla Alcatraz, he had discovered a cave about a half mile from camp. It was hidden in the cliff along shore and visible only at low tide. "Trust me," our guide said playfully. "You'll enjoy this much more than any regular shower."

Nearing the beach, he pointed out a small round portal at the bottom of a rough escarpment. "That's it," he said. "You've got about an hour before the flood tide."

Lois and Hi and Judy and I pulled our boats ashore and crawled into the cool dark hole. The passageway was about twenty feet long and three feet high, fairly level with an ankle-deep stream gushing from a crevice at its far end. We squeezed together near this natural fountain and, with plastic bailing scoops, took turns dunking bucketfuls of icy water over our heads. When Rod showed up, he said it sounded as if the cave were an opening to a subterranean world inhabited by screeching supernatural beings.

We spent the afternoon hiking a section of Curú's 150 acres. The miniscule preserve was an enchanted garden inhabited by giant Morpho butterflies, which were unmistakable with their sudden flutters of neon blue, as well as many colorful birds. The terrestrial wildlife, however, was difficult to observe. The tropical wild is not the place of constant and spectacular animal sightings that Hollywood has made it out to be. Still, I was overwhelmed by the biodiversity in so small an area.

When we returned to camp for happy hour—our hair washed and our skin tingly clean—there was news. The panga was totally and hopelessly sunk, a sand-filled relic awash on the beach. Álvaro, who was busily recording the event on video, told us what had happened. "Rafael and Chino were out in the panga when it sprung a leak. They were fortunate to get to shore before it went down." At the moment, Rafael was paddling back to work out something with Linda, who was scheduled to shuttle us to Puntarenas the following morning in the *Banana Express*.

"This is how it starts," I thought. "The lure of the tropics. You miss your plane; you don't care, you figure you'll get one next week. ... "

As Álvaro's company tee shirt boldly proclaimed, "Such is Life in Costa Rica."

San Diego

UNITED STATES

N

BAJA
CALIFORNIA
NORTE

Guaymas

MEXICO

P
A
C
I
F
I
C

O
C
E
A
N

S
E
A

O
F

C
O
R
T
E
S

BAJA
CALIFORNIA
SUR

Bahia
Magdaléna

Isla Espíritu
Santo
La Paz

Mazatlán

Cabo San Lucas

# 9.▲

# Baja's Southern Reaches (Mexico)
## Of Whales and Desert Islands

## Of Whales

THE JANUARY SUN WAS HOT, the wind calm. Magnificent frigatebirds soared overhead, their long hook-shaped bills pointed down in search of a morning meal. A bottlenose porpoise surfaced, then silently submerged, creating wrinkles on the otherwise glassy surface. Brown pelicans eyed us warily from the shoreline dunes, not sure what to make of our colorful kayak armada.

Suddenly, a boil of bubbles erupted in the sea ahead. I pushed forward in my flame-red boat and pulled alongside our young Mexican guide, ready for my first close encounter with a California grey whale.

We approached the bubbles cautiously. Both good sense and Mexican law dictate prudence when kayaking near whales; a puny plastic boat is no match for a creature that may be forty-five feet long and weigh forty tons. A huge barnacle-encrusted back arched out of the water nearby, accompanied by a loud *whoosh* and a fishy-smelling plume of rainbow spray that wafted by. I reached for my camera, but before I could pull it out from under my lifejacket, the whale kicked up its ten-foot-wide flukes and dove.

"Keep your camera ready," advised Cristobal. "Soon it will surface to breathe." Now Cristobal, who grew up in these parts, may know a lot more about whale ecology than I do, but even he was startled by what happened next. Instead of merely coming up to breathe, the whale exploded out of the water, rolled over, and with a tremendous splash of cascading foam, landed on its back directly in front of us. Instinctively, I braced with my paddle as a wave of whitewater surged past.

I was too mesmerized by the event to photograph it. But I wasn't disappointed. After all, this was only our second day of sea touring in southern Baja's Magdalena Bay, "The place," said Cristobal, "where *ballenas* come to make love."

▲

We were a diverse gathering of mostly novice kayakers, but whether physician, lawyer, office worker, school teacher, actor, or writer, we all shared the same desire: to observe the California grey whale in its winter home. Judy and I met our group in the gulf city of La Paz, the capital of southern Baja, near the southern tip of the Sea of Cortés. Our San Diego–based outfitter had been leading whale-watching trips to Magdalena Bay for more than a dozen years. The company's brochure stated that the trip "is great for people who are adventurous and open to discovering new cultures. It's for people who love nature." Throw in the whales, and a warm break from winter, and it sounded perfect.

"Mag Bay" is one of the largest yet narrowest bays in the world, a skinny finger of water running north to south along Baja's Pacific coast for a hundred miles. Formed by a long chain of barrier desert islands, the bay is a vast landscape of mangrove estuaries, interconnected lagoons, and deserted beaches. Isla Magdalena, the principal barrier island, is less than a half-mile wide but nearly fifty miles long, with sand dunes, some forty feet high, rolling across its surface like storm-tossed ocean waves frozen in time.

From December until March every year, Mag Bay hosts one of nature's greatest spectacles when hundreds of grey whales gather in its warm, protected inner waters to mate, give birth, and nurture their young before returning north to the Bering Sea in the spring. Their round trip of ten thousand miles is the longest migration of any mammal in the world.

After years of being hunted by Japanese, Russian, and American whalers, the California grey whale was considered virtually extinct in the 1930s. But with international protection, the species has rebounded to numbers approaching its original population—an estimated fifteen thousand to twenty thousand individuals. Magdalena Bay is just one of three areas in Baja where the grey whales congregate to mate and calve; San Ignacio Lagoon and Scammon's Lagoon to the north are also used. The Mexican government has recognized the importance of these nurseries, and all of them have been afforded official protection. Entry is restricted to scientific researchers and a small number of permit-holding tourist boats. Only in Magdalena Bay are boats allowed without special permission from the Mexican authorities, and that, too, may one day change.

▲

Our first campsite was on Isla Magdalena, with the bay on one side and a vista of rippled, shifting dunes on the other. Puerto Lopez Mateos, a small fishing village, was only a few miles away, but our solitude on the island felt complete. I needed only to wade through the dunes, which lay a short distance from the ring of tents, to find a panorama of uninhabited desert.

The majority of Mag Bay visitors whale watch from motorboats, but the quiet, low-profile sea kayak was my choice for exploring the bay's inner sanctum. With only a couple of hours of daylight left, Judy and I took off in a double kayak and went paddling along the shoreline; we had been cautioned not to go in the middle of the channel because of strong tidal currents and the possibility of bumping into a whale. It seemed odd that we would be the only ones paddling that first afternoon. After all, I thought we were here to watch whales. But several of our group returned to the village in one of the support pangas (motorized skiffs) to see who was winning the Super Bowl game.

We may have been the only kayakers, but we didn't have the bay to ourselves. Several fishermen's pangas were buzzing back and forth inside the windless channel and a live-aboard tour boat was anchored a mile or so away. We pushed south against the tide, with the idea that on the return trip the current would be at our back. The paddling was easy. The sparkling light, the gentle sounds of water, and the rhythm of the paddle lulled us into a meditative state. We saw several whales, but they remained hundreds of yards away—indistinct, glistening grey forms blowing off steam.

We came in around 5:00 P.M. The Super Bowl panga returned soon after with the sad news that the TV reception in the village was poor. Only two channels were available, neither of which carried the game. I did not flaunt my low cultural IQ by asking which teams were playing.

The temperature in the winter Baja desert drops quickly with the sun. Although the low fifties were considerably warmer temperatures than we had left in Illinois, the night air was damp, and we were glad to have pile jackets and pants with us. Judy and I walked off by ourselves beyond a dune to the water's edge. It was snug and refreshing to sit in the cool breeze and listen to the pounding and crashing of the surf on the Pacific side of the island. Occasional soft exhalations told of giant whales swimming in close to shore.

While mingling with our group at happy hour—a cocktail-party atmosphere on the beach, as opposed to our intimate little get-togethers in Costa Rica—we chatted with Barb, who, at fifty-something, was probably the oldest member of our group. Over pistachio nuts and red "doodle" chips, washed down with Mexican beer and potent rum punch, she told us about some of her experiences with outfitted trips. Not all of them were good.

Her previous mail-order adventure involved hooking up with a well-known travel company to go to Peru. "I should have known right from the start that there would be trouble when I was the only woman among eight men," she said. Her leader was the macho type, who chastised her for not walking fast enough. A few of her companions were cultural misfits. One of them carried a huge rucksack of expensive camera equipment and, when walking through towns, asked her to stand behind him to guard against pouncing thieves. "As if I had nothing better to do," Barb grunted. While they were in Cuzco, about to depart for Machu Picchu, another in her group wanted to buy coca leaves for tea. He asked the Indian vendor for a kilo (it was so cheap) and ended up getting a giant trash bag full of dried leaves. Barb was mortified as people stared at them carrying the hefty bag back to their hotel.

"That's the thing about group traveling," she observed. "You can find special companions with whom you share sensibilities and values, and who add immeasurably to your enjoyment of a place, or you can get stuck with jerks."

Judy was sympathetic. At the beginning of this trip she had almost bugged out when she learned that the majority of our trip mates were physicians. "I work with them every day," she had whined. "I don't want to vacation with them!" She regretted her initial bigotry when none of them turned out to be pompous bores, and most were even amiable and interesting.

The next morning Judy and I were out of the tent at 6:45, a half hour before sunrise. The howling of coyotes had awakened us from a sound sleep; their fresh tracks were everywhere in the damp sand. The camp staff was already up preparing breakfast. They waved as we took a boat down to the shoreline for a daybreak paddle.

A low fog hung in patches over the mirror-smooth surface. The birds were already busy trying to procure breakfast. As pelicans flapped overhead, we could hear the whoosh of their wings. Frigatebirds prowled the sky looking to pirate a hard-won catch. Grebes, gulls, and cormorants flew and swam, but there were no whales. We were beginning to wonder if we'd ever see a cetacean up close.

Later, as we broke camp and paddled north toward Boca de Soledad, a gap between the islands where the bay opens into the Pacific Ocean, we found our whales—a regular leviathan freight train. Scores of broad, smooth backs moved rhythmically in and out of the bay's mouth; geyserlike spouts of vapor reached high into the air. Female greys escorted their young, while others rolled, playing and slapping flukes and flippers on the surface during unhurried courtship. It was tempting to try to paddle for a closer look but Cristobal and another guide herded us toward shore, well away from the whale traffic and the outgoing tide. They were not being overly protective. Boats have been capsized by excessively close encounters with the whales, and females are very protective of their young. Often, as we kayaked along, we would be reminded to tap our boats to announce our presence.

At dinner that evening, conversation naturally centered on the animals we had come to see. Most of us had never observed a whale in the wild before, but now we were "experts," having counted dozens of greys surfacing and blowing, nursing their calves, and, most spectacularly, breaching. We liberally used newly acquired terms like "spy hopping," "fin slapping," "tail lobbing," and "foot-prints" (big flat spots on the water from the displaced water of the flukes driving down), to describe the more unusual whale behavior. Tom, a physician from Indianapolis, reminded us that he had videotaped much of the action and, for a small fee, would send us edited tapes. We stared at him blankly. After seeing the real thing, it would be a let-down to watch whales on TV; however, one guy did offer to buy a tape of the Super Bowl if Tom could find it.

Once camp chores were over, our camp assistants and cooks knew how to have a good time. At around seven o'clock, they began playing guitars and singing nonstop. They were very good—and loud—and as the evening wore on they became more and more animated. They never seemed to tire. Sometimes they were joined by one of the kayakers who had brought his fiddle and played Cajun tunes, or by our group as we twirled and clogged and swayed to the music. I played drums on the water jugs, but I didn't dance. My body was embarrassingly stiff and unrhythmic compared to Cristobal's smooth lambada moves.

▲

Our itinerary for the week-long trip was slow-paced and relaxed. We paddled three to four hours each morning in search of whales or whatever caught our interest. When the afternoon breezes picked up, creating a chop on the water, we were free to birdwatch, read, play volleyball, snooze, or watch whales from skiffs or shore.

I didn't even feel guilty about being so pampered and lazy on this backcountry trip; my week with Rafael in Costa Rica had already given me a taste of how easy life can be in the wilderness. Pangas carried all provisions of food, water, and camping gear, allowing paddlers the luxury of carrying only a daypack. The support boats could also be used if tides or winds made kayaking impractical, and served as a safety net in the event of a medical emergency or a kayak getting damaged or lost.

At first I thought the skiffs would be a hindrance. Why paddle a kayak when a motorboat was at our disposal? However, I was quick to change my mind. The Mexican drivers—local fishermen—maintained a discreet distance from the kayakers, so as not to intrude with motor noise. They also enjoyed the opportunity to show off "their" whales. The continued protection of the grey whale in Mexico hinges on the support of its citizens. By hiring local townspeople as guides and skiff drivers, the outfitter provided us an opportunity to learn something about the local culture as well as about whales. I was glad we had chosen to travel here with an organized group, with the chance to learn so much from their experiences.

▲

After a morning of whale watching, a group of us left the main channel to explore a part of the immense labyrinth of mangrove passages on Mag Bay's eastern side. The waterways were much too shallow for whales but were a paradise for birds and bird watchers.

Wheeling overhead, often plummeting into the sea, were the usual assortment of frigatebirds, gulls, and brown pelicans, now joined by blue-footed boobies, black brant geese, egrets, herons, ospreys, ibises, and other birds—a total of thirty-one species in less than two hours.

Compared to the saltwater lagoons and brackish swamps, which are oases of vitality and life, Isla Magdalena and the other Pacific desert islands are harsh, barren places—hot by day; cool and foggy at night. The only plants that can take hold are specially-adapted grasses, euphorbias, and other sand-loving species. In the full heat of the day, the dunes appeared lifeless, but etched across them each morning were signs that another world emerged with the setting of the sun.

Once, I was awakened around midnight by the sound of scratching outside the tent. As I sat up and looked around, the mysterious noisemaker appeared. Through the mosquito netting of the front door, inches from my own face, I stared into the eyes of a coyote, plainly visible even on this dark, moonless night. "What are you doing here?" I mused aloud. The animal jumped backward and was enveloped by the blackness.

At first light I crawled outside the tent to look for clues about the coyote's activity. The animal's tracks went from tent to tent. It didn't take a brain surgeon (although there was one in our group) to deduce that it wasn't scratching I heard, but rather the coyote licking the dew-dampened tent to quench its thirst. Also, for some reason or another, the animal made off with several bars of soap and a roll of toilet paper.

Later that afternoon, when the winds and waves ruled out paddling, Judy and I went hiking across the dunes to a seemingly endless Pacific beach of pavement-hard, surf-packed sand where shells, driftwood, porpoise skeletons, and even the remains of a forty-five-foot grey whale were found washed ashore. I had heard that a whale's penis is large, but this one's was the length of a small canoe; the same applied to its fleshy tongue, swollen and rotting in the sun. The smell was getting bad. Bird droppings streaked the sides of the carcass, but no carnivores had yet managed to tear through the tough skin and get to the blubber underneath. Easier pickings lay down the beach, where turkey vultures sat atop a dead pelican.

We climbed a sand dune and panned the ocean with our binoculars. Out to sea, beyond the dumping surf, we could see dozens of whale spouts, their vaporous plumes shooting into the sky and carried sideways by the wind. There had to be at least fifty whales out there, and for every one we saw there was probably another two or three below.

We were back in time for hors d'oeuvres, but a fellow traveler we had befriended had not yet shown up, and we were getting a little concerned because it was almost dark. He was the same guy who had taken a full half hour to set up his tent (and never did get it quite right), while most campers took ten minutes.

Dinner was in full swing when he finally showed up, looking exhausted. He had been dropped off by one of the pangas on the beach by the dead whale, but it was a different dead whale from the one near our camp. His "little hike" turned out to be seven miles long over waterless, rolling terrain. He had walked to the wrong kayak camp, and then had to backtrack around a mangrove swamp. To add insult to injury, he was admonished by one of the staff to "be more careful" in the future.

▲

Early morning was the magic hour. Except for the hushed voices of the camp staff, who were busily preparing breakfast, the only sounds were the unmistakable blows and inhalations of whales as they passed nearby in the fog. Judy, Tom, and I, with our commuter cups of coffee nestled between our knees, launched our solo kayaks just as the gauzy mist began to lift. Tom had his camcorder ready to roll, but all we saw were whales from afar, spouting, spy hopping, and tail lobbing: a great show, but not what Tom, a frustrated Marty Stouffer, was looking for.

We had some fleeting up-close glimpses of whales from our kayaks that morning, but, when it became too windy to paddle later in the day, some of us went out in the pangas. We motored north of our camp to a spot just inside the breaker line where the water in the bay mingles with the Pacific: whale heaven. At times, it was like a geyser basin out there. The horizon was full of spouts. The whales would seem far away, then all of a sudden they would surface next to our boat, while the outboard quietly idled. Several times they submarined beneath the skiff—appearing as shadowy, zeppelinlike bodies which took several seconds to pass by.

I had always thought it corny to want to touch a whale, viewing it as a bit of human hubris impelling us to impose ourselves on another creature. Here, however, the whales seemed to be interested in us. I had read that such curious behavior is relatively recent, evident for only the last twenty or so years. Were they conscious that we were not there to do them harm? Had they been close enough, I would have touched them. I wanted to make contact.

The best incident all day was the half-dozen breaches one whale repeated for us very close to the boat. Each time, Cristobal chanted, "Again ... one, two, three!" Then the animal would shoot out of the water as if trained by the guide for our entertainment. Watching the action from the relative security of the panga, I thought back to that earlier incident with Cristobal, and felt lucky the whale hadn't belly-flopped on top of our kayaks.

The panga ride was exciting, but there was a disturbing side too. Since this was a whale "hot spot," there were other boats besides ours, and not all drivers were as concerned and alert as our thoughtful guides. We saw one whale with propeller scars; and it seemed that some whales were being herded by overenthusiastic drivers for the benefit of their clientele. If the whales are being disturbed, then you would think that it should be stopped, but the drivers and guides would then lose the economic benefits of the wildlife resources in their area and might begin to care less about their survival. I asked our driver about this cetacean Catch 22, and whether he thought Mag Bay would be closed to tourists some day. "If the government wants to do this then it will be done," he said with a shrug.

▲

On the last morning I sat in the center of the channel, an ebb tide slowly pulling my kayak toward the break between the islands. Several of my campmates were stirring on shore, emerging from tents perched atop the dunes; but on the bay I was alone, except for a solitary fisherman.

I scanned the watery horizon. Soon, a small group of whales, numbering maybe four or five, circled my boat, softly exhaling each time they surfaced. Then, one by one, the whales began spy hop-ping—vertically pushing their massive grey and white heads out of the water while slowly spinning around. The eeriest thing of all, however, was not this graceful aqua ballet, but the deep, dark eyes that seemed to stare into my own. Maybe they were merely curious, yet I couldn't help hoping that they were also trying to reach out to this stranger in their midst.

▲

# AND DESERT ISLANDS

I didn't want to leave the clear, emerald green water; it was so refreshing, so teeming with life. On my snorkeling excursion I was seeing striped sergeant majors, big-lipped parrotfish, electric-blue damselfish, elegant angelfish, rainbow wrasses, odd-shaped gobies and blennies, and sinister moray eels. Huge schools of reef fish swam in front of me. When the sun glinted on their bellies they turned into a Milky Way of underwater stars.

I thought back to my first trip to Baja. In Magdalena Bay, in January, I wouldn't even wade in the chilly water, although Judy had often gone for a morning dip. Now, at a different time of year, in a different location, the situation was reversed: It was the heat of the land that I dreaded.

I bobbed to the surface to get my bearings. The glare was intense, almost blinding, made more so by the thick lens of my dive mask. At the far end of the small cove, pelicans dive-bombed, ospreys soared, gulls swooped from rocky perches, and, high up, magnificent frigatebirds floated, motionless against the afternoon sky. I scanned the water for Mike. His orange-tipped snorkel and splashing flippers let me know that he was near the cliff wall about fifty feet ahead. Satisfied that my buddy was close, I spun around to check the beach. Near camp was a great blue heron, standing motionless in the sun-dappled shallows, waiting for a meal. Behind the heron was a dry, mean desert basin, forested with spiny cacti and dessicated brush. The barren cliffs that edged the island's shores were almost white in the brilliant wash of light.

Mid-October means autumn to me—cooling temperatures, changing leaves, shorter daylight. But here in Baja California Sur, only ninety miles from Cabo San Lucas up the east coast of the Sea of Cortés, it felt more like a Saudi Arabian summer. The view, the pace, and the calm were invigorating to the spirit and cast a sense of enchantment over me, but I had no desire to leave the water until the fireball in the sky went down.

▲

A small, red-haired man named Pollo, or "Chicken," had delivered Mike and me to Isla Espíritu Santo earlier that morning from La Paz. We had met Pollo on the city's beachfront malecón, a palm-shaded boulevard that stretches for blocks along the harbor. A shrewd operator, he had wanted U.S. $100 for the sixteen-mile, one-way ride in his panga—a trip I knew couldn't take more than an hour and a half. I offered him forty; we settled for sixty and shook hands. It was 11:00 A.M. when Pollo deposited us on the southwestern corner of the desert island, separated from the mainland by the five-mile-wide San Lorenzo Channel. Espíritu Santo, meaning "Holy Spirit," was named by Spanish explorers in the 1600s. Written records show that they visited the island often for its abundance of pearl oysters.

Espíritu Santo, however, is actually two islands. Isla Partida is its detached northern end, separated by a narrow channel only a few feet wide at its narrowest point and only ankle-deep at low tide. Together the two islands are about twelve miles long, graced with numerous azure bays, white sand beaches, and clear water—nothing short of paradise for paddlers. Except for a few visiting yachts and ramshackle fishing camps, both islands are uninhabited. While paddling with the whales in Mag Bay earlier in the year, the guides had talked about the beauty of the islands, and I had concluded that I would visit as soon as I could.

Due to conflicting schedules, Judy couldn't make the trip, meaning for the first time in a long time I'd be traveling to Latin America without my interpreter-wife. However, Mike, my longtime friend and paddling companion, was ready to come along. Mike had turned forty-three in May. A Vietnam vet, biologist, teacher, and custom woodworker, this was his first journey to a Spanish-speaking country. I guess that was why even my limited knowledge of the language and customs was enough to impress him.

After Pollo left, we stood on the beach gazing after him like a couple of bewildered castaways. It was hot. Just how hot was confirmed by my thermometer: 98 degrees Fahrenheit in the sliver of shade behind the duffle bags; 112 degrees in the open. The sun was radiant against a blue sky as it baked the desert. I began to feel vulnerable, my pale skin sweltering and sweating. Suddenly, our sixteen gallons of drinking water in plastic folding jugs seemed inadequate for the seven days of paddling that lay ahead. My throat felt parched and I wanted to start guzzling, even though we had just arrived. "C'mon, let's get off the beach," Mike said, jolting me out of my reverie. We jumped in the ocean without bothering to strip off our clothes.

The water was warm but infinitely cooler than the scorching land. We swam over to a narrow inlet and followed a sinuous channel into a green grove of mangroves. The overhanging ten-foot-tall trees offered a welcoming tunnel of shade. The water was belly-button deep and aquarium-clear. Beneath us darted a colorful explosion of exotic fish. And tiptoeing among the mangrove roots were beautiful Sally Lightfoot crabs; their red, blue, and brown shells gleaming like baked enamel.

We waded in about a hundred yards, until the mangroves closed ranks to form an impenetrable, impassable screen. On the mud bank to my right I found a whale vertebra the size of a dinner plate. I was reaching for it when a loud squawking startled us. "Yellow-crowned night heron?" Mike asked in a whisper. "Black-crowned night heron," I replied. The foliage was far too dense to see more than a few feet.

It was tempting to hole up in the labyrinth a while longer, but we had chores to do back at camp. We emerged onto the beach to find the sun still fierce and unrelenting. Long-sleeved shirts, wide-brimmed hats, and legs basted in sunscreen weren't enough: shade was a priority; more than that, it was essential to our well-being. Using the kayak paddles for supports, we erected a twelve-by-twelve-foot tarp, which proved to be a passable awning. Thus protected, in the hour or two remaining before sundown we organized our gear and assembled the Klepper kayak, the same boat Judy and I had used on our first trip to South America.

Mike was no stranger to my old Klepper. We had been together on a trip to Alaska a few years earlier, which involved paddling a stretch of the Bering Sea to reach a large haulout of Pacific walrus. The voyage had been a humbling experience. Persistent high winds forced us to carry the heavy kayak and far too much gear over a tundra pass that led to a sheltered bay. The portage took two days. Mike is a true aficionado of wild places, but that episode made him wary of listening to my ideas about idyllic paddling. I had taken field trips to the Sea of Cortés while in college and promised him desert beauty, clear skies, and calm water. And I got him to read Steinbeck's *The Log from the the Sea of Cortez*, written when he and a friend sailed in a sardine boat to collect marine invertebrates along the beaches of the gulf. Steinbeck and I were too much to resist. Mike's only stipulation was that on no account was he going to carry, drag, or otherwise schlep the Klepper any farther than from beach to campsite.

After a final burst of fire, the sun dropped beneath the watery horizon. Instantly, the sky turned from blue to orange to blood red. The world quickly became dark.

"God, it's freezing!" Mike said, pretending to shiver. I checked the thermometer. "You're right!" I said, my teeth chattering. The temperature had plummeted to a numbing eighty-seven degrees.

Mike got the stove going. We weren't exactly hungry, but we needed to eat something. I tore open one of my freeze-dried dinners and examined some of my other provisions. "What a mess!" I moaned. The margarine was a total disaster. I'd have to pitch it. My chocolate bars, one for each night in the desert, were also suffering from meltdown. I sampled the oily glop anyway, dipping into it with a spoon. "Mmmm, not that bad," I said, smacking my brown-smeared lips, to Mike's disgust.

That night, the campsite seemed perfect: a magnificent sunset, gentle waves lapping against the beach, the gritty comfort of molded sand on a peaceful desert island. But even paradise can have its bugs. "Are you getting bitten?" Mike asked, scratching his legs. As a matter of fact I was—all over. Only later did we learn one of Baja's caveats: Don't camp near mangrove trees, home of *jejenes*, the dreaded Mexican no-see-ums.

We did a quick jig, trying to brush the critters off our bodies, then made a dash for the tent and zipped up the netting behind us. The air inside the poorly ventilated, cone-shaped shelter was thick. I stretched out naked atop my old Polarguard bag like a warrior awaiting the final passing. "Maybe we should have gone to Canada instead," I sighed. But Mike was already asleep.

▲

Despite our best efforts for an early start, it was eight o'clock, two hours after sunrise, when we finally nudged the kayak out into the still waters of the gulf. Packing the boat had slowed us down. The problem was space, or lack of it. We tried to make all our cargo magically disappear below but ended up with a medium-sized dry bag and a couple of two-gallon water jugs lashed on deck. Even so, there was almost no room for us in the cockpit. Mike had it the worst. At six feet and 185 pounds, it required a contortionist act for him to squeeze into the bow seat among the water containers, tent, and food bags.

We pointed the bow to the north, digging the paddles deeply and slowly into the glassy swells. To the east were uplifted, ochre-colored cliffs, glowing desert canyons, and steep *arroyos*; to the west, far across the water, was the Sierra de la Giganta, forming the dusty backbone of Baja's eight-hundred-mile-long peninsula. A few fishermen's skiffs sped past a mile or more offshore; otherwise we were alone. The world seemed reduced to the simplest elements: the sun, the rock, the cactus, the wind, the ocean, the kayak … and us.

About an hour into our journey, we stopped for a snorkel break near a sweeping shoreline of wave-sculpted rock. The water was soothing on our skin after the heat but the fish-watching was poor, so we slipped into running shoes and took a short hike up a slickrock arroyo that shelved into a rugged escarpment.

Not a hundred yards from shore, in a side gulch that twisted around a bend of pink and tan stone, were a couple of waterpockets. These pits and depressions in the rock fill every time it rains, which isn't often in a place that gets only about four inches of rain a year, barely enough to keep a cactus happy. The pools of old seepage were covered with organic scum, teeming with crawling, creeping, jumping things hatched from waiting eggs. The yellow-flowered bushes nearby hummed with a horde of bees. All this activity, in turn, would attract snakes, birds, jackrabbits, ringtailed cats, and other creatures that feed on the fleeting banquets and slake their thirst. The thought of drinking from the waterpockets was disgusting, but the pre-Columbian people who once lived here no doubt would have thought differently. They would have found the yellow, overused water to be the very stuff of life.

And, amazingly, people *have* lived here. Overlooking the waterpockets was a dry, shallow cave with half its opening walled in by carefully placed rocks. We climbed up to investigate. There was room inside the cave for two, maybe three, adults. Mike, who has done his share of deer hunting with bow and arrow, theorized that the cave may have served as a blind, allowing primitive hunters to shoot down on unsuspecting animals with spears, arrows, or even rocks. Additionally, there were a tremendous number of ancient sea shells, clams mostly, casually scattered nearby, the way modern man scatters beer cans.

There were many questions prompted by our find. Why would anyone have wanted to live here, on a bleak desert island? When did they come? Where did they come from? Did ancient man migrate here when the area was still fertile and well watered and then, as years of drought turned the land into a desert, find his retreat cut off? Did enemies drive him south into the peninsula? Did they arrive by mistake from across the sea? We searched the site for arrowheads, worked stones, potsherds, cave art etched into the stone wall or ceiling—anything that might serve as date and culture indicators. Nothing. No trace. Just as well. The nomadic Indians of Baja are gone, and anthropologists still have not come up with any conclusive and satisfying answers to the questions we posed.

We returned to the familiarity of our well-stocked boat and settled into the hypnotic punch and pull, slice and rise of the paddles. A series of rocky headlands slipped past us, their great heights gauged by the recognizable dimensions of the mangroves edging the shore. The sculpted cliffs were striped with pink volcanic ash and brown river rocks that revealed the island's past. Eons ago, immense forces pulled Baja away from mainland Mexico, shaped the Sea of Cortés, and thrust volcanic islands like this one up from its floor. Pounding wind and waves, and occasional catastrophic floods, did the rest.

Shafts of sunlight bouncing off the bottom turned the water lime green when the bed was sandy, and deep blue when coral reefs lay below. The liquid world looked inviting as we skimmed the surface; however, there was no good place to land the boat. We consoled ourselves with frequent dunks of our wide-brimmed hats, which we plopped dripping wet on our heads.

We cut a sleek wake past Islas Gallo and Gallina, which appeared close by on our port side. The islets bristled with giant cardon cacti, their squat, thorny trunks as gnarled as ancient oaks. In between the cacti, the rocks were white with the excrement, or guano, from countless generations of nesting seabirds. The pelicans, gulls, and blue-footed boobies were gone now, having already raised their young, but I could easily imagine what a screaming, pungent place this must have been.

We rounded Punta Ballena next. Across from it was Isla Ballena, a massive swale-backed rock rising out of the warm belly of the sea— a Baja rendered in miniature. We paddled into a snug cove directly opposite the island, searching for another place to camp. We had come only six miles since breakfast, but with the sun at its zenith, it made sense to rest in the shade, to go swimming, to snooze, anything to protect our skin and keep dehydration at bay.

The sand was still too hot to walk barefoot, so the moment we beached the kayak, we gathered our snorkel gear and eased into the slick turquoise water. Purely by luck, we had chosen a windless campsite cove where the undersea life was extravagant and bold. The bottom was a patchwork of sandy areas with rock piles and larger sections of reef that varied in depth from three to fifty feet. Sea fans and gorgonian coral were abundant, and small neon fish darted about the channels and fissures. I watched as coronet fish, as sleek as arrows, shot into huge schools of sardines, sending waves of panic through the silvery masses. I played with a large puffer fish, which responded to capture by inflating into a spiny balloon. And there were good numbers of angelfish, snappers, groupers, triggerfish, butterflyfish, and, my favorite, the boxy trunkfish.

Sharks are uncommon in the waters off Espíritu Santo, but there are some sea creatures that can hurt you. We were wary of the poisonous stonefish and spiny purple sea urchins. But the greatest natural danger for a Baja snorkeler is the stingray, which loves to burrow in the warm sand of the shallows. The wader who steps on one is likely to get a very painful puncture wound from the bony spike in the ray's tail. For this reason, whenever entering or leaving the water, we always slid and shuffled our feet, giving the stingrays plenty of warning to move along.

One sea creature we couldn't avoid was the small, gelatinous jellyfish. About the diameter of quarters, they drifted with the currents in untold numbers and were virtually invisible until their long, trailing tentacles brushed against our exposed skin. I always knew when I had made contact with them because of the irritating, tingling sensations their toxins produced, similar to low-voltage electrical jolts.

We were in the water so long that even with a shortie wetsuit on I was actually shivering when we returned to camp. My goose bumps quickly faded, though, when I learned that it was ninety-two degrees in the shade, a dozen degrees warmer than the sea surface temperature.

Relief finally came when the sky in the west turned brilliant red. The air cooled slightly when a soft breeze blew in from the pastel mountains behind us. Bats flitted over our heads, some coming so close I could hear the high-pitched clicks of their sonar, which is used as a means to echolocate prey. A great-horned owl hooted from somewhere in a nearby canyon. Flying fish skipped across the sparkling water, perhaps to escape a pursuing barracuda. Silhouetted against the horizon, a great blue heron pumped its wings in slow, graceful arcs as it flew over our beachside camp. It was a peaceful, beautiful night, with no *jejenes* to bother us—a perfect, moonless night to watch the stars swirl and to enjoy the camaraderie of a best friend.

My only regret was that Judy was not here to share and enjoy it. A rush of images came to me when I thought back to all our times together wandering in wild places. We've paddled down Patagonian rivers and across high-altitude lakes and along tropical shores. Searching the southern reaches, we've trekked through faraway mountains, steamy cloud forests, and lost worlds. We've been fortunate enough to see flamingos and condors, guanacos and vizcachas, monkeys and great whales. We've faced the horizons in strange surroundings and have been immersed in cultures far different from our own. Like all travelers, we had been pulled from confining routines by a need to stretch and seek.

In 1940, Steinbeck wrote in his *Log* about the reasons for his trip to the Sea of Cortés. A little boy had asked him what he was looking for, and he had had to consider that simple question for quite a while. "We search for something that will seem like truth to us," Steinbeck wrote. "We search for understanding; we search for that principle which keys us deeply into the pattern of all life; we search for the relations of things, one to another. ... " I don't expect to find any answers, but I enjoy looking.

Going to rinse my cup after dinner, I noticed faint green sparkles in the shallows—starlight playing on the water, I thought. But then I realized I was looking at bioluminescent blinks, phosphorescent jade bursts that pulsed on and off. Mike came over with his flashlight and shined it on the bottom. "There are the culprits," he said. Frozen within the yellow beam were several tiny, nearly transparent fishes that glowed like fireflies on a warm, summer evening.

If ever there was a night to go paddling, this was it. The luminosity grew in intensity the farther out we went. It seemed as if we were dipping the paddles into buckets of phosphorescent paint. We edged up to a cliff face that was lined with a jumble of submerged boulders. "Watch this," said Mike, ever the science teacher. He held his waterproof torch beneath the translucent water. Within seconds, the ray of light attracted scores of fish, mostly small ones, but some a foot long. I don't know who was more mesmerized by the incandescent beacon, the sea life or us.

Suddenly, the quiet of the cove was jarred by the *put-put-put* of a motorboat. Mike instantly cut the torch. We scrunched low in the kayak as a spotlight beam shined our way. There were three or four men. We could see them outlined against the sky about a hundred yards away. Their voices carried easily over the open water. They talked in Spanish, none of which I could understand. They searched the inky bay for a few minutes, but we were a small target. Finally, they gave up and doused their light. The motorboat lurched forward and chugged away into the dimness.

"What gives?" Mike whispered, squirming around in his seat.

"Probably only curious fishermen," I said. "But you never know." As a practical matter, there aren't any bandits in Baja. Baja residents, by and large, are law-abiding and friendly. It's in the honky-tonk border towns and tourist zones that the usual travel precautions apply. Still, we weren't interested in testing the supposition on a dark and lonely night.

Several uneventful minutes passed. I triggered off my camera flash while taking a picture of Mike paddling in the bow. Suddenly, Mexican voices erupted out of the darkness, "*¡¡Yeeeeaaa!! Yeeaaaaa!!*" I was startled. They were still at the mouth of the cove! Doing what?

Again, they trained their spotlight on us. And again, our low profile and muted colors helped us escape detection (no wonder folding kayaks have long been favored by commandos to sneak into enemy harbors, after being dropped offshore by submarines!). When the light off their skiff dimmed, we paddled furtively back to camp.

▲

We were up at five-thirty, watching the first tinge of sunshine creep over eroded ridges at least a billion years old. The temperature stood at seventy-nine degrees—another hot day. Since we weren't moving camp, we decided to take advantage of the relative coolness by taking a long hike up a boulder-filled canyon. First, though, was the morning stretch to limber up our tightened muscles, then the meditation of sipping coffee while waiting for the caffeine to kick in.

Shortly after sunrise we scrambled up the steep arroyo. Far beneath the cave-pitted canyon walls, we found rocky amphitheaters sheltering leafy wild fig trees, survivors of a wetter age. Also in the dry creek beds and topping the slopes, were white-barked elephant trees, *ocotillos*, fairy dusters, catclaws, *palos blancos*, agaves, various desert grasses, and many species of cacti. Etched in the sandy washes was the spoor of ringtail cat, called *babisuri* in these parts, along with the tracks of lizards and toads, rodents and birds, and wild goats and jackrabbits that roam the brushy interior.

In terms of color, Espíritu Santo's jackrabbits are unique: the island's landscape ranges from white to sandy to the dusty green of cactus and the dull red of old lava flows, yet the jackrabbits are jet black, making them startlingly conspicuous against the muted colors of their environment. This, and other examples of strange evolutionary processes on secluded desert islands, offer proof, as some biologists contend, that Baja is a "poor man's Galapagos," where original populations of organisms evolved in such a way as to be very different from other species of the same genus living elsewhere.

The bewildering variety of bizarre plants and the abundance of animal life contradict the popular conception of the Baja desert as dead and useless place, and that what little life it supports is wholly inimical to man. But, as we discovered, one is well advised to tread carefully.

There are eighteen species of rattlesnakes in Baja; the most common being the lower California rattlesnake, *Crotalus enyo*, found virtually everywhere in the lower three fourths of the peninsula: in the desert, in the mountains, along the seashore, *and* on the islands in the Sea of Cortés. Effectively colored and marked to blend with its surroundings, the snake is easy to miss. I passed right by one while hiking through the dense brush back to camp. I didn't hear the rattler's warning buzz, but fortunately Mike did.

After a late breakfast, we loaded up the kayak with a gallon of drinking water and some trail mix and paddled across a choppy sea to Isla Ballena, where we planned to spend the day exploring underwater. On the islet's north side was a quiet lee along a sheer rock face, perhaps no more than a city block long. Because there was no place to land or tie up, we would have to dive directly out of the beamy kayak and take turns towing it; some refer to this activity as "kanorkling." I sat on the gunwale and fell backward into the water. It took a moment to orient myself, to let my body adjust to an alien world, but when I cleared my mask the sight that greeted me was beyond imagination: a dreamlike experience in which the outlines of reality changed with every moment, depending on the angle and intensity of the light. Visibility approached the one-hundred-foot mark.

There was a straight drop-off of about twenty feet, quickly sloping to forty, sixty, and beyond into the murky depths. The fish were the central actors: schools of flashing mullet; darting hordes of goatfish and torpedo-shaped sierra mackerel; so many tiny silver fish that it was like an incredible sequinned dress waving before my eyes. Less flashy, but integral to the stage, were the corals, sea fans, starfish, green-flecked sea cucumbers, and small intensely colored sponges. The "web of life" was obvious here: myriad miniscule plankton thrive; fish flourish on the plankton; and sea birds and sea lions feast on the fish. The result is an almost unmatched variety of marine life. Of the more than eight hundred known fish species and one thousand species of invertebrates in the gulf, all but about ten percent are found close to the shores of either the peninsula or the islands.

Proceeding cautiously, we entered a catacomb of sea caves created by huge rocks and boulders along the face of the steep drop-off. The crevices were a perfect breeding ground for scores of fish; many were new and unfamiliar to me. Restricted to a single lungful of air, I couldn't explore the caves to my satisfaction, but the view looking up from ten feet down was as good as any I've seen while scuba diving in the Caribbean.

▲

A passing front moved in during the night, kicking up threatening waves. We ate breakfast in the dark and set off just as the rising

sun glared fiercely from between lingering clouds, creating a vermil-
ion path across the gulf and outlining the dark island with a rim of
fire. Our final stop before crossing *la partida*, the narrow tidal passage
separating Espíritu Santo from Isla Partida, was a port of call at
Candelero Bay. This is where the abandoned Mexican navy camp is
located and where a trail behind the beach leads to a small well. Our
drinking water supply was in good shape, but we figured it couldn't
hurt to fill up one of our empty jugs.

The tin-roofed, cement-walled building had been stripped of
anything of value; we found a dusty table and not much else.
According to Pollo, the marines had been stationed on the island to
protect the goats from poachers, but the troops were pulled off when
they were found to be killing what they were supposed to guard. The
marines were doing the island a favor, I told Pollo, since native
ground cover usually disappears under the goats' onslaught. Pollo
didn't reply. Either he didn't understand my Spanish, or maybe he
was too polite to tell me he didn't agree.

"Check this out," Mike called from a small room off to the side.
Like TV handyman Bob Vila, he was always poking his head into old
houses to get fresh ideas. This time, though, his discovery was a
bathroom equipped with a flush toilet, of all things. He pointed to
a water tank perched on the hillside. "That's where they got the
pressure. Probably filled the tank with gravity flow from the well." I
sat on the creaky crapper seat. The view wasn't bad.

We hiked up the side canyon to find the well, the source of the
miracle flush. The small, square shaft was located about two hundred
yards away at the end of a faint trail. It had been chiseled out of solid
bedrock and, judging from the rope I dangled below, was at least
twenty feet deep. I filled up the jug. The water looked sweet, perfectly
clear, with no insects or scum. We treated it with a couple of iodine
tablets anyway.

Waves broke over the kayak on our next leg to the north. The
roiled sea may explain why we didn't see the giant manta rays at first,
but as large as they are it was a wonder we could miss them. Shaped
like great kites, fifteen to twenty feet wide and weighing a ton or
more, a pair of rays repeatedly catapulted their huge bodies out of the
water and landed with a resounding splash. Scientists are unsure
whether their breaching is courting ritual, dance, or just showing off.
In any case, it was one of nature's grand shows. We also kept
searching for blue whales. The previous year, a group of kayakers had
seen sixty of the goliaths cavorting and breaching around some
islands farther up the gulf.

We looked for a camp at the northern end of Isla Partida, which would put us near Islas Los Islotes, a couple of rocky pinpoints famous for their sea lions and excellent diving. The only convenient take-out we could find, however, was a small trilobed cove a couple of miles to the south. We'd have to put off swimming with the sea lions until the following day.

▲

It was midafternoon, twenty-four hours later, when the winds finally subsided, allowing us to depart for Los Islotes. Mike was kind enough to refrain from needling me about my prediction of calm water. We headed for the easternmost, and smaller, island first. The sun-blasted mass of arid rock jutted straight up from the ocean, seeming to float on the water. What made the sea pinnacle even more peculiar was a wave-hollowed arch directly in its center. The absence of manmade reference points made it difficult to judge its true size, but even from a distance the opening appeared enormous. We paddled under the cathedrallike ceiling. The wave-hollowed cavern was mysterious, timeless, womblike. The boat was rocked by rebounding waves that sloshed against the smooth walls. It was with some regret that we left the cool dark cave for the garish light outside.

Once clear of the echo chamber, we heard the unmistakable roars of sea lions. Hunted for their oily blubber in the early nineteenth century, California sea lions are now protected in Mexico. Los Islotes is one of several thriving rookeries in the Sea of Cortés. The animals are attracted to the gulf by the abundant fish, anchovies, octopus, and squid.

"There must be hundreds of them," Mike said, as we crossed the gap to the neighboring islet. The rock-rimmed shore was crowded with what looked like big hairy slugs.

"Not only that," I added with relief. "We've got the whole place to ourselves." Sharing the sea lions with a bunch of scuba divers would have been a distraction.

Rather than beach the kayak, we decided to go kanorkling again. To get to the sea lions we had to first run the gauntlet of seabirds perched on the foul-smelling ledges exposed at low tide. With just our heads poking above the water, we managed to get so close to the trusting birds that I could have reached out and grabbed them by the legs. There were gulls, the noisiest of the lot, marching up and down; comical-looking boobies; awkward and indifferent brown pelicans; and a few black cormorants, wings outstretched to dry in the afternoon sun.

*Underwater shot of Mike frolicking with a sea lion pup, near Los Islotes in the Sea of Cortés.*

Next came the barking and belching sea lions sunning on the rocks. All our stealth was for naught. As we arrived, the lounging pinnipeds honked a noisy welcome before flopping into the water to play.

Swimming with a face mask, I glanced below into the clear, green water and found a brown female and her baby whizzing under my dangling legs. Their speed was astonishing, almost a blur. A couple of pups zipped up to me, as sleek as dolphins. One of them was especially curious and playful. Time and again it hovered face to face with me, wanting to stare at me through my mask. Maybe it was a diversion, because in my peripheral vision I caught sight of another youngster rocketing directly at me. It veered off at the last second, did an underwater somersault, then returned to tug on my fin in the same way it had nipped at the other pup's flippers.

Moving on, we encountered another family group consisting of a dozen or so brown-eyed females and their half-grown young. They shuffled back and forth on their front flippers, watched over by a bellowing, swollen-necked bull swimming at the water's edge. The half-ton specimen was not particularly pleased with the intruders in neoprene suits. In response to my drifting too close to his harem, the huge black male charged me, blowing a mask of bubbles in my face to enhance his bluff attack. The next pass it made a mock grab for my flipper. The warning was heeded. My heart was pounding as I made a hasty retreat.

During my shift towing the kayak, I noticed an inordinate amount of drag. Initially, I thought it was due to contrary currents, but when I looked back I saw an adolescent sea lion nipping at the trailing red stern line like a kitten pouncing on a string. Two could play this game. The next time the pup grabbed the end of the line, I hauled it in, hand over hand, as though reeling in a big fish. The sea lion stayed "hooked" long enough for me to stroke its soft belly, then spit it out the line and did a back flip so that we could start the fishing derby over again.

We traversed nearly the entire length of the island and were ready to repeat the swim, when we noticed an abrupt change in the weather. The sky had that peculiar clarity of light that frequently accompanies a storm, and the wind was raising whitecaps on the water. It was time to turn back to our campsite. We scissor-kicked up and into the kayak, stowed our snorkel gear, and paddled back through the arch. Out at sea again, away from the cacophony of the sea lions, we grew silent, absorbed by the rhythms of nature—wind, waves, arcing sun, flying fish, and diving birds.

We reached camp with little daylight to spare. The sun had already set and a storm was definitely on its way. Foamy rollers, heaped up by the stiff winds, broke onto the slanting beach. The landing would have to be quick if we wanted to avoid damaging the boat. We nosed closer and closer to shore and, in one coordinated motion, jumped out and carried the kayak ashore.

That evening was pure bliss, in part because we were still buzzing from our wildlife encounters of the day. Our isolated camp was ideal. The winds were tropical and refreshing. The sound of the surf was soothing and mellow. Even our dinner of rice and beans washed down by tepid Gatorade tasted better than normal. I looked at my partner under the bright starlight, and I examined myself. Our hair was salt-soaked, our skin sun-baked, our clothing stained beyond recognition. But it felt good to be dirty and sandy, surrounded by solitude, inhaling the hot, dry air of the desert. Things couldn't get much better—unless, of course, my chocolate bars had still been edible.

Mike took out a book and read by flashlight. I didn't want to read just yet. Instead, I wondered where to go next, now that this journey was coming to a close. As long as my compass pointed south, the choices were endless: from the Amazon to the Andes, from the rivers and rainforests in Costa Rica to the glaciers and golden grasslands in Patagonia. There were so many areas of beauty and fascination in Central and South America. But where to go?

When I asked Mike's advice he made me laugh, chiding me as Judy might have done. "Aren't you getting a little ahead of yourself?" he said. "Here you are jabbering about your next trip, and we still have three days to go on this one."

"You're right," I concurred, as I put away my notebook and lay back to look at the stars and listen to the ocean. No need to worry about where I'm going when I'm perfectly happy where I am.

# SELECTED BIBLIOGRAPHY

This list includes many, but by no means all, of the existing English-language publications about Latin America's wilderness, fauna and flora, history and exploration.

## BOOKS

Several of these books are out of print, and may only be available through secondhand book stores, libraries, and mail-order catalogs; some of the older titles have recently been republished in paperback.

Andrews, Michael A. *The Flight of the Condor*. Boston: Little, Brown, and Company, 1982.

Bates, Marston. *The Land and Wildlife of South America*. New York: Time-Life Books, 1964 (revised 1975).

Box, Ben, ed. *The South American Handbook*. London: Trade and Travel Publications, revised annually. Published in North America by Prentice-Hall Trade.

Bradt, Hilary. *Backpacking and Trekking in Peru and Bolivia*. London: Bradt Publications, 1987. Published in North America by Hunter Publishing.

Bradt, George, and Hilary Bradt. *Backpacking in Venezuela, Colombia, and Ecuador.* Boston: Bradt Enterprises, 1980.

Bradt, Hilary, and John Pilkington. *Backpacking in Chile and Argentina.* Boston: Bradt Enterprises, 1980 (revised 1991).

Bradt, Hilary, and Rob Rachowiecki. *Backpacking in Mexico and Central America.* Boston: Bradt Enterprises, 1982.

Bridges, E. Lucas. *Uttermost Part of the Earth: Indians of Tierra del Fuego.* New York: Hodder & Stoughton, 1949 (renewed 1988, Dover).

Chatwin, Bruce, and Paul Theroux, photos by Jeff Gnass. *Nowhere Is a Place.* San Francisco: Sierra Club Books, 1992.

Darwin, Charles. *The Voyage of the Beagle.* 1836.

Dorst, Jean. *South and Central America: A Natural History.* New York: Random House, 1967.

Fons, Valerie. *Keep It Moving: Baja by Canoe.* Seattle: The Mountaineers, 1986.

Frazier, Charles, with Donald Secreast. *Adventuring in the Andes: The Sierra Club Travel Guide to Ecuador, Peru, Bolivia, the Amazon Basin, and the Galapagos Islands.* San Francisco: Sierra Club Books, 1985.

Glassman, Paul. *Costa Rica.* Champlain, N.Y.: Passport Press, 1989.

Goodall, Natalie P. *Tierra del Fuego.* Buenos Aires: Ediciones Shananaiim, 1970 (revised 1975). Bilingual.

Hemming, John. *The Conquest of the Incas.* New York: Harcourt Brace Jovanovich, 1970.

Johnson, William Weber. *Baja California.* New York: Time-Life Books, 1972.

Krutch, Joseph Wood. *The Forgotten Peninsula.* William Sloane Associates, 1961.

Leitch, William C. *South America's National Parks: A Visitor's Guide.* Seattle: The Mountaineers, 1990.

Lindenmayer, Clem. *Trekking in the Patagonian Andes.* Berkeley: Lonely Planet Publications, 1992.

Macinnes, Hamish. *Climb to the Lost World.* London: Hodder and Stoughton, 1974.

Matthiessen, Peter. *The Cloud Forest.* New York: Viking Press, 1961.

McIntyre, Loren. *Exploring South America.* New York: Clarkson N. Potter, Inc., 1990.

Meisch, Lynn. *A Traveler's Guide to El Dorado and The Inca Empire.* New York: Viking Penguin, Inc., 1977 (revised 1987).

Morrison, Tony. *The Andes.* New York: Time-Life Books, 1975.

———. *Land Above the Clouds.* London: Andre Deutsch, 1974.

Perry, Roger. *Patagonia: Windswept Land of the South.* New York: Dodd, Mead, 1974.

Samagalski, Alan. *Argentina: A Travel Survival Kit*. Berkeley: Lonely Planet Publications, 1989.

———. *Chile: A Travel Survival Kit*. Berkeley: Lonely Planet Publications, 1987.

Searby, Ellen. *The Costa Rica Traveller*. Juneau: Windham Bay Press, 1988.

Shipton, Eric. *Tierra del Fuego: The Fatal Lodestone*. London: Chas. Knight and Co., 1973.

Simpson, George Gaylord. *Attending Marvels: A Patagonian Journal*. Chicago: The University of Chicago Press, 1934 (renewed 1982).

Steinbeck, John. *The Log from the Sea of Cortez*. New York: The Viking Press, 1951.

Swaney, Deanna. *Bolivia: A Travel Survival Kit*. Berkeley: Lonely Planet Publications, 1988.

Theroux, Paul. *The Old Patagonian Express*. Boston: Houghton Mifflin, 1979.

# PERIODICALS

These are just a few of the periodicals that contain articles about Latin America.

*Américas*. 19th Street & Constitution Avenue, N.W., Washington, D.C. 20006 (bimonthly). Focusing on the Organization of American States member nations, the articles in each issue cover a wide variety of topics including culture, history, literature, arts, architecture, travel, science, the environment, and economics.

*Baja Traveler*. P.O. Box 81323, San Diego, CA 92138 (bimonthly). An authoritative guide to the Baja peninsula, covering sports, travel, maps, and adventures.

*Great Expeditions*. P.O. Box 18036, Raleigh, NC 27619 (quarterly). A journal of adventure and off-the-beaten-path travel, with frequent articles on socially responsible travel to Latin America.

*National Geographic*. 17th and M Streets, N.W., Washington, D.C. 20036 (monthly). Back issues are an excellent source for articles on all aspects of Latin America.

*South American Explorer*. 126 Indian Creek Road, Ithaca, NY 14850 (quarterly). The journal of the South American Explorers Club. A serious and authoritative source of information about travel, science, and culture in Latin America.

# About the Author

LARRY RICE HAS BEEN EXPLORING wilderness for more than twenty years. His fascination with the outdoors led him to obtain a wildlife biology degree at the University of Arizona, which he puts to work as manager of the Marshall State Fish and Wildlife Area near Lacon, Illinois. He is the author of *Gathering Paradise: Alaska Wilderness Journeys* and is a contributing editor to *Backpacker* and *Canoe* magazines. His writing has appeared in *Outside, Men's Journal, Explore,* and *Américas.* He recently traveled to Panama to join an expedition trekking across the Darien Gap.

# Whether you travel

By kayak, canoe, cruise ship or car,
On foot, bicycle or bush plane,

# Whether you travel

Alone, with family or friends,
Or simply in your imagination,

# However you travel,

Fulcrum Publishing has books
For the **Adventuresome You.**

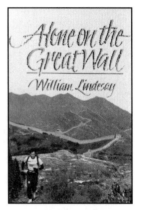

## GATHERING PARADISE
### Alaska Wilderness Journeys
### Larry Rice

Larry Rice shares the joy of traversing ten of Alaska's most remote wilderness areas. Whether it's by kayak, rubber raft or on foot, he vividly conveys the experiences of those backcountry days.

"And like all the best armchair adventure books, in *Gathering Paradise* we learn not only about Alaska, but about the heart of the man who has taken us there."
—Donovan Webster, *Outside* magazine

"*Gathering Paradise* has placed the name of Larry Rice solidly on the map of nature writers. It is a fine book."
—*The Bloomsbury Review*, May/June 1990

ISBN 1-55591-057-2
5 1/2 x 8 1/2, 318 pages, paperback, b/w photos, maps, $14.95

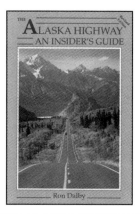

## THE ALASKA HIGHWAY
### An Insider's Guide
### Ron Dalby

The greatest driving adventure remaining in North America awaits you with this easy-to-use guide to the entire Alaska road system.
• **New Revised Edition,** featuring a new chapter devoted to flying the highway.

"Ron Dalby is one of those few people who talk like they write.... Dalby's book has side trips and insider tips for those who want to make their drive a leisurely one."
—*Los Angeles Daily News*, 1/91

ISBN 1-55591-171-4
6 x 9, 220 pages, paperback, b/w photos, maps, $15.95

## THE ALASKA GUIDE
### Ron Dalby

Alaska: the name sparks our nation's collective imagination, conjuring up endless vistas of mountains, fjords and tundra in the "Land of the Midnight Sun." Now award-winning author Ron Dalby has written a complete travel guide to Alaska.

More than just a collection of lists, *The Alaska Guide* provides history, lore and description of the natural landscape, thoroughly introducing readers to the many-faceted jewel that is Alaska.

ISBN 1-55591-131-5
6 x 9, 240 pages, paperback, b/w photos, maps, $15.95